2.00

INSPIRED BY

INGREDIENTS

Market Menus and Family Favorites
from a Three-Star Chef

BILL TELEPAN
and ANDREW FRIEDMAN

Simon & Schuster
New York London Toronto Sydney

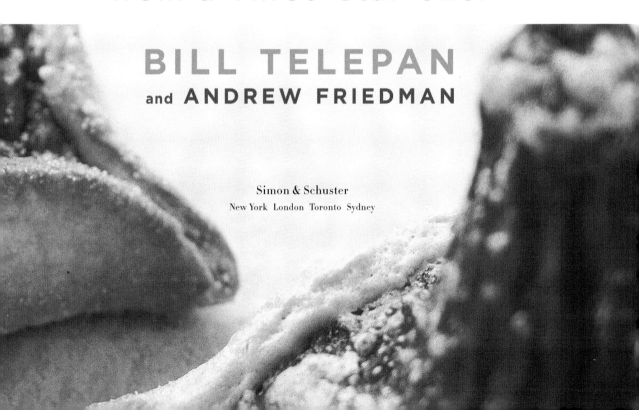

SIMON & SCHUSTER
Rockefeller Center
1230 Avenue of the Americas
New York, NY 10020

For information regarding special discounts for bulk purchases, please contact
Simon & Schuster Special Sales at 1-800-456-6798 or business@simonandschuster.com

Designed by Joel Avirom and Jason Snyder
Design assistant: Meghan Day Healey

Manufactured in the United States of America

10   9   8   7   6   5   4   3   2   1

Library of Congress Cataloging-in-Publication Data

Telepan, Bill.
     Inspired by ingredients: market menus and family favorites from a three-star chef /
Bill Telepan and Andrew Friedman.
     p. cm
     Includes index.
     1. Cookery. I. Friedman, Andrew. II. Title.
TX714.T446 2004
641.5—dc22   2004052148

ISBN 0-7432-4387-0

To Beverly—
You still know how to make
me laugh and smile.

To my parents—
You've done a great life's work:
you raised a good family.

To Leah—
How I love to watch you grow.

Always, every minute, grateful.

CONTENTS

Acknowledgments

This book seemed incredibly easy, thanks to the contributions of these fine people: Andy Boy Friedman, my new friend, thanks for the great effort and letting me shoot my mouth off about the state of the world; Sydny Miner, extraordinary editor, your guidance gave me confidence; Janis Donnaud, super agent, for believing in it in the first place; Quentin Bacon, sensational photographer, your seemingly effortless work made it all the more beautiful; Allison Ehri, tester of recipes with the perfect palate, your energy made it move along swiftly; Anne-Michele Andrews, dessert diva, your incredible skills and knowledge helped create the yummy sweets that people will be enjoying for years to come; Beth von Benz, my wine hero, I know I drive you crazy, but you know that I think you are simply the best; Margo True, my proposal pilot, thank you for your early work in getting this project off the ground; Charles Brassard, Matthew Schaefer, Josh Lawler, Andre Volik, Jennifer Lanza, and the kitchen crew at JUdson Grill for helping with the recipes and the photo shoot; *everyone* at JUdson, for putting up with the extra work and time; JUdson Grill owners Jerry Kretchmer and Jeff Bliss, for the opportunity and guidance; Wendy Roltgen at Amana, thank you for the stove on which the recipes were tested; John Weintraub and Joel Somerstein at Riviera Produce, thanks for getting me the produce I needed, even when there were two feet of snow on the ground (this book definitely owes *no* thanks to the winter of 2003); Mark Scaffati at Scaffati and Company, Maureen Cole at Minner's Design, and Bill Kelly of Cristal Marketing for the plates for the photos; and to the food press of New York City, thanks for all the kind ink you've spilled in my name over the past seven years.

And to all my customers, past, present, and future: it's an honor to cook for you.

INTRODUCTION

THERE'S AN OLD SAYING THAT YOU ARE WHAT YOU EAT. But I've always thought that for chefs, the expression should be "We are what we cook." The dishes that my colleagues and I serve in our restaurants and prepare for friends and family at home sum up the lives we've lived up to that moment. Our palates are formed in childhood, refined in cooking school, honed and personalized as we work for other chefs and dine in other restaurants, and finally shared with the public when we begin composing menus in our own restaurants.

But I'm getting ahead of myself. Unless you've eaten at JUdson Grill, the restaurant in midtown Manhattan where I was the executive chef from 1998 through 2004, or read the food magazines that have reviewed my work and featured my recipes, you might not know who I am.

These are the bare facts: I was born and raised in Sayreville, New Jersey, schooled at the Culinary Institute of America, trained in a number of three- and four-star restaurants in New York and France, and now have the privilege of serving a menu of my own design to some of the most discriminating diners in the world.

Laid out in broad strokes, my biography sounds a lot like most New York City chefs' biographies. But, as with cooking, the difference is in the details.

The first thing you should know about me is that I'm a proud New Jersey native. I had a happy childhood, love my parents and siblings, and don't have a bad word to say about Bruce Springsteen. I didn't grow up in a family of "foodies," but we had it pretty good when it came to food. My father kept a modest garden in the backyard from which we picked cucumbers, tomatoes, peppers, and corn. The memories of those vegetables and the cooking we did with them led me years later to develop such dishes as Cucumber-Dill Soup with Scallions (page 76), Pan-Fried Summer Jersey Vegetables (page 91), and Boiled Lobster with a Corn Salad and Grilled New Potatoes (page 103).

The next thing you should know about me is that the Telepans are descended, in part, from Hungarians, and nowhere do we show our pride more than at the dinner table. My mother has always been one of my favorite cooks, making me and my siblings countless Hungarian-influenced dishes featuring cabbage—including a noodle one called Káposzta Teszta (page 340)—and poppy seeds, which show up in my repertoire in dishes like Lemon–Poppy Seed Bars (page 79). Some of Mom's most beloved recipes have been adapted for the menu at JUdson Grill. Some have become favorites of my wife, Beverly, and my daughter, Leah. All of them are represented in this book.

The next and in some ways the most important thing you should know about me is about the strawberries. Every chef can point to a moment early in his or her life or career that qualifies as an epiphany. For me the Big One came while I was working for the great chef Alain Chapel at his eponymous restaurant in Mionnay, France. One afternoon, I was going about my business, hauling a crate of strawberries into the walk-in refrigerator. It was a perfectly normal day until I glanced down at the berries—in the dim, romantic light they looked like a chestful of precious, edible jewels—and found myself mesmerized. I had never seen such beautiful, plump, perfect strawberries. To look at them was to taste them; you could actually *see* how good they were. Since I'm trying to bare my culinary soul here, I'll confess that I sneaked about a dozen of them just to be sure and, yes, they were the best I've ever had.

I had always known that raw ingredients were important, but that was the moment when I began to revere them.

When I returned to New York, I started going to the Union Square Greenmarket and shopping for produce for the restaurants where I worked. This is when I first met some of the farmers you'll encounter in this book and began appreciating how much their hard work influences any cook's success.

Never Have So Few Fed So Many For So Little
—POPULAR FARMER BUMPER STICKER

As far as I'm concerned, farmers are the ultimate prep cooks. The decisions they make and the work they do are the first building blocks of every dish we serve at my restaurant. So I make a point of getting to know the farmers from whom we buy our ingredients. I want to make sure they observe practices that I believe in. For example, I want to know that they don't use pesticides or, if they do, that they use natural ones.

But more than anything, I want to get to know the person or people behind the farm. I like to surround myself with passionate professionals, and that extends to these men and women who grow our food. Farming, like cooking, is hard work. For some, it's a way of making a living. Then there are those who flat-out love it, who feel about being in their fields the way that I do about being in the kitchen. There's one farmer I work with who tries something a little daring and unconventional every year. When I check in with him by phone at the end of winter, he'll say something like "I'm growing these new purple carrots. I don't know how they're going to turn out, but, man, am I excited." People like him are the ones I want to be in business with. I'll tell him to put me down for a few crates of those purple carrots, just to support his effort and encourage his enthusiasm.

You can make this same commitment at home: cooking with in-season fruits and vegetables is the simplest way to ensure that you get great raw ingredients and support the efforts of farmers who really care about what they're doing.

Some might consider sticking to seasonal ingredients a limitation. But consider this: cooking seasonally means cooking with the best fruits and vegetables available. It means always having something waiting for you around the next season's corner. Sure, you can get your hands on any ingredient you want at any time of year if you're willing to shell out more money for inferior fruits and vegetables that have traveled from thousands of miles away. But I think that part of the fun of food is anticipating the next season. I get excited every year when I stroll into the market and all of a sudden there's locally grown corn piled high in a barrel at the end of the summer, or the fava beans, peas, and asparagus that signal winter has finally become spring.

This applies to fish, shellfish, livestock, and cattle as well as to fruits and vegetables. Just about every ingredient you can think of has a season, whether it's based on its natural cycle or on external factors. For example, diver scallops are most abundant from November through April. Because they're fed on grass, lamb and veal are considered spring foods; they're fed on hay in the winter, which makes for a less tasty product. True story: The most idiosyncratic and amusing season is halibut; it is scarce in the winter because so many of the Canadian fishermen have gone moose hunting.

A Passion for Seasonal Foods and Cooking

I wanted to write this cookbook for the same reasons I love to cook and eat—to celebrate the seasons and the ingredients they bring, and to show off the work of the farmers for whom I have developed such respect and affection over the years. Of course, I also want to do for you what some of the great chefs I worked with early in my career did for me: to inspire you to be the best cook you can be by sharing my love of cooking and some of the most important knowledge I've picked up along the way.

I love everything about cooking. I love the physical act of cooking. I love serving people and seeing them take satisfaction in the food I've made. I love creating original dishes. But I'm not looking to reinvent the wheel; I take as much pleasure in cooking steak and roasted potatoes for me and my wife at home as I do in preparing an elaborate tasting menu for eight people in a restaurant.

I also love to eat, and the foods I appreciate run the gamut from simple to complex. My taste leans toward two primary ingredients in balance, like peanut butter and jelly sandwiches or a good martini with lots of olives. I also go wild for one perfect ingredient on its own, like sweet purple beets, late-summer tomatoes, or a prime, aged rib-eye steak. As for my favorite dishes, most of them are season-specific, like Striped Bass with Shell Beans and Garlic Kale (page 93) in the summer or Lamb Shanks with Mashed Parsnips, Caramelized Shallots, and Dried Cherries (page 305) in the winter. I'm fond of great red and white Burgundy and a sucker for homemade ice cream. Oh, and eggs. I can't get enough of eggs; they turn up over and over again in my cooking in dishes like Fettuccine "Carbonara" with Asparagus and Lemon Zest (page 20). I even offered shirred eggs on the lunch menu at JUdson Grill.

I'm proud of being a three-star New York City chef, but I'm not a food snob; there are recipes in this book based on my fond memories of such guilty pleasures as Pop-Tarts (Peach Jam Crostata, page 24) and fried chicken (Brined Fried Chicken, page 77). Like I say, you are what you cook, and these delicious, homey dishes are as much a part of my culinary identity as more sophisticated dishes such as the Black Sea Bass with a Lobster Champagne Broth, Lobster Dumplings, and Baby White Turnips (page 252) or the Muscovy Duck Breast with Creamy Polenta, Baby Spring Onions, and Black Pepper–Rhubarb Compote (page 67).

I believe that anyone can learn to cook great food. You don't have to have spent a childhood eating freshly netted lobsters in Brittany or wild boar killed by your grandfather in the hills of Tuscany. If you have some curiosity and are eager to learn about and try new ingredients and patiently improve your skills, both in the market and in the kitchen, there's no end to how good a cook you can become.

I'm living proof that this is true. As a teenager, my first job was stacking sandwiches in a delicatessen. My next was at a local Italian-American restaurant where we made eggplant parmigiana, veal piccata, fettuccine Alfredo, and other traditional dishes. It's safe to say that I became an expert on chicken francese.

Between high school and college, I landed the first of several jobs that would change my life. It was at Garfunkel's, which sounds like one of those generic American bierhaus-bistros. But Garfunkel's was something else altogether. It was run by some guys who had graduated from the Culinary Institute of America and were trying very hard to do something special. Their enthusiasm was contagious.

For some reason, it didn't occur to me to keep cooking at that point, and for a short time I studied engineering in college. But then I returned to Garfunkel's and all was right with the world. I was starting to get "the bug," the feeling that I, too, could become a professional chef. And that maybe I wanted to.

The Garfunkel's gang encouraged me to pursue cooking professionally; I applied to and was accepted by the Culinary Institute of America. I was pretty excited, until I told my mother the news. Cooking wasn't as glamorous then as it is today, and she was very concerned about my prospects. But I'm happy to report that she's come around. At the Culinary Institute (known to my fellow alums as the "CIA" or "the Culinary"), I learned all the formal basics in every area, from butchering to pastry. I took courses devoted to French, Italian, and Asian cuisine, as well as to nutrition, and American produce. There was even an experimental kitchen where we were encouraged to take new ideas out for a test drive.

When I graduated from the Culinary in 1987, I was incredibly fortunate: my first Manhattan job was at a restaurant that is now an institution but at that point was only three years old, Gotham Bar and Grill. Working under Alfred Portale, I spent time at every station on the line. This was a wonderful continuation of my education, and I also found strength in the fact that the kitchen team was made up of exclusively American cooks. It's no big deal today, but in those days the prevailing wisdom was that you had to be French to be a great cook. Seeing that Americans could do what I wanted to do was invaluable. And not only were these guys cooks; every single one of them wanted to be a chef. Have you ever heard women athletes describe how Billie Jean King inspired them by beating Bobby Riggs in the "Battle of the Sexes" back in the 1970s? Well, that's how it felt to see a kitchen full of ambitious American cooks in the late 1980s. It was inspiring and empowering.

At the Gotham, Alfred thought about vegetables in a more specific way than any other chef I knew. Every dish had a well-thought-out accompaniment that wasn't only logical in taste but fit right into his famously beautiful presentations.

In 1990, I left Gotham to do what all of my peers still felt we had to do, even though we had kitchens full of compatriots to teach us: I went to France to apprentice with a great French chef. This would be the second job that changed my life, where lightning struck and I began to see things in a different way. At Alain Chapel's Michelin three-star restaurant in Mionnay, just north of Lyons, I first learned to appreciate the importance of cooking with locally grown, seasonal ingredients, like those magnificent strawberries I told you about earlier.

Chapel changed his menu every month. "This is what we have *now*," was his personal mantra. I worked with him for six months, so I was privileged to see him transition from the wintry foods of January to the late-spring and early-summer offerings of June.

Chapel's entire way of life was a revelation to me, from the small food stands where he shopped for his restaurant to the fresh-cut flowers he and his wife arranged around the dining room every day of the week.

When I returned to New York, I went to work at the four-star seafood temple Le Bernardin under its founding chef, Gilbert Le Coze. There, I learned how wonderful fish could be if you purchased the best and let its natural beauty and flavor shine. From Le Bernardin, it was on to Le Cirque, where I spent five months working as saucier for the great Daniel Boulud. Daniel taught me two big lessons that I still think about all the time. The first was balance. Daniel was brilliant at offsetting acidity and sweetness with other complementary elements to make sure that no single flavor overwhelmed the dish. This could be achieved with little decisions, like how carrots were cooked to control their sweetness or adding sorrel to a sauce for an elusive herbaceous quality that was missing. If possible, his preference was to bring out each ingredient's natural flavor, a preference that he passed on to me.

Daniel also taught me a valuable lesson about the much-debated subject of presentation. He had a very simple slogan, "If it tastes good, it'll look good," and I've adopted that guiding principle. When I'm working up a new dish, I just worry about flavor—if the elements are sound, then by the time I get to plating it, it comes out looking just fine. Don't ask me why; all I know is that it works every time.

In 1991, I returned to Gotham Bar and Grill and became Alfred Portale's sous chef, a job I held for four years. This was another life-changing position: I started going to the Union Square Greenmarket, just two blocks from Gotham, every day it was open—my version, I guess, of Chapel's market visits.

In 1996, I became the executive chef at Ansonia on Manhattan's Upper West Side, where I had my first opportunity to develop my own menu. I began to try out my own dishes, focusing on the seasonal produce I loved so much, honing and improving them all the time.

I also got reviewed for the first time. This is a nerve-racking experience that can turn even the most confident chef into a warbling bundle of nerves. But it worked out all right. Ruth Reichl, who was the food critic for *The New York Times,* said that customers were "captivated" by the food, that "Mr. Telepan lets his ingredients dictate the terms of each plate," and that all of my dishes "honor the season." I don't know what put a bigger smile on my face, those comments or the fact that I was being called "Mr. Telepan" in *The New York Times.*

But it wasn't until I came to JUdson Grill in 1998 that I really found myself as a chef. During my years there, I continued to forge my own style, calling on all of the great produce available, keeping dishes simple and balanced, and cooking food guided by a combination of personal history and contemporary influence and inspiration.

A lot of the reviews we received at JUdson Grill talked about our devotion to seasonal produce and local farmers. In *New York* magazine, Hal Rubenstein said that I was "inspired by vegetables" and called my vegetable plate "the best in town." And Ms. Reichl, still writing at *The New York Times,* said that my food was "extremely eloquent" and "roars with flavor," and pointed out that "the secret of Mr. Telepan's cooking is in the quality of his products. He seems to have made an extraordinary commitment to freshness." Jonathan Gold, *Gourmet* magazine's New York restaurant critic at the time, wrote that my cooking is "grounded in an American classic but lifted beyond it by absolute devotion to the quality and sourcing of produce, the smack of sharp fragrance, and the confidence to exploit subtle variations in flavor and texture."

These observations still make me very happy. I think back to those strawberries, and all the farmers I'm proud to call my friends, and the family dishes and culinary traditions I'm carrying on, and feel like—in my own modest way—I'm keeping the faith.

Bill Telepan
New York City

BILL-OSOPHIES

When I think back on the great chefs I worked with early in my career, I remember each of them primarily for one or two major lessons. I don't think of myself as a chef-philosopher, but there are some strongly held ideas I've developed over the years. Here are the Top Ten:

1   *Ask questions.* I think it's important to question tradition whenever it doesn't make sense to you. Ask. "Why pepper?" Salt, I understand: it brings out the flavor of an ingredient. But I don't think pepper should automatically be used in every recipe; it adds a heat that can detract from other ingredients, especially delicate ones like eggs, spring vegetables, and light broths. Many of the recipes in this book don't include pepper.

   In the same spirit, I have an unusual method of cleaning mushrooms (see page 19), sometimes eschew the blanching of vegetables, and season meats after braising rather than before. I encourage you to take nothing for granted: read as much as you can, ask cooks questions at cooking demonstrations and by e-mail, try new things, and do what *you* think works best.

2   *Relax.* When cooking at home, don't worry about presentation. Keep things nice and simple. I don't worry too much about it at home, even with more formal dinners, and neither does any chef I know. Remember what Daniel Boulud taught me: if it tastes good, it'll look fine.

3   *Splurge for some extra equipment.* There are some basic kitchen tools that you should have on hand. For example, I call for a ricer in many places throughout the book. Now, you might not own a ricer, but it can make a big difference in the quality of the finished dish. One can be bought for about ten dollars.

4   *Know what you like and cook what you love.* Cook the food you remember most fondly and crave most often. My favorites? A dish of summer berries, a Warm Carrot Pudding with Milk Chocolate (page 35), a menu of Grilling, Italian Style (pages 109–115), and all the recipes based on recollections of my mother's home cooking. Those are all things that I simply adore. Morel and Spring Onion Toasts (page 18), was inspired by how much I love mopping up the sauce on a plate with a piece of bread.

5 *Find techniques you can use over and over.* I can't remember the first time I used Parmigiano-Reggiano cheese as a more full-flavored alternative to salt for seasoning, or mascarpone in place of ricotta, or discovered the benefits of brining meats and poultry. But I use all of those in my cooking so often that they've become a part of my own personal style.

6 *If it ain't broke, don't fix it.* The food in contemporary restaurants is so adventurous that many home cooks are ashamed to make good old-fashioned recipes. But there are times when there's nothing better, or more appropriate. For example, my Thanksgiving menu (pages 262–77) almost exclusively features traditional recipes like Brussels Sprouts with Bacon (page 264), Glazed Carrots and Pearl Onions (page 266), and Cranberry-Orange Sauce (page 269), because that's what we want to eat on Thanksgiving. Don't feel as if you need to be inventive every time you step into the kitchen.

7 *Follow your bliss.* The great scholar of mythology Joseph Campbell coined the phrase "follow your bliss" to describe his belief that you should pursue whatever appeals to you on a gut level. This applies to cooking as well. For example, there are a number of Italian-influenced recipes in the book that I developed without ever visiting Italy. I became interested in Italian food, read a lot about it, talked to Italian chefs, and found that I had absorbed enough information to cook in that style.

8 *Appreciate the simple things.* Cooking doesn't have to mean turning out a three-course dinner. Some of the most pleasurable cooking can be as easy as preserving summer fruits and vegetables, which I describe on pages 157–63. It can also be as easy as not cooking at all, just savoring a perfect apple, pear, or tomato.

9 *Fear nothing.* This is the corollary to numbers 7 and 8. Cooking can and should be simple and fun. But if you're intrigued by something as ambitious as a Foie Gras Terrine (page 182), then buy the ingredients, read the recipe carefully, turn off the ringer on the phone, and go for it. It's just another recipe. It may ask you to do more than you usually do, but—trust me—you can handle it.

10 *Cook for others.* Finally, I think there's nothing more important when cooking for others than to really try to please your guests. I'm not a vegetarian, but I've included several vegetarian menus because you should be able to make something delicious

for anyone. I'm used to cooking food for others in my restaurant. But I also do the same thing at home, like with the make-ahead Pasta with Mushrooms, Arugula, and Peas (page 82), a homemade TV dinner I make for my wife, Beverly, all the time, leaving it for her to reheat and enjoy while I'm off working. She loves it, and—even though I never get to eat it myself—I love making it for her. That's what cooking is all about.

YOUR OWN PURCHASING DEPARTMENT

If you do a lot of cooking, you should shop around the same way I do. Even though you don't have dozens of purveyors to choose from, you do have a choice.

Visit each of the markets in your community that has a good reputation and check out what it seems to do best. Make a mental note, and next time you're thinking of cooking a recipe using that category of food, give it a try. Before long, you'll find that you know all the best places in town to shop: who has the freshest fish; who really knows how to butcher meat and honors rather than resents special requests; who sells farm-fresh eggs; and who has the best locally grown tomatoes.

If that sounds like more of a time commitment than you're inclined to make, then pick one good market. If I were going to depend on just one market, I'd be looking for the following signs: friendly and knowledgeable employees; produce and meat departments that are replenished and cleaned throughout the day; and no inferior specimens hiding at the bottom of a bin. Your market should take as much pride in its meat and produce as you do in your cooking.

Do this and you'll find that your cooking has instantly improved, because you'll have a new team of prep cooks helping you create great dishes in your own kitchen.

How to Use This Book

In this book, we'll spend a year cooking together, reveling in the fresh foods that come around every few months and creating menus for specific occasions. I've taken this approach for the simple reason that many of the home cooks I meet find menu planning stressful and mystifying. In the introduction to each menu, I've shared the logic behind each meal to help you put your own menus together.

Chapters

The book is divided into five recipe chapters, one for each season and one of "Dishes for All Seasons." Within each chapter there are several menus: three themed menus, a special occasion menu, and a make-ahead menu. There are also recipes grouped by ingredient or technique, like peas in the spring, preserving in the summer, and cabbage in the winter. Profiles of some of my favorite farmers and suppliers are scattered throughout, near recipes or groups of recipes that remind me of them.

Recipes

Although most of the recipes in the book are part of a menu, they can (and should!) be served individually or with other dishes from the book or from your own repertoire.

EDIBLE FLOWERS
CALENDULA: SWEET FLAVOR: YELLOW/ORANGE
BORAGE: PRETTY PURPLE
NASTURTIUM: SPICY FLAVOR
CHAMOMILE: TEA · DECORATIVE
DILL FLOWER: YELLOW · SPICY
FEVERFEW: DRY FOR TEA

FRESH ~ HERBS ~ FRESH
BASIL ~ SAUCES · PESTO · TOMATOES
CHERVIL ~ PARSLEY LIKE · SOUPS · SALADS
CHIVES ~ ONION FLAVOR ·
CHAMOMILE DRY FLOWER · TEA ·
CILANTRO ~ SALSA · COLD SALADS ·
DILL ~ SOUPS · FISH · PICKLES
LEMON BALM / LEMON FLAVOR · TEA
LOVAGE ~ SOUPS · STEWS ·
MINT ~ DESSERTS · TEA · DRINKS
OREGANO ~ MEAT DISHES, SAUCES
PARSLEY ~ SOUPS, VEGETABLES
SAGE ~ STUFFING, SAUSAGE
SAVORY ~ BEANS, SALADS ·
TARRAGON ~ FISH, VINEGARS
THYME ~ SAUCES, MARINADES
ROSEMARY ~ VEGETABLES, LAMB

Ingredients

A number of the ingredients I use most often come in a number of forms: salted and unsalted, bleached and unbleached, coarse or fine, fresh or dried. Unless otherwise stated, here's what I mean when I call for the following:

Butter is unsalted butter, sometimes called sweet cream butter.

Cream is heavy cream, also sold as whipping cream.

Eggs are large and preferably organic.

Flour is unbleached, all-purpose flour.

Herbs such as basil, chervil, parsley, and thyme are fresh. Bay leaves are dried.

Milk is whole milk.

Salt is fine sea salt, not to be confused with iodized table salt.

Sugar is granulated sugar.

Wine

Following each recipe, you'll find a wine recommendation from Beth von Benz, who was the wine director at JUdson Grill and Ansonia. I love Beth's passion for wine and her tireless effort to constantly learn about new ones. At JUdson, she managed a list of more than three hundred wines and received an Award of Excellence from *Wine Spectator* magazine. She's been pairing wines with my food for more than ten years, so I can't think of a better person to advise you in this area. As with a meal at the restaurant, if you follow her advice, your experience will be significantly enhanced.

A NOTE FROM
THE WINE DIRECTOR

I worked with Bill in two restaurants for more than a decade. As you are about to discover, his food is an ideal vehicle for wine. The fresh, clean-flavored ingredients he uses, and will encourage you to use in the pages that follow, are a sommelier's dream come true.

Just as Bill has nurtured relationships with the upstate "mushroom man" or heirloom tomato farmer, my wine list favors the "little guy," the lesser-known winemaker who makes a limited number of cases of so-called boutique product. Many of the wines I recommend hail from out-of-the-way places or hard-to-find producers. Again, just as it's worth a special visit to a roadside farm stand or greenmarket, I feel that these wines are worth the effort it may take to find them. And thanks to Internet wine shops and relaxed wine laws, it's not as difficult as it once was to obtain these gems.

But if you cannot find a recommended wine, look for another from the same country, or region when indicated. Or simply convey my description to your wine merchant and ask her to help you make an informed substitution. Tell her what dish you plan to serve it with and watch the wheels start turning in her head; wine merchants love to play sommelier.

As I do in restaurants, I have shied away from big, rich, fruit-driven, oaky wines when pairing with food. The wines suggested have a cleaner, more elegant style that does not overwhelm the often delicate flavors of Bill's dishes.

A few hints on pairing wine with food. When a particular wine is used as an ingredient in cooking, pour that same wine at the table. And always remember that wine is meant to be an enjoyable component of the total dining experience. Moreover, it is part of the *everyday* dining experience. Therefore, most of the wines I recommend represent a very good value; you will find no famous châteaux or domaines listed, nor any prized vintages. On my many wine trips to Europe, some of the most memorable food matches have been with some of the simplest wines.

Bottom line: The wine suggestions are included in this book as a guideline. Use them if you can find them, but substitute accordingly. Enjoy yourself.

—*Beth von Benz*

Spring

o me, the first day of spring isn't March 21. It's not the first day that sunny, blue skies reappear over New York City and roller skaters and joggers fill the streets and paths that run through Central Park. It's not even Easter Sunday, when my daughter hunts for pastel-painted Easter eggs in the grass.

No, my seasons begin when their first ingredients show up at my kitchen door. So for me, the first day of spring is the day that the first crate of morels arrives from Oregon, the mushrooms still lightly caked with the dirt from which they were foraged. Like other spring vegetables, these cone-shaped, honeycombed mushrooms appear as the snow thaws into the softening earth and the sun shines warm for the first time since last year. After morels come the intense wild leeks called ramps, followed in quick succession by watercress, peas, asparagus, nettles, and fiddlehead ferns.

This happy little parade of green signals it's time to shift culinary gears. I love root vegetables, but by the end of winter I feel as if I've got them coming out of my ears. It's also nice, after a season of slow roasting, stewing, and braising, to do some quick cooking again. When there's so much to be enjoyed outside—perhaps including the food itself—even a passionate chef like me doesn't want to spend too much time in the kitchen. A brisk sauté or blanching takes asparagus and peas from raw to perfectly cooked, leaving all of their natural flavor and color intact.

First Signs of Spring

Morel and Spring Onion Toasts

Fettuccine "Carbonara" with Asparagus and Lemon Zest

Peach Jam Crostata

This menu features spring onions and morel mushrooms, two of my favorite early-spring arrivals, and also relies heavily on fresh herbs and lemon zest, which are not, strictly speaking, seasonal but feel springlike to me because they're so light and fragrant.

But the Most Valuable Player in this menu isn't light at all. In fact, it's heavy cream, which contributes to and unites the savory dishes in important ways. In the Morel and Spring Onion Toasts (page 18), cream is the only source of body, rounding out the other flavors and making the dish feel substantial. In the main course, Fettuccine "Carbonara" with Asparagus and Lemon Zest (page 20), a variation on the classic Italian pasta, bacon, and egg dish, the cream is both a conduit for and complement to the egg's richness.

The dessert, a Peach Jam Crostata (page 24), is something I start craving on the first warm day of the year. Based on a supermarket pastry treat that I used to eat right out of the box as a child, it strikes me as the perfect spring dessert, because this season never fails to reawaken childhood memories and appetites.

Morel and Spring Onion Toasts

SERVES 4

orel mushrooms are one of the truest spring ingredients. I love them for their one-of-a-kind appearance, meaty texture, and deep, nutty flavor. In addition to finding a signature way to celebrate morel mushrooms, this dish grew out of an old habit I've never outgrown: using a piece of bread to mop up the sauce on a plate after the other food is gone. Here, the toast is already on the plate, so if you're like me in this regard, you don't have to be shy about it. It also uses one of my favorite effects: arranging greens alongside something warm that causes them to wilt just the slightest bit, almost melting them into the other ingredients.

In the market, seek out morel mushrooms so dry that they feel like little stones. Because they are especially sensitive to temperature and moisture, morels are often kept in the refrigerated section of the market. When storing morels, or any mushrooms, moisture is the enemy, especially after cleaning (see page 19). To protect them, line a plate with several layers of paper towels, set the mushrooms on the paper, and wrap them tautly with plastic wrap but do not crush them. Perforate the plastic with a fork. The mushrooms should stay dry in the refrigerator for up to three days.

If you can't find fresh morels, it's okay to use dried, which, because they reconstitute so well, are the only dried mushrooms I eat.

2 tablespoons butter	1 cup cream
1 medium shallot, minced	4 slices sourdough bread, 1/3 inch thick, 3 by 3 inches
8 ounces morel mushrooms, bottoms trimmed, larger ones halved, washed	1 tablespoon sherry vinegar
1 bunch ramps, root trimmed, white part cut to 3 inches, green portion thinly sliced and set aside separately (see page 19)	3 tablespoons extra-virgin olive oil
	Freshly ground black pepper
Salt	2 cups mesclun greens

1   Preheat the oven to 350°F.

2   Melt the butter in a sauté pan set over medium heat. Add the shallot and cook, stirring occasionally, until softened but not browned, about 5 minutes. Add the morels and white portions of the ramps, season with a pinch of salt, and cook, stirring occasionally, until softened but not browned, about 8 minutes.

3   Add the cream to the pan, stir, and cook over medium heat for 8 minutes while you toast the bread and make the vinaigrette.

4   Set the bread slices directly on the center rack of the oven and bake until crisp and lightly browned on both sides, about 5 minutes.

5   Pour the vinegar into a large bowl. Whisk in the olive oil and season with salt and pepper. Add the greens to the bowl, toss well, and set aside.

6   To serve, divide the greens among four salad plates. Place 1 slice of toast atop the greens on each plate. Stir the green parts of the ramps into the mushroom mixture and spoon some mushrooms and cream over the bread.

RAMPS

Ramps, or wild leeks, look a lot like scallions, but they are available for only a few weeks every spring. Don't be fooled by their wispy, frail appearance; they have a pleasingly powerful onion flavor that makes quite an impact.

SOURDOUGH BREAD

Tart sourdough bread brings more personality to a dish than lighter, fluffier choices. Here, the sourdough's density lets it soak up an incredible amount of sauce.

CLEANING MUSHROOMS

To clean morels and other mushrooms, I use an unusual method that removes any dirt that may have found its way into the mushroom's crevices. Put cold water in a bowl, add the mushrooms, and quickly shake the bowl to agitate the mushrooms, then remove them by hand to a colander or strainer. Repeat once or twice to loosen and remove any hidden dirt. If not using them immediately, gently pat them dry with paper towels or a clean kitchen towel.

Wine

Match the creamy mushroom notes in this starter with a white Burgundy; try a Meursault or a single-vineyard Mâcon Milly-Lamartine from Comtes Lafon.

Fettuccine "Carbonara" with Asparagus and Lemon Zest

SERVES 4

ne of my favorite ingredients is eggs, and one of my favorite ways to enjoy them is in a decadent pasta carbonara, where a raw egg is tossed in right before serving and just barely cooked by the heat of the pasta, coating the noodles with rich flavor and texture. In this variation, the voluptuous egg is offset by asparagus and lemon zest, lighter alternatives to the original's bacon. The strips of green asparagus and white fettuccine are the same size and shape, making a tangle of color when tossed.

I use a lot of asparagus every spring, but I must say that I value it as much for the crunch it brings to a dish as for its flavor. When I can, I use small asparagus that I get from Ray and Sue Dare, the farmers profiled on page 124. In this recipe, we use the entire vegetable, including the peelings, which help infuse the sauce with a green, spring flavor.

When shopping for asparagus, test them by bending them. You don't want to break your grocer's asparagus, but you want to have the impression that the stalk would snap if you applied enough pressure. If you pinch asparagus, they should be firm; softness indicates age.

To store asparagus, cut half an inch off the bottoms and stand them up in half an inch of water in a cylindrical vessel in the refrigerator as you would a bouquet of flowers. They will keep this way for three or four days. The "bouquet" is such an appropriate greeting when you open your refrigerator in the spring.

(continued)

12 ounces large asparagus stalks (about 8 stalks), bottoms trimmed, peeled, and peelings reserved separately

1 cup cream

2 tablespoons cold butter, cut into small cubes

Salt

Freshly ground black pepper

Egg Fettuccine (recipe follows), or ½ pound store-bought dried fettuccine

Zest of 1 lemon, chopped

2 eggs, beaten (see Note)

2 teaspoons chopped flat-leaf parsley

2 teaspoons chopped chervil leaves

2 teaspoons chopped chives

2 teaspoons chopped tarragon leaves

½ cup tightly packed mixed herb leaves (parsley, chervil, tarragon, and/or ½-inch chive segments)

Freshly grated Parmigiano-Reggiano cheese, optional

1 Put the asparagus peelings and cream in a medium-size pot. Set the pot over high heat and bring the cream to a boil, being careful to not let it boil over. Immediately remove the pot from the heat and let rest for 30 minutes to let the asparagus flavor infuse the cream.

2 Bring a pot of lightly salted water to a boil. Fill a large bowl halfway with ice water.

3 Return the cream to high heat and bring it to a boil again, then immediately remove the pot from the heat and strain its contents through a fine-mesh strainer set over a bowl, pressing down on the peelings with a wooden spoon to extract as much flavorful liquid as possible. Discard the peelings. Whisk the butter into the asparagus cream, 1 piece at a time, season to taste with salt and pepper, and set aside, covered, to keep warm.

4 Add the asparagus stalks to the boiling water and blanch until tender, 3 to 5 minutes. Remove the stalks from the water using tongs or a slotted spoon and plunge them into the ice water for 2 minutes to stop the cooking and preserve their bright green color. (Leave the boiling water on the stove; you can use it to cook the fettuccine.) Remove the stalks from the ice water and pat them dry with paper towels.

5 Lay 1 asparagus stalk in front of you on a cutting board. Holding the top inch of the stalk in your hand, use a vegetable peeler to shave it into fettuccine-like strips, then quarter the 1-inch piece in your hand and set the tips aside in a small bowl. Repeat with the remaining stalks, gathering the strips in one bowl and the quartered tips in the other.

6   Add the fettuccine to the boiling water and cook until al dente, 2 to 3 minutes for fresh, 8 to 10 minutes for dried. Drain the fettuccine and turn it out into a wide, deep sauté pan. Add the infused cream, asparagus strips, and lemon zest to the pan, and set the pan over low heat. Bring the cream to a simmer and toss well. Remove the pan from the heat, immediately add the eggs, season with salt and pepper, and toss. Toss in the chopped parsley, chervil, chives, and tarragon.

7   To serve, divide the pasta among four warm dinner plates. Add the quartered asparagus tips to the pan, set the pan over medium heat, and sauté for 1 minute to reheat them. Spoon the asparagus tips over the fettuccine and top with the whole herb leaves. Serve at once, passing the grated cheese alongside, if desired.

NOTE: Eating raw eggs carries the risk of salmonella. Foods containing raw eggs should not be eaten by the very young, the very old, pregnant women, or anyone with a compromised immune system.

Wine

An herbaceous, grassy sauvignon blanc is a perfect accompaniment to the asparagus. Pick one from California (but no oak, please). Or, for a creamier style to match the fettuccine and lemon, turn to the Mason sauvignon blanc from Napa.

Egg Fettuccine

MAKES ½ POUND FETTUCCINE

I grew up eating egg noodles. I love them because they have more body and flavor than semolina pasta and taste more like home to me. I also find that they have the all-too-rare ability to enhance a dish without distracting from the other ingredients. These are one of the treasured personal favorites that I want to share with my customers, and they've always been present in one dish or another in every restaurant where I've had final say on the menu.

4 teaspoons butter	¼ teaspoon salt
1½ cups flour	1 whole egg plus 4 egg yolks

(continued)

1   Crumble the butter, flour, and salt between your fingers into a bowl, breaking the bits into a coarse meal.

2   In a small bowl, beat the whole egg and yolks with 1 tablespoon cold water. Form a well in the middle of the flour mixture and pour the eggs into the well. Incorporate the eggs by stirring in the flour mixture from the sides of the well a little at a time. If the dough is too dry and begins to crumble, add some more water. When most of the flour has been mixed in, form the dough into a ball, transfer it to a clean flat surface, and knead for 10 minutes.

3   Wrap the dough in plastic wrap and chill in the refrigerator for 1 hour.

4   Use a pasta machine to roll the dough to a ¹⁄₁₆-inch thickness, then cut it into fettuccine strips. (If you don't have a pasta machine, use a rolling pin to roll the dough to the desired thickness, then cut fettuccine strips with a knife or pizza cutter.) Lay the noodles out on a cookie sheet and let them dry for 15 minutes. Cook within a few minutes, or refrigerate by wrapping the entire cookie sheet in plastic wrap and refrigerating it for up to 2 days.

Peach Jam Crostata

SERVES 4

first served this at a JUdson Grill special event, where it went over very well. But I didn't tell anyone my secret inspiration for the dish: Pop-Tarts. As a child, I ate them all the time. I ate every flavor. I ate the ones with frosting and the ones without. I ate them toasted and I ate them cold. This crostata, a classic Italian dessert pastry, is easy to make, with a crust that's dense yet flaky, just like the one I snacked on as a kid. Keep in mind that using homemade or good-quality commercial jams or preserves is a good shortcut to capture the essence of a season.

10 tablespoons (1 stick plus 2 tablespoons) butter	Grated zest of ½ lemon
⅓ cup sugar	2 eggs
Pinch of salt	1¾ cups flour, plus more for dusting work surface
½ teaspoon vanilla extract	1 cup peach jam

1 Preheat the oven to 400°F.

2 Put the butter and sugar in the bowl of an electric mixer fitted with the paddle attachment. Add the salt, vanilla, and lemon zest, and paddle until incorporated. Add 1 egg and paddle just to combine. Slowly add the flour and paddle until crumbly. Turn the dough out onto a lightly floured surface and knead briefly using the palm of your hand. Pat the dough into 2 flat pieces, wrap them in plastic wrap, and chill in the refrigerator for 1 hour.

3 Set a 10-inch flan or tart ring with a removable bottom by your work surface. Dust your hands with a little flour, and roll out 1 piece of dough into a circle, 11 inches in diameter.

4 Lay the dough in the bottom, but not up the sides, of the flan ring and trim it to fit. Spread the jam over the surface of the dough, leaving a ½-inch border of undressed dough all around. Beat the remaining egg lightly and combine with 1 tablespoon of cold water in a small bowl. Roll out the second piece of dough into an 11 by 6-inch rectangle. With a paring knife or rolling cutter, cut six ¾-inch strips from the rectangle. Lay 3 strips across the filling, leaving room for the jam to peek through. Lay the remaining 3 strips at a diagonal to the bottom strips, to form a lattice. Roll the remaining dough into a rope about 20 inches long. Place the rolled dough around the edge of the crostata, flush to the tart ring. Press it down with your fingers to flatten it. Brush the strips and edge with egg wash.

5 Bake the crostata until golden, about 25 minutes. Remove from the oven and let cool. Remove from the pan and serve warm or at room temperature within 24 hours.

Wine

Emphasize the fruit in this dessert by serving it with an American vidal blanc grape with ripe, peachy notes such as the Sakonnet *eiswein* (literally, ice wine) from Rhode Island. Yes, you heard right: Rhode Island.

A Simple but Satisfying Spring Menu

Mixed Beet Salad with Buttermilk-Chive Dressing and Purslane

Maine Halibut with Herb-Caper Oil, Warm Cucumbers, and Red Onion

Warm Carrot Pudding with Milk Chocolate

Generally speaking, spring cooking can and should be quick. Here's a three-course menu you can pull together in about an hour, not including the time it takes to marinate the fish.

In many ways, the dishes that follow trick the palate, telling it delicious white lies. Because they're so small, the baby beets in the Mixed Beet Salad with Buttermilk-Chive Dressing and Purslane (page 27) roast in half an hour or less but have the same depth of flavor as fully grown beets. Similarly, the technique for roasting the fish fillets in the Maine Halibut with Herb-Caper Oil, Warm Cucumbers, and Red Onion (page 31)—first marinating the fillets with fresh herbs—produces a flaky texture and herbaceous flavor that is as full as that of whole roasted fish stuffed with herbs.

This very light meal really needs dessert to feel complete. Warm Carrot Pudding with Milk Chocolate (page 35) will satisfy any lingering appetite.

Mixed Beet Salad with Buttermilk-Chive Dressing and Purslane

SERVES 4

'm so fond of beets' sweet bite and beautiful deep-purple color that whenever I meet people who don't like them, I'm baffled. I usually assume that they must never have had a fresh one and are basing their opinion on canned beets or store-bought pickled beets.

Full-grown beets are the stuff of fall, but baby beets belong to spring. I look forward to them every year. When they're small, they're extra-sweet, like little candy drops, and are perfect for roasting, boiling, or pickling. This dish perfectly balances them with tangy buttermilk tinged with lemon and a drizzle of olive oil.

In the market, beets should be rock-hard, not the least bit spongy. If you can, buy them with the tops intact; the greens are beautiful, crunchy, and edible, and you can use them in my Beet Greens Pierogi with Mixed Summer Beets, Brown Butter Sauce, and Ricotta Salata (page 139), or cook them like the Swiss chard on page 69.

If you've never eaten purslane, please don't be put off by the fact that, technically, it's a weed. Thick-branched, the leaves have a waxy texture that gives way to a watery burst when you bite into them and a mildly lemony flavor, the perfect contrast to the sweet beets and creamy dressing.

4 bunches baby beets (ideally 4 each of small white, chioggia, golden, and red beets, but any combination, or just one type, is fine), tops and bottoms trimmed

¼ cup olive oil

Salt

Freshly ground black pepper

¼ cup buttermilk

2 tablespoons freshly squeezed lemon juice

2 tablespoons thinly sliced chives

2 ounces (about 2 cups loosely packed) purslane or baby greens

2 tablespoons extra-virgin olive oil

(continued)

1   Preheat the oven to 450°F.

2   Put each type of beet in a separate baking pan. Drizzle each pan with 1 tablespoon of the olive oil and 3 tablespoons water, and season lightly with salt and pepper. (If using just one type of beet, put them all in one pan and drizzle with all of the oil and 9 tablespoons water.)

3   Cover each pan with aluminum foil and roast the beets until they are tender when pierced with a sharp, thin-bladed knife, 25 to 30 minutes, depending on type. As each type of beet is done, remove its pan from the oven and set aside to let the beets cool.

4   Pour the buttermilk and lemon juice into a small bowl. Add the chives, whisk, season with salt, and whisk again. Set aside.

5   When the beets are cool, peel by rubbing them with a clean, dry kitchen towel; the skins should come right off. Quarter the beets lengthwise.

6   In a medium bowl, dress the purslane with 1 tablespoon of the extra-virgin olive oil and sprinkle it with salt. Add the beets to the bowl with the purslane.

7   To serve, spoon a shallow pool of dressing over the surface of four salad plates. Pile an assortment of beets and purslane in the center of each plate on top of the dressing. Drizzle the remaining tablespoon olive oil around the edges of plates.

Wine

A Loire Valley sauvignon blanc would pair well with the beet and purslane in this salad.
Or try the Hubert Lamy Saint-Aubin "La Princée."

Maine Halibut
with Herb-Caper Oil,
Warm Cucumbers,
and Red Onion

SERVES 4

his preparation imitates the delicate, flaky flesh and herbaceous flavor produced by roasting a whole fish but does it in less time and eliminates the need to carve around the bones when you're done cooking. The technique couldn't be easier: fillets are marinated, then oil is rubbed into the flesh before roasting the fish on a bed of herbs.

I developed this recipe to use cucumbers as a cooked vegetable; they're unusual and delicious. Buy unblemished cucumbers that aren't soft or mushy. Before peeling cucumbers, cut about ½ inch off each end; the ends are bitter, and if you drag a peeler across them, you'll draw the bitterness across as well. Check out how the lemon juice really perks up their flavor and ties all the components together.

8 sprigs rosemary

8 sprigs thyme

8 sprigs flat-leaf parsley

4 skinless halibut fillets, 6 ounces each

Extra-virgin olive oil

Salt

2 tablespoons butter

½ medium red onion, ends trimmed, thinly sliced lengthwise

1 hothouse cucumber or large regular cucumber, peeled, halved lengthwise, seeds or soft center scooped and discarded, and cut crosswise into ¼-inch slices

¼ cup Vegetable Stock (page 344) or water

1 tablespoon freshly squeezed lemon juice, plus ½ lemon for squeezing

1 tablespoon finely sliced chives

1 tablespoon minced flat-leaf parsley

Herb-Caper Oil (recipe follows)

(continued)

1   Arrange half the rosemary, thyme, and parsley sprigs on a baking sheet. Put the fish fillets, skinned side down, on top of the herbs. Scatter the remaining herb sprigs over the fish. Cover the fish with plastic wrap, molding the wrap around the fish to keep it moist, and gently press the herbs into the flesh. Place the fish in the refrigerator and chill for at least 1 hour and up to 4 hours.

2   Preheat the oven to 450°F.

3   Remove the fish from the refrigerator and let come to room temperature, about 15 minutes.

4   Remove the plastic wrap from the fish. Remove the herbs from above and below the fillets and set aside. Rub 1 teaspoon olive oil into each side of the fillets and season both sides with salt. Spread all of the herbs on the baking sheet and place the fillets on the herb bed in a single layer. Roast until just opaque in the center, 10 to 15 minutes, depending on the thickness of the fillets (pry apart the flesh on 1 fillet to check for doneness). Squeeze some lemon juice over the fillets as soon as they come out of the oven; this is when they will take on the most flavor.

5   Meanwhile, cook the cucumber: Melt the butter in a sauté pan set over medium-low heat. Add the onion, season with salt, cover, and cook until softened but not browned, about 5 minutes. Raise the heat to high, add the cucumber, and sauté for 2 minutes. Pour in the stock and cook until reduced and the vegetables are nicely glazed, 2 to 3 minutes. Add the lemon juice, chives, and parsley, and season to taste with salt. Remove the pan from the heat and set aside, covered, to keep warm.

6   To serve, divide the cucumber and onion mixture among four dinner plates, mounding it in the center. Top each mound with a fish fillet. Drizzle Herb-Caper Oil over and around the fish and vegetables on each plate. Serve at once.

Wine

An Italian wine with character and Mediterranean flavor would be a classic pairing with the capers and herbs in this dish. If you can find it, try the Furore bianco from Marissa Cuomo, a falanghina from the Amalfi coast.

HALIBUT

Halibut flesh should be pale white. If it looks snowy white, it's either been stored in a lot of ice or actually frozen, and it will fall apart when cooked.

Herb-Caper Oil

This oil would be delicious with any white-fleshed fish, and is also wonderful with chicken and pork.

2 teaspoons finely chopped flat-leaf parsley

2 teaspoons finely chopped chives

1½ teaspoons finely chopped chervil leaves

1 teaspoon finely chopped tarragon leaves

2 teaspoons finely chopped shallot

2 teaspoons capers, rinsed and drained

2 anchovy fillets, rinsed

¼ teaspoon minced garlic

¼ cup extra-virgin olive oil

Salt

1 Put the parsley, chives, chervil, tarragon, and shallot in a small bowl.

2 Finely chop the capers, anchovies, and garlic together on a cutting board, then mash them together with the side of a large, wide-bladed knife to form a paste. Add the paste to the bowl with the herbs and shallot.

3 Slowly whisk in the olive oil. Taste and add salt if necessary; the anchovies and capers may be salty enough. This can be made ahead on the day you plan to serve it. Cover tightly and store in the refrigerator. Let come to room temperature before using.

RON BINAGHI

Ron Binaghi is the fifth generation of his family to run Stokes Farm, which has been operating on eighteen acres of land in Bergen County, New Jersey, since the 1870s. Because it's only twenty-four miles from the Union Square Greenmarket (you can see the Empire State Building from the farmhouse), it has the distinction of being the closest farm to New York City in any direction. Like so many of the farmers who supply New York City restaurants, Ron's family grew very basic vegetables when he was a kid—tomatoes, peppers, eggplant. Heirloom tomatoes and Thai basil weren't even in the family vocabulary.

Today, it's just the opposite. "We specialize in anything that's different," says Ron. In particular, the family grows forty unusual herbs, from Vietnamese cilantro to Texas tarragon to black peppermint (which, by the way, is the herb that makes Altoids mints curiously strong).

Ron treasures the relationship he and his Greenmarket customers enjoy. "There are old ladies there who have literally watched me grow up during their weekly visits," he reminisces. He also loves bringing food to the people in this concrete jungle: "These customers depend on us," he says. Then, after a thoughtful pause, he adds, "I don't know how much they realize it, but we depend on them, too."

Warm Carrot Pudding
with Milk Chocolate

SERVES 4

ere's another personal memory that's been turned into a restaurant dish. Most carrot cakes have cream cheese frosting, but my mother's is topped off with chocolate icing, a variation that my siblings and I adore for the way the semisweet chocolate and subtly sweet carrots play off each other. This recipe takes that unusual combination and turns it into a pudding. Trust me, it's delicious.

1¾ cups thinly sliced carrots

¾ cup finely ground gingersnap crumbs

⅓ cup almond flour (see page 36)

8 tablespoons (1 stick) butter, softened at room temperature

¾ cup sugar

4 eggs, separated

¼ teaspoon salt

½ teaspoon ground cinnamon

⅓ cup grated carrots

2 tablespoons raisins

4 ounces semisweet chocolate

¾ cup sour cream

1 Preheat the oven to 375°F. Line the bottom of a 5-cup soufflé mold with a round of parchment or waxed paper.

2 Bring a pot of salted water to a boil over high heat. Add the sliced carrots and cook until very soft, about 15 minutes. Strain the carrots, transfer them to a blender, and puree. Set aside.

3 Stir the gingersnap crumbs and almond flour together in a bowl. Set aside.

4 In the bowl of an electric mixer fitted with the paddle attachment, cream the butter and ½ cup of the sugar until very light. Add the egg yolks one at a time, beating well after each addition. Add the crumb mixture, the salt, and cinnamon to the butter mixture. It should be very soft. Add 1 cup of the warm carrot puree and the grated carrots and mix to combine.

(continued)

5   Using a fresh bowl of an electric mixer, whip the egg whites to soft peaks on medium-high speed. Slowly add the remaining ¼ cup sugar and beat to a medium-stiff peak. (If beaten too stiffly, the whites will fall during steaming and your pudding will be too dense.) Fold a bit of the butter mixture into the whites, then fold the whites into the remaining butter mixture. Sprinkle the raisins over the surface of the mixture and fold lightly to incorporate. Evenly spread the carrot mixture into the soufflé mold.

6   Place a baking dish slightly larger than the soufflé mold into the oven. Loosely cover the mold with aluminum foil and put it in the center of the baking dish. Pour hot water to a depth of 2 inches around the soufflé mold. Steam the pudding in the oven until it springs back when gently touched, about 65 minutes. Take care when peeling back the foil to test for doneness. While the pudding steams, make the chocolate topping (Step 7).

7   Fill a small pot with water to a depth of 1 inch and bring to a simmer over medium heat. Chop the semisweet chocolate into corn flake–size pieces. Place the chocolate in a small mixing bowl and set the bowl over the pot of simmering water. When the chocolate has completely melted, remove the bowl from the heat and whisk in the sour cream, ¼ cup at a time. Set aside at room temperature.

8   Remove the pudding from the water bath and cool until warm. Run a knife or metal spatula around the edge of the pudding, flush to the mold. Place a serving dish over the top of the soufflé mold and invert. Peel away the parchment or waxed paper and discard. Serve immediately with the chocolate topping.

Wine

Serve this unusual dessert with a brown muscat from the Rutherglen area of Australia. A perfect selection for the carrot cake–like flavors and the chocolate in this pudding would be Campbell's Rutherglen Muscat, from Victoria.

ALMOND FLOUR

Almond flour is baker-speak for almonds that have been pulverized into a powder. For the ⅓ cup needed here, grind 30 to 35 whole almonds.

A Celebration of Lemons Menu

Carrot Soup with Maine Crabmeat, Carrot Slaw, and Dill Croutons

Marinated Poussin with Mâche and Radishes

Lemon Verbena Custard with Rhubarb Compote

If you find the prospect of putting a menu together daunting, one way to hedge your bets is to select one flavor to use in all of the courses of the meal to subtly unite them.

The following menu illustrates this principle, as lemon appears in every dish, though it doesn't dominate any of them. The slaw in the Carrot Soup with Maine Crabmeat, Carrot Slaw, and Dill Croutons (page 39) and the mâche salad in Marinated Poussin with Mâche and Radishes (page 41) are both dressed with creamy lemon dressing, one of my favorite condiments, and the dessert, Lemon Verbena Custard with Rhubarb Compote (page 45), also features lemon very prominently.

Carrot Soup with Maine Crabmeat, Carrot Slaw, and Dill Croutons

MAKES ABOUT 7 CUPS

his soup takes full advantage of the often overlooked sweetness of carrots, playing it off against sweet Maine crabmeat. It is best made with small carrots, which have a more sugary flavor than fully grown ones. When I say "small carrots," I'm not talking about large carrots cut into bite-size pieces and sold in a bag; I'm talking about medium carrots with their tops intact. But the real key to this soup's success is the addition of carrot juice at the end. If you don't have a juicer, get some from a heath food store, a juice bar, or even your gym, but don't leave it out.

The carrot slaw is delicious on its own or with cold shrimp; you will probably want to double the recipe. The croutons are versatile as well. You can use them to garnish almost any recipe where dill would be an appropriate addition or substitution; for example, in place of the garlic croutons in the Romaine Salad with Bacon and Garlic Croutons (page 180) or to embellish Braised Beef Short Rib Borscht with Horseradish Oil (page 327).

Carrot Slaw

1 cup packed grated carrots	Salt
¼ cup Creamy Lemon Vinaigrette (page 192)	Freshly ground black pepper

Put the carrots in a bowl. Drizzle the Creamy Lemon Vinaigrette over them, season with salt and pepper, stir well with a wooden spoon, cover, and chill in the refrigerator for 1 hour or overnight.

(continued)

Dill Croutons

3 or 4 slices sourdough bread, crusts removed, cut into ½-inch cubes (about ¾ cup cubes)

1 tablespoon chopped dill

2 tablespoons extra-virgin olive oil

Salt

1 Preheat the oven to 300°F.

2 Place the bread cubes on a cookie sheet in a single layer. Toast in the oven until the bread is completely dried but not browned, about 20 minutes.

3 In a bowl large enough to hold the croutons, stir together the dill and olive oil and season the mixture with salt.

4 When the croutons are crisp, remove them from the oven, transfer them to the bowl with the dill oil, and toss well. The croutons can be made up to 2 hours ahead of time and kept at room temperature.

Carrot Soup and Assembly

¾ pound carrots (3 to 5 small or medium carrots), thickly sliced crosswise

Salt

1 tablespoon olive oil

1 small leek, white and light green parts only, split lengthwise, thinly sliced crosswise, well washed in several changes of cold water, and drained

½ small onion, sliced

1 clove garlic, sliced

2 cups Vegetable Stock (page 344) or water

1½ cups carrot juice (see headnote)

¼ pound Maine crabmeat (Jonah or peekytoe), cold

4 sprigs dill

1 Put the carrots in a bowl and sprinkle with 1 teaspoon salt. Set aside to let the salt draw out the carrots' moisture while you begin making the soup.

2 Warm the olive oil in a 2-quart pot set over low heat. Add the leek, onion, and garlic, and season with salt. Cook until the vegetables are softened but not browned, about 7 minutes. Add the carrots, cover, and cook until they are tender but not browned, and they release their liquid, about 30 minutes. Pour in the stock, raise the heat to high, and bring the stock to a boil. Lower the heat and let simmer for 10 minutes.

3   Carefully transfer the contents of the pot to a blender or food processor fitted with the metal blade and puree; process in two or three batches. Transfer the soup to a bowl.

4   Stir, taste, and adjust seasoning if necessary. Let cool to room temperature, then cover and chill for at least 1 hour or for up to 4 days.

5   When ready to serve, stir the carrot juice into the soup.

6   To serve, divide the soup among four chilled bowls. Use a spoon or tongs to put some of the slaw in the middle of the soup. Top the slaw with some crabmeat and a sprig of dill. Scatter the croutons over the surface of the soup.

Wine

This dish needs something aromatic yet subtle enough not to overpower the delicate crab flavors. A viognier from the northern Rhône region, from the village of Condrieu, would be a good choice, as would a simple Vin de Pays d'Oc from Alain Paret.

Marinated Poussin with Mâche and Radishes

SERVES 4

âche, also known as lamb's tongue, is a beautiful, tender green with an appealing, bitter bite offset by just a hint of sweetness. These qualities are best appreciated when mâche is paired with something a bit crunchy and peppery, like the radishes here. When you buy mâche, make sure the leaves are standing up rather than wilting. It's my fervent hope that, in a few years, mâche will be more commonly available than it is today; until then, if you can't find it, substitute other baby greens or roughly chopped mesclun mix.

In keeping with the seasonal theme of this menu, I've used poussin, or spring chicken, for this dish. I originally developed it as a restaurant showcase for quail, and you could substitute eight quail for the four poussin. In either case, the deglazing of the pan with lemon juice just after the bird is cooked really picks up the flavors of the marinade and the roasted meat.

(continued)

2 lemons, halved crosswise and thinly sliced, plus 1 large lemon

4 cloves garlic, crushed and roughly chopped

1 tablespoon coriander seeds, crushed

1 tablespoon black peppercorns, crushed

8 sprigs parsley, roughly chopped

½ cup plus 2 tablespoons extra-virgin olive oil

4 boneless poussin, 10 to 12 ounces each, butterflied by your butcher or mail-ordered (8 boneless quail can be substituted)

½ cup canola or other vegetable oil

Salt

Freshly ground white pepper

2 tablespoons freshly squeezed lemon juice

½ pound mâche or mesclun greens

1 bunch radishes (about 8 radishes), washed and thinly sliced

¼ cup Creamy Lemon Vinaigrette (page 192)

1   In a small bowl, stir together the sliced lemons, garlic, coriader, peppercorns, parsley, and the ½ cup olive oil. Pour half of the marinade over the bottom of a large glass baking dish. Place the poussin in a single layer on top of the marinade. Drizzle the remaining marinade over the poussin. Cover the dish with plastic wrap and refrigerate for at least 4 hours or overnight.

2   When ready to proceed, preheat the oven to 450°F.

3   Segment the lemon: Cut off the top and bottom through to the flesh. Stand the lemon up on a cutting board and use a paring knife to cut from the top down to the flesh, removing the rind and pith in strips. Then, cut along the membrane dividing each segment to remove whole segments of lemon. Remove any seeds and cut each segment crosswise into 3 pieces. Set aside.

4   Warm the canola oil in a large overproof sauté pan set over high heat. Remove the poussin from the marinade and brush off as much of the marinade as possible. Season with salt and pepper. Place 2 of the poussin skin side down in the sauté pan and cook for 3 minutes until browned. Put the pan in the oven and roast for 10 minutes. Remove the pan from the oven, turn the poussin over, and fold the breast up over the legs. Continue to cook the legs for 2 minutes more on the stovetop over low to medium heat. Transfer the poussin to a plate and cover with aluminum foil to keep warm. Repeat with the 2 remaining poussin.

5   When the poussin are finished, drain and discard the oil from the pan. Return the pan to the stovetop over high heat, add the lemon segments and lemon juice, and gently scrape off any bits cooked onto the bottom of the pan. Add the 2 tablespoons olive oil, warm the contents of the pan, season with salt and pepper, and set aside.

6   In a small bowl, dress the mâche and radishes with the Creamy Lemon Vinaigrette and season with salt and pepper.

7   To serve, divide the mâche and radishes among four plates and top each serving with 1 poussin. Drizzle with the warm lemon juice and segments.

Wine

A white Priorat made from the Grenache grape (known as garnacha blanco in Spain) from an up-and-coming wine region just southwest of Barcelona has the body to stand up to the poussin and the acidity to blend with the lemon-spice notes. A favorite of ours is the Palacios Remondo Plácet Priorat Blanc. A simple Côtes-du-Rhône blanc would be delicious as well.

Lemon Verbena Custard
with Rhubarb Compote

SERVES 4

here's no surer sign of spring than the first neon-red stalks of rhubarb. When cooked right, it can be a source of simple perfection. Though it's actually a vegetable, we usually use rhubarb as a fruit, baking it into tarts and other desserts. Rhubarb is so tart that even in the rare savory dish, it needs to be sweetened.

As with asparagus, when shopping for rhubarb look for stalks that feel as if they would snap if you bent them. Don't be thrown by the look of local or organic rhubarb: it's green-to-red, as opposed to bright red, in color. This is perfectly fine; you'll get the same rhubarb flavor. Be very careful when cooking rhubarb; the pieces can turn to mush if you overcook them by even just a few seconds.

A natural for infusing milk and cream, lemon verbena also makes great ice cream, crème brûlée, and a dynamite flavored whipped cream topping for strawberries. Here, it's used in a cool, creamy lemon verbena custard that provides the perfect foil for the tart, acidic rhubarb compote, creating a dessert that, to my mind, is a high-class variation of yogurt with fruit on the bottom.

These custards will last for days covered in the refrigerator; I usually get a good four days' worth of snacking from one batch.

2 large stalks rhubarb, cut crosswise into 1/4-inch pieces (about 2 cups)	1½ cups milk
2/3 cup sugar	4 lemon verbena leaves, or 1 lemon verbena tea bag
Pinch of ground cinnamon	1 whole egg plus 3 egg yolks
1/4 cup freshly squeezed orange juice	

1   Put the rhubarb, 1/3 cup of the sugar, the cinnamon, and the orange juice in a small non-reactive saucepan. Cook over medium-low heat, stirring occasionally. After 5 to 8 minutes, the rhubarb will become a thick, pulpy compote. Divide the compote among four 6-ounce ramekins. Place the ramekins in a shallow baking dish and set aside to cool.

2   Preheat the oven to 350°F.

(continued)

3 Put the milk and lemon verbena leaves in a medium saucepan and bring to a boil over high heat, then immediately remove the pot from the heat, stir in the remaining ⅓ cup sugar, set aside, and let the mixture steep until its temperature drops to lukewarm. Pour the milk through a fine-mesh strainer set over a bowl. Discard the leaves and rinse the strainer. (If using a tea bag, skip the straining step and simply discard the tea bag.)

4 Lightly beat the whole egg and yolks together in a medium bowl. Slowly add the milk, whisking as you do. Strain this custard mixture through a fine-mesh strainer set over a bowl. Gently pour equal amounts of custard over the rhubarb in each ramekin, taking care not to dislodge the compote.

5 Put the baking dish on a rack in the center of the oven. Carefully pour cold water into the baking dish, nearly to the top of the ramekins. Bake the custards until just set, about 55 minutes; a good custard should "shimmy" a bit when tapped.

6 Remove the baking dish from the oven and let it stand a moment. The custards must be taken from the water to stop the cooking; a quick grab with your bare fingertips is the easiest way to remove them, but an offset spatula underneath each ramekin works just as well. Let the custards cool to room temperature, then cover with plastic wrap and chill. The custards will keep in the refrigerator for up to 2 weeks.

7 To serve, simply remove the plastic from the ramekins and serve the custards cold from the refrigerator.

Wine

The rare moscato rosa grape from the Alto Adige region in northern Italy has the aromatic red fruit flavors with just the right balance of sweetness to balance the rhubarb. You could go with the moscato rosa from Abbazia di Novacella. A sparkling brachetto or moscato d'Asti from Piedmont would go nicely as well.

Peas, Glorious Peas

Pea Soup

Pea Ravioli with Mascarpone
Cheese and Basil-Mint Pesto

Pea Pancakes

Glazed Peas with Morels,
Nettles, and Fiddlehead Ferns

Twice a week at the office at JUdson Grill, we received a fax from Blooming Hill Farm, in Blooming Grove, New York. It was a handwritten list from Guy Jones, one of my favorite farmers, of what was available for the next delivery his team had scheduled to New York City restaurants. The lists always took me back to my visits to Guy's farm and home, where the fax machine sits on the counter that divides his open kitchen from his living room. The logo at the top of the page is a very simple line drawing of a hill with the farm's name under it and the phrase "Organically Grown," and Guy scrawls whatever idea happens to be on his mind that day, something brief but meaningful, like "Buy Local."

I've known Guy for a long time and I've always thought of him as one of the cooler farmers at the Union Square Greenmarket. He's very opinionated, always ready to share his radical thoughts about the government and politics, but also very friendly. People gravitate to him; his stand at the Greenmarket is a gathering place for most of the farmers I know.

Guy is a big man with an easygoing demeanor and real warmth that shows in the big smile that spreads across his face when you tell him some good news or a good joke. He has curly blond locks, a round face that's usually red from his hours in the sun, and he often wears a straw hat that has a button pinned to it that reads FARMS, NOT ARMS. Guy got his first taste of farming when he was twenty-one through his work as a community organizer for Cesar Chavez and his United Farm Workers group. As part of his responsibilities, Guy had to go out and work in the fields. At the time, he was "looking for something honest to do," he recalls, and farming became it.

"In those days," he says, "organic didn't mean anything." Today, *organic* pretty much defines what Guy and most of the farmers you'll meet in this book do. He works without the aid of artificial pesticides, which is a huge commitment of time and energy. But Guy thinks it's worth it. "We started to realize that agriculture was in a bad way," he says, "which forced farmers to do things that were bad for the earth and bad for the community." Some of Guy's most strongly held opinions have to do with pesticides. "If you go into a field after it's sprayed," he warns, "you'll die."

And his crops? "There's nothing in them but the rain," he says, one of those big grins spreading across his face. One of the ways he maintains his organic vegetables is through crop rotation: each season he moves each vegetable to a different part of his field, never allowing the predatory insects a chance to really establish a bulkhead in their ongoing battle with Guy and his crew.

Guy started coming to the Union Square Greenmarket in the mid-1980s. It was there that he began to meet New York City chefs. "They were asking for lettuces this big," he says, pinching an inch of space between his thumb and forefinger. "They wanted haricots verts, and so on." Guy was one of the people who took real pleasure in this challenge, and he was a vital part of the evolution of New York dining in the 1980s and 1990s.

These days, Guy grows fifty kinds of tomatoes and six types of squash, not to mention amaranth, escarole, fingerling potatoes, cardoon, and every herb you could imagine. Some chefs give him seeds, hiring him to grow the vegetables just for them.

It makes me feel good to learn that Guy has gotten as much out of working with chefs like me as we've gotten from him. He says that contemporary American cuisine has been the "tide that raises all ships." The fact that restaurants like JUdson Grill have been introducing people to better food makes them want that food for themselves at home. This leads to customers for farmers' markets and even to these items being in demand in supermarkets. Everybody wins.

In addition to buying peas, I used to buy a lot of Guy's mesclun (Guy's Greens) and his sauté mix (Mess O'Greens). Guy's an easy person to do business with. You call him up, tell him what you want, and

you know that when it shows up, it'll be good. In addition to what I know I want, I also trust his instincts: when he gets excited about something new, I go with it, tasting it and then finding a way to get it onto my menu.

If you ever find yourself in the area of Blooming Grove, New York, look up Blooming Hill Farms. They run a shop during the peak times of spring and summer where you can buy vegetables and herbs from big basket-bins, and occasionally host Saturday dinners for which they turn the shop into a small mess hall. You might even get to meet Guy. He's the big man with the gleam in his eye. Introduce yourself, and tell him I sent you. I don't know if you'll get that big grin when you do, but I'd like to think you might.

Pea Soup

haven't really settled into spring until I've made that first pot of pea soup. Is there anything else that so perfectly captures the tender colors and flavors that define this season? I've always found pureed soups a bit monotonous, so I include some solids along with the puree, just as you would in a brothy soup. If you can get your hands on only a few fresh peas, use frozen peas for the body of the soup and garnish it with the fresh ones.

6 cups shelled fresh peas (about 5 pounds in shells) or 1½ pounds defrosted frozen peas

2 tablespoons olive oil

1 leek, white and light green parts only, split lengthwise, sliced thinly crosswise, well washed in several changes of cold water, and drained

½ medium onion, sliced

2 cloves garlic, sliced

Salt

4 cups Vegetable Stock (page 344) or water

4 thin slices bacon

3 tablespoons crème fraîche

1 tablespoon cream

2 tablespoons chopped chervil or mint leaves (see page 52)

1   Bring a pot of lightly salted water to a boil. Fill a large bowl halfway with ice water. Add the peas to the boiling water and blanch until just tender, 4 to 6 minutes for fresh, 1 minute for frozen. Drain the peas in a strainer and immediately plunge them into the ice water for 2 minutes to stop the cooking and preserve their color. Drain, transfer them to a bowl, cover with plastic wrap, and chill in the refrigerator. (The easiest way to do this is to keep the peas in the strainer while they are shocked in the ice water. After lifting them out of the ice water, empty the bowl and quickly dry it, then use it for chilling the peas.

(continued)

2   Fill a bowl halfway with ice water and set another bowl over the ice water. In a 2-quart pot, warm the olive oil over medium heat. Add the leek, onion, and garlic, season with salt, and sauté until softened but not browned, about 7 minutes. Add the stock, raise the heat to high, and bring it to a boil, then lower the heat and let the stock simmer for 10 minutes to let the flavors develop. Taste, adjust seasoning, and transfer the mixture to the bowl set over the ice water to cool it as quickly as possible. Once the mixture is cold, cover the bowl with plastic wrap, and chill in the refrigerator.

3   Put the bacon in a sauté pan and cook over medium-high heat until crisp, approximately 7 to 8 minutes. Transfer the bacon to a paper towel–lined plate to drain, then to a cutting board. Chop it and set aside.

4   In a small bowl, stir together the crème fraîche and cream. Season with a pinch of salt and set aside.

5   In a blender or food processor fitted with the metal blade, puree 5 cups of peas and the vegetables. Pour the soup into a large bowl, taste, and adjust seasoning.

6   To serve, ladle the soup into four chilled bowls and garnish with the remaining peas and a dollop of the crème fraîche mixture. Scatter some bacon and chervil over the top.

Wine

The fresh, herbal pea flavors would pair with a crisp Italian white from the cooler climate of the north of Italy. An aromatic wine like the moscato gialla from the Alto Adige region of northern Italy would be a likely match or a clean pinot bianco would do as well. Try Alois Lageder's Vogelmeier Moscato Gialla.

CHERVIL

Chervil isn't as popular an herb in the United States as it is in Europe, but it is well worth discovering. I think of it as a delicate, sophisticated alternative to parsley. It's sometimes difficult to find, so where possible, I've offered alternatives when I call for it.

Pea Ravioli with Mascarpone Cheese and Basil-Mint Pesto

SERVES 4 TO 6 (MAKES ABOUT 48 RAVIOLI)

hen I developed this recipe, the challenge was the pea filling; the texture of peas alone can be a little coarse, but some traditional binding elements, like egg yolk, overwhelm their delicate flavor. The solution was mascarpone cheese (page 55), which provides a velvety mouthfeel without distracting from the peas. I also use finely grated Parmigiano-Reggiano cheese to help bind the filling and provide a nice salty seasoning. Indeed, I sometimes use the cheese instead of salt as a seasoning because a little of it melts right into hot dishes, providing a more complex flavor.

Filling and Ravioli

2 cups shelled peas (fresh and or defrosted frozen)

2 egg yolks

½ cup mascarpone cheese (about 5 ounces)

½ cup freshly grated Parmigiano-Reggiano cheese (about 2 ounces)

Salt

Pasta Dough (page 56)

Flour for dusting work surface

Cornmeal

1　Bring a pot of lightly salted water to a boil. Fill a large bowl halfway with ice water. Add the peas to the boiling water and blanch until just tender, 4 to 6 minutes for fresh, 1 minute for frozen. Drain the peas in a strainer and immediately plunge them into the ice water for 2 minutes to stop the cooking and preserve their color. Drain. (The easiest way to do this is to keep the peas in the strainer while they are shocked in the ice water. After lifting them out of the ice water, empty the bowl and quickly dry it, then use it for chilling the pea puree in Step 2.)

(continued)

2   Puree the peas in a blender or food processor fitted with the metal blade. Transfer the puree to a bowl, scraping down the sides of the blender or processor bowl to remove all of it, and cover with plastic wrap. Fill a slightly larger bowl with ice water and set the bowl with the puree on the ice. Place both bowls in the refrigerator and chill until very cold, 30 minutes to 1 hour.

3   Whisk the egg yolks in a separate bowl. Fold the mascarpone, Parmigiano-Reggiano, and pea puree into the yolks. Season generously with salt and chill.

4   Assemble one-fourth of the ravioli at a time to prevent them from drying out; keep the filling refrigerated to prevent it from softening. Use a pasta machine to roll the dough to a $\frac{1}{16}$-inch-thickness (or use a rolling pin to roll the dough to the desired thickness) and as wide as possible. Transfer the sheet of dough to a lightly floured work surface and cut it into $2\frac{1}{2}$- to 3-inch-wide strips. Place 1 scant tablespoon of filling at regular intervals, 2 inches apart, down the strip. With a damp pastry brush, moisten around the filling with a little water. Lay another strip of pasta over the top and, working down the strip one mound at a time, gently press down the pasta between the mounds. Then, press the air out the sides and seal the sides. Cut squares around the mounds with a pastry cutter or knife. Transfer the ravioli to a baking sheet generously sprinkled with cornmeal. Repeat with the remaining pasta and filling. Place the sheet in the freezer for at least 1 hour.

Garlic Broth

2 tablespoons extra-virgin olive oil	1 cup Vegetable Stock (page 344) or water
¼ medium onion, thinly sliced	Salt
2 cloves garlic, thinly sliced	Freshly ground black pepper

Warm the olive oil in a small pot set over medium-low heat. Add the onion and garlic and a pinch of salt, and sauté gently until tender but not browned, about 7 minutes. Add the stock, raise the heat to high, and bring it to a boil, then lower the heat and let the stock simmer for 5 minutes. Remove the pot from the heat, season with salt and pepper, and set aside.

Basil-Mint Pesto and Assembly

½ cup tightly packed basil leaves plus 2 teaspoons thinly sliced basil leaves

¼ cup tightly packed mint leaves plus 1 teaspoon thinly sliced mint leaves

¼ cup tightly packed flat-leaf parsley

¼ cup extra-virgin olive oil

Salt

½ cup fresh peas

1 Bring a pot of lightly salted water to a boil. Fill a large bowl halfway with ice water. Blanch the whole basil, mint, and parsley leaves in the boiling water for 20 seconds. Remove the leaves with tongs or a slotted spoon, and shock in the ice water for 2 minutes. Drain the herbs, dry them on a clean towel, and squeeze out excess water.

2 Put the blanched herbs and olive oil in a blender with a pinch of salt and puree until smooth. Set aside.

3 Bring a large pot of lightly salted water to a boil. Fill a large bowl halfway with ice water. Add the peas to the boiling water and blanch until just tender, 3 to 4 minutes. Remove the peas with a slotted spoon and shock in the ice water for 5 minutes, then drain and set aside. Keep the water boiling for the ravioli.

4 Add the ravioli to the boiling water and cook until they rise to the surface, about 4 minutes. Meanwhile, pour the garlic broth into a pot, warm it over medium heat, and add the peas.

5 To serve, stir the pesto into the broth and spoon ¼ cup or so of broth into each of four shallow bowls. Remove the ravioli with a slotted spoon and divide them among the bowls. Sprinkle with the thinly sliced basil and mint.

Wine

The fresh pea taste and basil and mint flavors are a good match with a clean, dry, yet slightly aromatic and spritzy white such as a Vinho Verde or a blend from the Douro area of Portugal called Evel Blanco. An albariño from the Galicia region of northern Spain would be a fine match as well.

MASCARPONE CHEESE

Mascarpone is a smooth Italian cow's milk cheese that's not as runny as crème fraîche and not as gummy as cream cheese. It's often used in desserts but can also replace ricotta in savory contexts.

Pasta Dough

MAKES JUST UNDER 2 POUNDS

If you don't want to make pasta dough from scratch, purchase ready-made pasta dough, which is increasingly available from Italian markets and gourmet grocery stores. Do not use wonton wrappers; they're too thin for my recipes that use this dough.

3 3/4 cups flour, plus more for dusting work surface

1 teaspoon salt

6 eggs

1 tablespoon plus 2 teaspoons extra-virgin olive oil

1 Place the flour and salt in a large bowl.

2 In a separate bowl, beat the eggs with the olive oil and 1/2 teaspoon water.

3 Form a well in the middle of the flour mixture and pour the eggs into the well. Incorporate the eggs by stirring in the flour mixture from the sides of the well a little at a time. If the dough is too dry, add another 1/4 teaspoon water. When the dough begins to come together in clumps, transfer it to a clean flat surface sprinkled with a little flour and knead for 10 minutes. Wrap the dough in plastic wrap and chill in the refrigerator for 1 hour.

Pea Pancakes

SERVES 4

y restaurant vegetarian plates always include at least one kind of pancake. This version can be the basis for a vegetarian main course: start with a soup or salad and finish with the pancakes. For a more complex dish, add some sliced, sautéed mushrooms to the topping.

Pancakes

4 ounces sugar snap peas, strings removed

½ cup shelled peas (fresh or defrosted frozen)

2 tablespoons milk

1 tablespoon cream

1 egg

¼ cup flour

¼ teaspoon sugar

¼ teaspoon kosher salt

½ teaspoon baking powder

1 tablespoon plus 1 teaspoon butter

1 Preheat the oven to 450°F.

2 Bring a pot of lightly salted water to a boil. Fill a large bowl halfway with ice water. Add the sugar snap peas to the boiling water and blanch for 2 minutes. Remove the peas with a slotted spoon, and shock in the ice water for 2 minutes. Remove the peas with a slotted spoon and set aside.

3 Add the shelled peas to the same boiling water and blanch until just tender, 4 to 6 minutes depending on size for fresh, 1 minute for frozen. Transfer them to the ice water and shock for 2 minutes. Remove and set aside.

4 In a blender, puree the sugar snap peas with the milk and cream. Transfer the puree to a mixing bowl, scraping down the sides of the blender. Stir in the egg, then add the flour, sugar, salt, and baking powder. Coarsely puree the shelled peas in the blender, then mix them into the batter.

(continued)

5   Melt ½ teaspoon of the butter in a medium ovenproof nonstick pan over high heat, swirling the butter around the pan. Make 2 pancakes, 3 inches in diameter, using 2 tablespoons of batter for each. When the edges start to lightly brown, 1 to 2 minutes, transfer the pan to the oven and bake for 2 minutes. Flip the pancakes and return the pan to the oven until the upward-facing side is lightly brown, about 4 minutes. Transfer the pancakes to a plate and cover with aluminum foil to keep them warm. Repeat with the remaining batter.

Topping and Assembly

1½ cups shelled fresh peas (about 1 pound in shells)

½ pound sugar snap peas, strings removed and cut into 3 pieces on the diagonal

3 tablespoons butter

½ cup Vegetable Stock (page 344) or water

Salt

1 ounce pea leaves, optional

2 teaspoons finely sliced mint leaves

1   Bring a pot of lightly salted water to a boil. Fill a large bowl halfway with ice water. Add the shelled peas to the boiling water and blanch for 30 seconds. Remove the peas with a slotted spoon, transfer them to the ice water, and let chill for 2 minutes. Drain and set aside.

2   Put the sugar snap peas, butter, stock, and a pinch of salt in a pot and bring to a boil over high heat. Add the shelled peas and pea leaves, if using, and cook until the peas are nicely glazed, 3 to 5 minutes. Season to taste with salt.

3   To serve, divide the pancakes among four plates. Top with the pea mixture and sprinkle with the mint. Serve immediately.

Wine

Serve these with a flavorful and aromatic Greek white, like Domaine Gerovassiliou Malagousia from northern Greece in Epanomi. Or a zesty wine from the Greek island of Santorini or a northern Italian white such as pinot bianco.

Glazed Peas with Morels, Nettles, and Fiddlehead Ferns

his recipe captures the gentle essence of spring. It showcases my favorite technique for glazing vegetables by stewing them in butter rather than blanching them, which can rob them of their flavor. Use it as an accompaniment to fish or chicken, or toss it with pasta.

Nettles are a spinach-flavored herb that strike me as quintessentially spring; they are so alive before cooking that they can "sting" you with their coarse hairs. This is no joke—wear latex gloves when handling them. This dish also features fiddleheads, which are the tender sprouts of spring ferns.

1 cup shelled peas (fresh or defrosted frozen)

2 cups nettles

2 tablespoons extra-virgin olive oil

4 ounces morel mushrooms, trimmed, cleaned (see page 19), and thickly sliced

4 ounces fiddlehead ferns, washed in several changes of cold water

½ cup Vegetable or Chicken Stock (pages 344, 343)

4 tablespoons (½ stick) butter

1 tablespoon chopped flat-leaf parsley

1 tablespoon chopped chives

Salt

Freshly ground black pepper

1 Bring a small pot of lightly salted water to a boil. Fill a large bowl halfway with ice water. Add the peas to the boiling water and blanch until just tender, 2 minutes for fresh, 1 minute for frozen. Drain the peas in a strainer and immediately plunge them into the ice water for 2 minutes to stop the cooking and preserve their color. Drain, transfer to a bowl, cover with plastic wrap, and chill in the refrigerator. (The easiest way to do this is to keep the peas in the strainer while they are shocked in the ice water. After lifting them out of the ice water, empty the bowl and quickly dry it, then use it for chilling the peas.)

(continued)

2   Bring another pot of lightly salted water to a boil. Wearing latex gloves (see headnote), remove the nettle leaves from the stems. Add the leaves to the boiling water and blanch for 30 seconds. Remove them with tongs or a slotted spoon and shock in the ice water for 2 minutes. Drain the leaves, squeeze out any excess water, and roughly chop them. Set aside.

3   Heat the olive oil in a sauté pan set over medium-high heat. When the oil is hot but not smoking, add the morels and fiddleheads and cook until browned well on one side, about 2 minutes. Add the peas, nettles, stock, butter, and a pinch of salt, and cook until the liquid is reduced to a glaze, about 5 minutes. Stir in the parsley and chives and season with salt and pepper.

4   Serve as a side dish to fish or chicken or toss with your favorite pasta.

Sprucing Up Spring

Asparagus with Pistachios
and Baby Greens

Bacon-Wrapped Monkfish
with Peas, Spring Potatoes,
and a Red Wine Sauce

Muscovy Duck Breast
with Creamy Polenta, Baby
Spring Onions, and Black
Pepper–Rhubarb Compote

Flummery with Warm Cherries
and an Oatmeal Fan

The challenge in creating a special-occasion menu with the ingredients that make spring cooking so unique is to showcase and enhance their delicate flavors without overwhelming them. Each dish here has a few embellishments that make it special.

In the first course, Asparagus with Pistachios and Baby Greens (page 62), that something is roasted pistachios and chopped hard-boiled eggs. In the second, Bacon-Wrapped Monkfish with Peas, Spring Potatoes, and a Red Wine Sauce (page 64), it's wrapping the monkfish in bacon and finishing the dish with an elegant red wine sauce. And, in the main course, Muscovy Duck Breast with Creamy Polenta, Baby Spring Onions, and Black Pepper–Rhubarb Compote (page 67), it's the compote that takes the dish over the top.

But it's the dessert, Flummery with Warm Cherries and an Oatmeal Fan (page 70), that pulls out all the stops. Though it's deceptively easy to make, it could end any meal, at any time of the year, with an elaborate flourish.

Asparagus with Pistachios and Baby Greens

SERVES 4

his is my take on a traditional combination of ingredients: asparagus, hard-boiled eggs, and lemon. I've added pistachios and hazelnut oil to the mix for the way they accent the nutty quality of asparagus.

2 tablespoons chopped unsalted roasted pistachios

1 tablespoon dried bread crumbs

4 teaspoons chopped hard-boiled egg

1 tablespoon chopped flat-leaf parsley

3 tablespoons freshly squeezed lemon juice (from about 1½ lemons)

2 tablespoons hazelnut oil

Salt

Freshly ground black pepper

1 pound small (not pencil) asparagus, peeled if thick, bottoms trimmed

2 tablespoons extra-virgin olive oil

2 ounces baby greens (chopped mesclun can be substituted)

1 In a bowl, stir together the pistachios, bread crumbs, 2 teaspoons of the egg, the parsley, 2 tablespoons of the lemon juice, and the hazelnut oil. Season with salt and pepper and set aside.

2 Fill a large bowl with ice water and set aside.

3 Bring a large pot of lightly salted water to a boil and cook the asparagus until tender, 3 to 5 minutes, depending on size. Use tongs to transfer the asparagus to the ice water for 2 minutes to stop the cooking. Drain the asparagus, pat dry, and chill in the refrigerator.

4 When ready to serve, put the asparagus in a bowl, dress them with the pistachio mixture, season with salt and pepper, and divide among four chilled plates. Mix the remaining 1 tablespoon lemon juice with the olive oil and season with salt and pepper. Dress the greens with half of the vinaigrette, adjust seasoning to taste, and place some dressed greens on top of the asparagus on each plate. Mix the remaining 2 teaspoons egg with the remaining vinaigrette and drizzle around the edges of the plates. Serve at once.

Lemon and asparagus can be challenging to pair with wine. A wine with tangy fruit notes and good acidity to match the lemon juice would be a sauvignon blanc from the Loire Valley. Try Domaine de Chatenoy from the village of Ménetou-Salon. A light Sancerre would do in a pinch.

HARD-BOILING EGGS

Here's my tip for perfect hard-boiled eggs: Use large, rather than extra-large or jumbo, eggs. Start with cold water and bring the water to a boil with the eggs already in the pot. Once the water comes to a boil, lower the heat and let it simmer for 11 minutes. This will give you perfectly cooked eggs.

Bacon-Wrapped Monkfish with Peas, Spring Potatoes, and a Red Wine Sauce

SERVES 4

Monkfish is one of those fish that needs a little help to taste good. Over the years, I've wrapped it with hearty herbs, roasted garlic, caul fat, and other enhancers. I even use herbed butter rather than plain old butter when I pan-roast it on its own. Bacon-wrapping it is one of my favorite ways to punch up the flavor of monkfish. When it's pan-roasted, the bacon flavor infuses the fish, an effect heightened by the bacon stock in the sauce. After you cut the monkfish, be sure to season the tails with a sprinkle of salt, just as you would roasted meat, to draw out as much flavor as possible.

Red Wine Sauce

³/₄ cup fruity red wine	4 black peppercorns
3 tablespoons red wine vinegar	4 tablespoons (½ stick) butter
1 teaspoon minced shallot	Salt
1 teaspoon minced garlic	Freshly ground black pepper

Put all of the ingredients except the butter in a small saucepan. Reduce over medium-high heat until syrupy, about 20 minutes. Swirl in the butter, season with salt and pepper, strain, and set aside.

Peas

1 cup shelled fresh peas (about 1 pound in shells)

12 ounces waxy red potatoes, cut into ¼-inch dice (about 2 cups dice)

4 ounces sugar snap peas, strings removed, cut crosswise into thirds (about ¾ cup)

Bacon Stock (recipe follows)

2 tablespoons butter

2 tablespoons cream

Salt

1 tablespoon finely sliced mint leaves

1 tablespoon finely chopped flat-leaf parsley

1 Bring a pot of lightly salted water to a boil. Fill a large bowl halfway with ice water. Add the shelled peas to the boiling water and blanch for 1 minute. Remove the peas with a slotted spoon, transfer them to the ice water, and let chill for 2 minutes, then remove with a slotted spoon and set aside.

2 Using the same boiling water, cook the potatoes for 2 minutes, then plunge them into the ice water for 2 minutes to cool. Drain and set aside.

3 Bring the stock, butter, and cream to a boil in a saucepan set over high heat. Add the peas, sugar snap peas, and potatoes. Season with salt. Cover, lower the heat to medium-high, and cook until the sugar snap peas are just tender, about 4 minutes. Adjust seasoning, add the mint and parsley, remove the pot from the heat, and set aside.

Monkfish and Assembly

8 to 12 thin slices bacon

4 monkfish tails, 7 ounces each

2 tablespoons vegetable oil

4 mint leaves for garnish

1 Wrap 2 or 3 slices of bacon, depending on length of fish and bacon, around the monkfish in a spiral, overlapping the ends by 1 inch. If using a third piece, make sure the overlapping seams are on the same side of the fish.

2 Do the following in two batches: Heat 1 tablespoon of the oil in a large sauté pan set over high heat. Just before the oil begins to smoke (when it begins to shimmer), carefully lay the monkfish in the pan, bacon-seam-side down, without crowding. Be sure the seam side of the bacon is very crisp so the seams hold together, then carefully turn the fish over, using

tongs. Cook until the bacon is golden and crisp on all sides, about 3 minutes per side, 6 minutes total for thinner pieces and 8 minutes for thicker. Remove to a cutting board.

3   To serve, divide the vegetable mixture among four plates. Cut the monkfish tails in half and place on top of the vegetables. Drizzle 1 tablespoon of the red wine sauce around the edge of each plate. Garnish with the mint tops.

Wine
The smoky notes and red wine sauce here demand a full-bodied rosé from the Bandol region of southern France. Try the famed Domaine Tempier with its robust strawberry-fruit made from the mourvèdre grape. Or select a bright, Grenache-based rosé from the southern Rhône Valley village of Tavel.

Bacon Stock

MAKES ABOUT 1½ CUPS

This is a wonderful stock for cooking collard greens or any vegetables that will be served alongside pork.

1 tablespoon vegetable oil

1 ounce double-smoked bacon, cut into chunks (a little under ¼ cup) (below)

¼ cup chopped onion

1 clove garlic, crushed

1 cup Chicken Stock (page 343)

Warm the oil in a medium sauté pan set over medium-low heat. Add the bacon and cook until it is rendered and lightly browned, about 5 minutes. Reduce the heat to low, add the onion and garlic, and cook until tender, about 5 minutes more. Add the stock and ½ cup water. Simmer for 20 minutes. Strain and set aside.

DOUBLE-SMOKED BACON
All bacon is both cured and smoked. Double-smoked bacon is bacon that undergoes a second, more intense smoking that produces a powerful smoky flavor. It must be mail-ordered or purchased from a well-stocked butcher or deli counter.

Muscovy Duck Breast with Creamy Polenta, Baby Spring Onions, and Black Pepper–Rhubarb Compote

SERVES 4

hen I put together a new dish, I usually start with one component and add others to it. This dish began with the rhubarb compote and duck followed right behind it because rhubarb is a perfect foil for this fatty bird. Usually it's the sauce that holds a dish together, but in this case it's the duck, which goes great with the compote, the polenta, and the onions.

Rhubarb Compote

4 ounces rhubarb, thinly sliced crosswise

1 tablespoon red wine vinegar

¼ cup sugar

½ teaspoon freshly ground black pepper

Put half of the rhubarb, the red wine vinegar, and the sugar in a pot and cook over medium heat until the rhubarb is soft, about 5 minutes. Puree in a blender (or use an immersion blender), return to the pot, add the remaining rhubarb, bring to a boil over high heat, remove from the heat, and add the pepper. Chill immediately in the refrigerator.

(continued)

Baby Onions

12 baby spring onions, trimmed to 2 inches from the bulb (green onions can be substituted)

1 tablespoon butter

1 cup Vegetable Stock (page 344)

Salt

Freshly ground black pepper

Put the onions, butter, and stock in a small sauté pan set over medium heat. If the stock does not cover the onions, add just enough water to cover. Season with salt and pepper. Cook the onions until tender and the stock is reduced to a glaze, 15 to 20 minutes. If the glaze reduces before the onions are tender, add a little hot water. Taste and adjust seasoning, remove from the heat, and let cool.

Polenta

2 cups half-and-half

1 clove garlic, crushed

2 sprigs thyme

3 tablespoons instant polenta

Salt

Freshly ground black pepper

1 Combine the half-and-half, garlic, and thyme in a medium pot. Bring to a boil over high heat, then immediately remove from the heat and let steep for 30 minutes.

2 Return the pot to the heat, bring to a boil over high heat, then strain through a fine-mesh strainer set over a bowl. Return the liquid to the pot, and bring to a simmer over medium heat.

3 Gradually whisk in the polenta and cook for 5 to 6 minutes, whisking constantly. Remove the pot from the heat, season with salt and pepper, and cover with plastic wrap. Set aside and keep warm. The polenta will thicken while sitting.

Duck, Swiss Chard, and Assembly

4 Muscovy duck breasts, 6 to 8 ounces each

Salt

Freshly ground black pepper

1 bunch Swiss chard (about 1 pound)

2 tablespoons butter

½ cup Vegetable Stock (page 344)

1 With a sharp knife, score the duck skin, making 4 diagonal slits through the fat but not into the meat. Season the duck with salt and pepper.

2 Put the duck breasts, skin side down, in a large sauté pan set over medium-low heat. After about 15 minutes, drain the excess fat from the pan and return the pan to the heat. Continue to cook until the fat is completely rendered and the skin is crisp, about 30 minutes total.

3 Meanwhile, prepare the Swiss chard: If the chard leaves are large, remove the thick part of the stems by cutting a V into the leaves, then chop them into 3-inch squares. Put the butter and stock in a large pan with a lid. Bring to a boil over high heat, add the chard, cover, and wilt until tender, about 3 to 5 minutes. Drain well and cover to keep warm.

4 Turn the breasts over and cook on the other side for 3 more minutes or until the juices run pink. Remove from the heat, let rest for 10 minutes, and slice.

5 Reheat the onions over low heat.

6 To serve, divide the Swiss chard among four dinner plates. Lean a few slices of duck against the chard on each plate. Spoon some onions next to the chard. Spoon some compote next to the duck and mound some polenta on the other side of the chard.

Wine

A fruity, unoaked barbera from the Piedmont region of Italy has the perfect balance. The maggiur barbera d'Alba from Cascina Luisin would go well with this dish. An unoaked barbera d'Asti is another option.

Flummery with Warm Cherries and an Oatmeal Fan

SERVES 4

flummery is a British oatmeal dish that's sweet and cold, not unlike the Scottish crowdie. This elegant but easy dish matches warm, sweet cherries with a crunchy, creamy concoction for an irresistible dessert served in brandy snifters. To really impress your friends, make sure they're around when you light the cherries in classic flambé style just before serving.

Flummery

3 tablespoons rolled oats	2 cups cream
Generous pinch of salt	½ cup sugar
Pinch of ground cinnamon	¼ teaspoon grated orange zest
1¾ teaspoons powdered gelatin	3 tablespoons brandy

1 Fill a large bowl with ice water and set aside.

2 In a blender or coffee grinder, finely grind the oats.

3 Toast the oats in a small saucepan set over medium heat, stirring constantly. When the oats are golden, add the salt, cinnamon, and ½ cup water, and cook as you would oatmeal. Set aside.

4 In a small bowl, sprinkle the gelatin over 3 tablespoons cold water and set aside to bloom (the predissolving step by which the gelatin's granules soften and swell).

5 Add 1 cup of the cream and the sugar to the oatmeal and warm over low heat. Add the bloomed gelatin to the warm mixture, remove the pan from the heat, and stir to dissolve.

6 Pour the remaining 1 cup cream into a large mixing bowl. Add the orange zest and brandy. Pour the warm oatmeal mixture into the bowl. Stir to combine. Cool over an ice bath, stirring frequently. (The oatmeal will sink to the bottom if the flummery is not stirred while setting.) When the flummery is softly set, pour into four brandy snifters and chill in the refrigerator until firm.

Oatmeal Fan Tuiles

1 cup rolled oats

¾ cup sugar

¼ teaspoon almond extract

Pinch of ground cinnamon

1 egg plus 1 egg white

2 tablespoons cherries, finely chopped

1 Preheat the oven to 350°F. Line a baking sheet with a Silpat or similar silicone mat.

2 In a blender or coffee grinder, finely grind the oats, but not to flour. Place the ground oats and the remaining ingredients except the cherries in a mixing bowl and combine well. This is your tuile batter.

3 Cut a fan stencil from a soft plastic lid; a coffee can lid is perfect. Trim the edges so the template will lie flat. Place the stencil on the Silpat so that 4 tuiles will fit on the sheet.

4 Using an offset metal spatula, spread the tuile batter over the stencil in an even layer. The tuile should be only as thick as the plastic lid. A thicker tuile will lose its shape when baked. Lift the stencil, move to another spot on the sheet, and repeat three times. Sprinkle the tuiles with half of the chopped cherries.

5 Bake the fans until tan, about 10 minutes. Remove the baking sheet from the oven and let cool for 2 minutes, and then run a clean spatula under each tuile to loosen it. The tuile is quite sticky; cooling briefly allows the sugar to firm up. Too cool and the tuiles will break as you slide the spatula underneath.

6 Once all the tuiles are loosened, return the sheet to the oven to rewarm the sugar for 2 to 3 minutes. Lift a warm tuile with the spatula and roll the sides in to form a cone. Set aside to cool. Continue with the remaining tuiles, rewarming them if necessary. Wipe the Silpat off and repeat. Only 1 tuile is needed per flummery, but accidents do happen; the batter makes many more than 8 tuiles, so if the tuiles are not as attractive as you wish, keep trying.

(continued)

Cherry Flambé and Assembly

2 tablespoons butter

2 tablespoons sugar

Juice of ½ orange

½ pound sweet cherries, pitted and halved

3 tablespoons brandy

1   Preheat a 10-inch sauté pan over medium-high heat. Melt the butter and sugar with the orange juice. Cook the sugar mixture for a few moments until thick and bubbling and the bubbles are of uniform size.

2   Add the cherries to the pan and toss to coat with the sugar glaze. Cook until warmed through but still firm enough to hold their shape. Add the brandy to the glazed cherries. Heat the brandy briefly, then lift the sauté pan to catch the tip of the cooking flame into the brandy glaze and flambé.

3   Immediately spoon the cherries over the flummeries, top with the tuiles, and serve.

Wine

A sparkling, off-dry brachetto would complement the pure cherry flavor without overpowering it. Choose the brachetto d'Acqui from Marenco in Piedmont, Italy, and make sure to get the latest vintage; it needs to be fresh. If it's not available, a sparkling wine with some fruity notes, like a demi-sec Champagne, would do.

The Year's First Picnic

Chickpea-Carrot Salad

Cucumber-Dill Soup with Scallions

Brined Fried Chicken

Lemon–Poppy Seed Bars

To qualify as great picnic food, a dish must pass a number of tests. First, it must be easy to cook, because it goes against the laid-back spirit of a picnic for the preparation to be a hassle. Second, it must be delicious cold; even if there's a grill available, you should have the option of not cooking at all once you arrive at the picnic spot. Third, it must be able to travel to the picnic easily and to travel *back home* easily where it can be snacked on at midnight in front of the tube, the next day for lunch, or—when no one is looking—for breakfast. And last but not least, it should be fun—tasty, maybe even indulgent food that's packed with flavor and some of which can be eaten by hand.

Here are four recipes that get an A+ on the Picnic Test. The Chickpea-Carrot Salad (page 74) is durable enough to be snacked on for days after you've made it; the Cucumber-Dill Soup with Scallions (page 76) is a very satisfying soup that you don't even have to turn your stove on to make; the Brined Fried Chicken (page 77) is quite simply the best fried chicken I've ever tasted. (I'm allowed to say this because it isn't my original recipe. If you know a better recipe, then maybe you should write a cookbook yourself.) And the Lemon–Poppy Seed Bars (page 79) are built to travel.

This is also a great menu for a spring lunch or dinner at home, especially if you have a table and chairs outside.

Wine

You gotta love a sommelier who's realistic enough to acknowledge that nobody's going to cart wines for each course out to the state park. The ever-pragmatic Beth suggests two wines that would go well with everything on the following menu. She says that rosé, her favorite picnic wine, offers refreshing strawberry notes and versatility. A classic rosé from the southern Rhône region of France would be the Domaine Trinquevedel from the village of Tavel, made from a Grenache blend. Or you can go with a versatile white; a fun and zesty choice would be a bright Priorat blanco from the region of Priorat, southwest of Barcelona, in Spain. Garnacha blanco is the main grape in this wine, and a good example of its charms can be found in a bottle of Plácet from Palacios Remondo.

Chickpea-Carrot Salad

SERVES 8

This recipe is a tribute to the chickpea salad they sell at the prepared-foods counter at Zabar's market in New York City, which my wife, Beverly, and I have always enjoyed.

The key to this recipe is letting the beans soak after they've cooked. Rather than seasoning the beans while they're cooking, which keeps them from softening, you season them after they've cooked and then give them time to absorb the salt and garlic. Ideally, this recipe should be made a day or so ahead of time to let the flavors develop even further.

A lot of people use parsley as a "default herb" to garnish a dish without really thinking about whether another herb might work better. But the flavor of parsley here truly matters; it completes the balance of the salad.

One 1-pound bag dried chickpeas, soaked overnight in cold water to cover

1 tablespoon crushed red pepper flakes

2 quarts Vegetable Stock (page 344) or water

Salt

1/4 cup freshly squeezed lemon juice

2 tablespoons red wine vinegar

3/4 cup extra-virgin olive oil

2 cups grated carrots (from 2 large or 4 medium carrots)

1 cup red onion, cut into 1/4-inch dice

1/2 cup chopped flat-leaf parsley

1 teaspoon minced garlic

1 Drain the chickpeas and transfer them to a pot. Add the red pepper flakes and stock and bring to a boil over high heat, then lower the heat and let simmer until tender, about 1 hour. Season with salt and let them rest, off the heat, for 20 minutes.

2 Drain the warm chickpeas (you should have 5 cups) and transfer them to a bowl. Add the lemon juice, vinegar, and olive oil. Season with more salt, cover with plastic wrap, and chill.

3 When ready to serve, remove the chickpeas from the refrigerator and stir in the carrots, onion, parsley, and garlic. Let rest for 1 hour so the flavors have a chance to develop. Taste and adjust seasoning if necessary.

CHICKPEAS

As with all dried beans and legumes, it's a good idea to experiment with several brands and then stick to one that you trust.

Cucumber-Dill Soup
with Scallions

MAKES 8 CUPS

This is one of my favorite soups. It has to be served really cold so that you can appreciate the buttermilk and yogurt tang and the sharpness they add to the cucumbers. The Tabasco is optional, but I recommend it to give a little kick at the end; it won't register as spicy, but you'll miss it if it's not there.

5 large cucumbers, peeled, quartered lengthwise, and seeded

1 bunch scallions

1 bunch dill, ends picked

1 clove garlic, chopped

Juice of 3 large lemons

4 cups buttermilk

1 cup plain yogurt

Salt

Freshly ground white pepper

Dash of Tabasco

1   Thinly slice half of the cucumbers crosswise. Thinly slice half of the scallions crosswise. Set aside.

2   Coarsely chop the remaining cucumbers and scallions and transfer to a large bowl. Add the dill, garlic, lemon juice, buttermilk, and yogurt, and give a good but gentle stir. Season with salt and pepper and puree in a blender until liquefied. (NOTE: You can use a food processor, but a blender will give a smoother, more pleasing result.)

3   Transfer the soup to a large bowl and add the reserved sliced cucumbers and scallions. Adjust seasoning with salt, pepper, and Tabasco to taste. Chill for at least 2 hours in the refrigerator.

Brined Fried Chicken

SERVES 8

This recipe, from my old sous chef Mitch SuDock, makes the best fried chicken ever. We used to make brined pork at JUdson Grill, and he started using the brine to make fried chicken for our nightly staff meal. The benefit of brine is that the batter keeps the seasoning from penetrating the meat, but the brine works its way in. Keep a close eye on the thermometer when frying; try to maintain a temperature of 300°F, which will cook the chicken through without burning the exterior.

Fried Chicken

2 chickens, 3 pounds each, cut into 8 pieces each (see page 78)

Brine (recipe follows)

3 cups buttermilk

2 tablespoons plus 1½ teaspoons kosher salt

3 cups flour

1 tablespoon plus 1½ teaspoons paprika

1 tablespoon plus 1½ teaspoons cayenne pepper

3 teaspoons freshly ground black pepper

Oil for frying (I cook 4 pieces of chicken at a time in 8 cups of oil in a 5-quart pot.)

1 Put the chicken in a glass baking dish and pour the brine over the chicken. Cover with plastic wrap and refrigerate for 12 to 24 hours.

2 Remove the chicken from the brine, remove any peppercorns stuck to the skin, and let the chicken dry slightly on a wire rack while preparing the buttermilk and flour.

3 In a large bowl, stir together the buttermilk with 1 tablespoon of the salt. In another large bowl, stir together the flour with the remaining salt and spices.

4 Dredge the chicken 4 pieces at a time in the flour. Transfer to the buttermilk, gently shaking the bowl to coat the chicken. Transfer the chicken back to the flour, being careful not to scrape off the batter. Gently shake the bowl to coat the chicken with flour, then transfer the pieces to a wire rack, again being careful not to scrape off the batter. Repeat with the remaining pieces of chicken and let dry on the wire rack for 30 minutes.

(continued)

5   Pour the oil into a 5-quart pot and heat it to a temperature of 350°F. Cook the white and dark meat separately over medium heat. The oil will cool to about 300°F after adding the chicken; this is the correct heat for cooking the chicken. Cook for 5 minutes, then turn the chicken over and cook for an additional 10 minutes for white meat and 12 minutes for dark meat. If the chicken gets too dark, lower the heat. Drain on a wire rack and repeat with remaining chicken. Serve hot or cold.

Brine

½ cup sugar	1 teaspoon black peppercorns
¼ cup salt	1 teaspoon coriander seeds
1 bay leaf	

Pour 4 cups cold water water into a pot and bring to a boil over high heat. Remove from the heat and add the sugar, salt, bay leaf, peppercorns, and coriander seeds. Allow to cool completely.

CHICKEN

Chicken skin should be clean with no drying and no odor. It shouldn't look or feel slimy. Do not use a wooden cutting board for chicken; I have a plastic board at home that I use only for meat and poultry, and I recommend that you do the same. Be sure to wash your cutting board thoroughly after cutting chicken.

Lemon-Poppy Seed Bars

come from a Hungarian-Czech background, which means I grew up on lots of things with poppy seeds, like poppy seed cakes and poppy seed rolls. I still look forward to visiting my parents in New Jersey during the holidays and getting my annual fix.

These portable bars combine my love of lemon desserts, specifically lemon meringue pie, with my culinary heritage. You can make them ahead of time, chill them, and then cut them up at the picnic. They hold together very well and are fun to eat.

Crust

8 tablespoons (1 stick) butter

Pinch of salt

¼ cup sugar

½ teaspoon vanilla extract

1 cup flour

1 Preheat the oven to 350°F.

2 In the bowl of an electric mixer fitted with the paddle attachment, beat the butter on medium speed. Add the salt, sugar, and vanilla, and continue to beat until light but not fluffy. Lower the speed and add the flour. Mix until just combined.

3 Spread the dough into the bottom of an 8 by 8-inch pan, patting with your fingers and smoothing the top with an offset metal or rubber spatula if necessary.

4 Bake until light golden brown around the edges, 18 to 20 minutes. Remove from the oven and let cool on a wire rack. Do not turn off the oven.

(continued)

Poppy Seed Layer

½ cup poppy seeds, finely ground in a coffee grinder or blender, or crushed with the bottom of a heavy pan

¼ cup sugar

2 tablespoons butter

Place the poppy seeds, sugar, and ¼ cup cold water in a small saucepan and bring to a boil over high heat. Let boil for 1 to 2 minutes, stirring occasionally, until the mixture is thick and glossy. Add the butter and stir until incorporated. Remove from the heat immediately and spread the poppy seed mixture evenly over the baked cookie crust. Set aside.

Lemon Filling

¼ cup cornstarch

1 cup sugar

3 egg yolks

¾ cup freshly squeezed lemon juice

Grated zest of 1 lemon

2 tablespoons butter, softened

1   Place ¾ cup cold water and the cornstarch into a medium nonreactive saucepan and whisk to dissolve the cornstarch.

2   Add the sugar and egg yolks and whisk to combine. Over medium heat, stirring constantly, bring the mixture to a boil and let boil for 2 minutes. Remove from the heat.

3   Add the lemon juice, lemon zest, and butter. Whisk until smooth. Pour the lemon filling evenly over the poppy seed layer.

Topping

3 egg whites

⅓ cup sugar

1 tablespoon cornstarch

1 tablespoon poppy seeds

1   Using a handheld mixer or in the bowl of an electric mixer, whip the egg whites on medium-high speed. When the whites peak softly, slowly add the sugar. Continue whipping until firm (but not stiff) peaks are formed.

2   Fold in the cornstarch, and then the poppy seeds. Cover the lemon filling completely, and dab the top to make attractive swirled points. Bake until the meringue browns, about 18 minutes. Cool and refrigerate until firm, at least 2 hours. Cut into 8 large bars.

Make-Ahead Meal

Pasta with Mushrooms,
Arugula, and Peas

Fresh Strawberry
Cream Roll

This make-ahead meal is one I've been preparing for my wife, Beverly, for the past fourteen years. It's essentially a sophisticated TV dinner. You cook the pasta only halfway; it finishes cooking when the dish is reheated.

Presented here for spring, it can be adapted to include your favorite vegetables and beans in each season of the year.

The jelly-roll-like dessert is made with whipped cream and fresh strawberries. The cake recipe can be used for making different jelly rolls year-round as well.

Pasta with Mushrooms, Arugula, and Peas

SERVES 8

1 pound dried penne

½ cup extra-virgin olive oil

3 cloves garlic, chopped

12 ounces cremini mushrooms, quartered

3 leeks, white and light green parts only, sliced into ½-inch rounds, well washed in several changes of cold water, and drained

½ to 1 tablespoon crushed red pepper flakes

Salt

4 cups Vegetable Stock (page 344) or water

1 bunch arugula, leaves coarsely chopped

1 cup shelled peas (fresh or frozen)

One 15½-ounce can white beans, drained and rinsed

Freshly ground black pepper

1 cup freshly grated Parmigiano-Reggiano cheese

1   Bring a large pot of salted water to a boil. Add the pasta and cook for half the time recommended on the box, about 4 minutes. Drain in a colander and turn it out onto a cookie sheet to let it cool as quickly as possible. Drizzle with ¼ cup of the olive oil. Transfer to an airtight container and refrigerate until ready to use.

2   Warm the remaining ¼ cup olive oil in a deep 12-inch sauté pan or Dutch oven set over high heat. Add the garlic and cook until it starts to brown, 3 to 4 minutes. Add the mushrooms in a single layer and cook until they start to brown, about 4 minutes. Add the leeks, red pepper flakes, and a generous pinch of salt. Cook, stirring frequently, until the leeks begin to soften, about 3 minutes. Add the stock and bring to a boil. Boil vigorously for 8 minutes to develop the mushroom flavor. If using fresh peas, add them and return to a boil. Add the arugula and beans (and frozen peas, if using). Return to a boil to wilt the arugula. Season to taste with salt and pepper. Remove from the heat, let cool, and refrigerate until ready to use.

3   To serve, reheat the pasta in the sauce. Taste and adjust seasoning and top with grated cheese.

Fresh Strawberry Cream Roll

SERVES 4 TO 6

Sponge Roll

⅓ cup flour

¼ cup potato starch

4 egg whites

⅓ cup plus 2 tablespoons superfine sugar

7 egg yolks

½ teaspoon vanilla extract

1 Preheat the oven to 350°F.

2 Line a 15 by 9-inch jelly roll pan with parchment paper, lining the long sides as well as the bottom.

3 Sift the flour and potato starch together.

4 Using an electric mixer on medium-high speed, whip the egg whites until soft peaks form. Slowly add the sugar, then whip to medium peaks. Quickly, but one at a time, add the yolks. Whip only until just combined. Whisk in the vanilla and fold in the sifted dry ingredients.

5 Spread the batter evenly into the jelly roll pan. Bake until golden, 12 to 15 minutes. The cake should spring back when touched lightly. Remove from the oven to the countertop.

6 Lay a dish towel on the counter, short side toward you. Run a small knife around the edges of the cake to release. With the tips of your fingers, pick up two corners of the parchment and invert the sponge cake lengthwise onto the dish towel. Carefully peel the paper from the cake. If the parchment sticks in a specific area, tear it away in small sections from a different direction. Once the paper is removed, roll the warm cake and towel tightly into a log and let cool.

Filling and Assembly

½ teaspoon powdered gelatin

⅓ cup moscato wine

½ vanilla bean, split lengthwise, soft seeds scraped out and reserved

3 sprigs mint

1 cup cream

1 tablespoon superfine sugar

⅔ cup good-quality strawberry jam

1 cup sliced strawberries

Confectioners' sugar

1   In a small bowl, sprinkle the gelatin over 2 tablespoons cold water and set aside to bloom (the predissolving step by which the gelatin's granules soften and swell).

2   In a small saucepan, place the wine, vanilla bean scrapings, and mint. Over low heat, reduce the wine by two-thirds. Discard the mint. Add the bloomed gelatin to the warm mixture, remove the pan from the heat, and stir to dissolve.

3   In the bowl of an electric mixer, whip the cream and sugar softly. Add the gelatin mixture in a thin stream and whip for a few seconds to incorporate.

4   Heat the jam in a small saucepan. Unroll the sponge cake. (It will not flatten completely, so don't force it.) With a pastry brush or small metal spatula, spread the jam over the entire interior of the unrolled cake. Cover the jam evenly with the whipped cream filling and sprinkle with the strawberry slices. Reroll the cake, and slide it from the dish towel onto a serving platter. Store in the refrigerator until ready to serve. Sprinkle with confectioners' sugar, slice, and serve.

Summer

Every summer I'm reminded that I just didn't appreciate how well my parents fed us when I was growing up. I don't think they appreciated it themselves, because our family wasn't self-conscious about food. We didn't make a big deal about ingredients, fuss over meals, or plan vacations around restaurants. But we did eat a lot, and when I think back on the meals my family enjoyed together, I remember some of them as deliciously as the best ones I've eaten in New York and France.

My mother influenced my palate more than she'll ever know or believe. But the person who'll *really* be shocked to learn of his impact on my culinary point of view is my father. Some of my fondest childhood memories are of the garden Dad kept in our backyard where he grew cucumbers, tomatoes, peppers, and corn. I didn't know it at the time, but in its own small way that humble little family resource was my introduction to the virtues of farming and the fresh-from-the-earth fruits and vegetables I celebrate in my restaurant today. I also learned how simple it was to have great food when you start with great ingredients. What could be better than the late-summer tomatoes we picked from the garden and ate like apples, with just a sprinkling of salt on the exposed flesh?

It must be those garden memories that make me want to get as close to the farming process as possible in the summer. I visit the Union Square Greenmarket more than at other times of the year, and even make an occasional pilgrimage to a farm in the tristate area. When I get back to the kitchen, I'll glance around at all the produce I've bought and won't know what to start chopping first, because everything looks so appealing. I think this is why I love eating in the summer more than at other times of year. There's so much great stuff to cook and it's all so easy to prepare.

I'm a New York City chef, but summer is when my inner Jersey boy comes out and my taste drifts back across the river. On that note, as much as I love wine, I also recommend beer as an accompaniment to just about every savory dish in this chapter, except those in the special-occasion menu. If you happen to have some wine on hand, that's fine, but if you've got some cold beer in the fridge, I think it's very much in the spirit of summer to keep it simple and pop one open to enjoy with these meals.

"Buy Local" Menu

Pan-fried Summer Jersey Vegetables

Striped Bass with Shell Beans and Garlic Kale

Berry Clafouti with Crème Fraîche

As you can tell, I'm a big fan of supporting your local farmers. When you buy locally, you get the freshest, best-tasting fruits and vegetables available and often the best value as well. Buying from farmers is the ultimate win-win scenario—you get the freshest ingredients, the farmers stay in business, and American cuisine gets better and better.

This menu invites you to discover the great foods available from your local roadside stand or farmers' market, using them in a starter of Pan-fried Summer Jersey Vegetables (page 91), a main course of Striped Bass with Shell Beans and Garlic Kale (page 93), and a Berry Clafouti with Crème Fraîche (page 97) for dessert.

Of course, the best seasonal produce in your region may differ from that in mine, so feel free to substitute the most appropriate vegetables, fish, and berries for the ones called for in the following recipes. But do try to get them from a local supplier.

Pan-fried Summer
Jersey Vegetables

SERVES 4

This dish came about when I wanted to do a fritto misto (mixed fried vegetables) at JUdson Grill. I decided to make it a celebration of New Jersey's finest, really focusing on the distinct flavor of each vegetable, and ordered a selection from Ray and Sue Dare, who are profiled on page 124.

Even when purchasing vegetables from a farmer, it pays to know the signs of optimum freshness. Eggplants should be bright and have a bit of give to them but should not be excessively soft. I recommend white or lavender eggplant, which have fewer seeds, which can be bitter. If using purple eggplant, avoid bitterness by using only the portion that spans from the top to the seedbed. In the case of squash and zucchini, try to get the firmest, most unblemished ones possible. When they're at their absolute peak of freshness, you'll notice a little moisture on the skin, almost as though they were sweating in the summer sun.

The mint oil adds a nice, sophisticated touch to this dish, but you could leave it out and it will still be delicious.

2 tablespoons thinly sliced basil leaves

1 tablespoon thinly sliced mint leaves

1 tablespoon chopped flat-leaf parsley

6 tablespoons extra-virgin olive oil

Salt

Freshly ground black pepper

8 squash blossoms, with the squash attached if possible

2 ounces fresh mozzarella, cut into 8 pieces small enough to fit into the bottoms of the squash blossoms

1 cup flour

4 eggs

4 cups fresh bread crumbs, preferably from brioche

Eight ¼-inch slices eggplant

Eight ½-inch slices zucchini

Four ¼-inch slices green tomatoes

Four ½-inch slices yellow tomatoes

Olive oil for panfrying

(continued)

1   Make the mint oil by combining the basil, mint, parsley, and extra-virgin olive oil in a small bowl. Whisk together and season with salt and pepper. Set aside.

2   Clean the squash blossoms by removing the stamen with fish tweezers or pliers; be careful not to rip the bottom cup of the blossom. Put a piece of mozzarella in each blossom and seal them by twisting the top closed and folding it under the blossom.

3   Spread the flour out on a plate. Beat the eggs with ¼ cup water and pour into a wide, shallow bowl. Spread the bread crumbs out on a third plate. Season all three with salt.

4   Bread the squash blossoms by dredging them in the flour, then in the eggs, and then in the bread crumbs, shaking off any excess crumbs. Repeat with the eggplant, zucchini, and green and yellow tomatoes.

5   Pour olive oil into a wide, deep-sided sauté pan to a depth of ¼ inch. Set the pan over high heat. When the oil begins to shimmer, add a few bread crumbs to see if they brown up. As soon as they sizzle, begin panfrying the vegetables in batches until golden brown, 2 to 3 minutes per side. As each batch is done, transfer to a paper towel–lined plate to drain, then season with salt.

6   To serve, arrange the vegetables decoratively on a platter and drizzle them with the mint oil.

Wine

A bold, fresh, herbal rosé would pair well with the vegetables and herbal notes in this dish. The vibrant Rosato Sangiovese from the famed Chianti producer Castello di Ama would do well and stand up to the tomato flavors in this dish.

Striped Bass with Shell Beans and Garlic Kale

SERVES 4

ike the halibut dish on page 31, this recipe gives you the same flaky texture and herbaceous flavor of a whole roasted fish by baking fillets in a pan with olive oil and herbs. Just as important as the fish here is the garlic kale, which isn't a variety of kale (although I wish it were because it sounds awesome) but kale sautéed with roasted garlic. I think kale is one of the most underrated vegetables. I myself turned up my nose at it until I became interested in Italian cooking and learned how appealing its texture and flavor are. Now I love it, and also love *cavolo nero* (black cabbage, its Italian cousin), and the green and red kale that local farmers have introduced me to.

When shopping for kale, look for bright green leaves, with firm stems that feel as if they would snap if you bent them. Another good test of freshness is that when you hold the bunch up vertically, the leaves shouldn't droop. When cooking kale, be patient; it needs more time in the pan than, say, spinach, in order for the leaves to soften up. Here's a nifty trick: Briefly freezing kale breaks down its fibers and makes it easier to cook; you can go right from the freezer to the pan. If you have time to plan to do this, I highly recommend it.

In this and other recipes, you can replace kale with Swiss chard, spinach, or broccoli rabe. Whatever greens you use, save this dish for late summer, when you can obtain fresh, locally grown shell beans.

(continued)

Mixed Shell Beans

¼ cup dried cranberry beans

¼ cup dried flageolets

¼ cup dried Great Northern beans

¼ cup dried scarlet runner beans

4 cups unsalted Vegetable Stock (page 344) or 2 cups Vegetable Stock mixed with 2 cups water

Salt

1 Soak the beans overnight in separate containers in cold water to cover. Drain.

2 In four separate heavy pots bring each type of bean and 1 cup stock to an active simmer over medium heat (the surface of the stock should be bubbling gently), uncovered. Do not let the liquid boil, or the bean skins will separate from the beans and the beans won't cook evenly. Resist the urge to stir, which will break the beans into pieces. If the liquid reduces enough to expose any beans to the air, add some hot water to the pot. When the beans are just tender (cooking time can vary from 30 minutes to 1½ hours depending on how dry the beans are), remove the pot from the heat. Always test more than one bean, as they do not always cook evenly. Add salt to taste, set aside, and let cool in their liquid to absorb even more of the flavorful stock. Beans keep about a week in the refrigerator, and up to a month frozen.

Bass, Kale, and Assembly

8 sprigs rosemary

8 sprigs thyme

8 sprigs flat-leaf parsley

4 skinless striped bass fillets, 6 ounces each, or a whole 1½-pound fillet

1 whole head garlic, unpeeled, cut in half horizontally

Extra-virgin olive oil

Salt

2 bunches kale, about 1½ pounds, preferably black Tuscan *cavolo nero*

2 cups cooked mixed shell beans (above)

1 tablespoon butter or extra-virgin olive oil, optional

1 lemon, halved

1 tablespoon finely sliced chives

1 tablespoon minced flat-leaf parsley

1   Preheat the oven to 400°F.

2   Arrange half the rosemary, thyme, and parsley sprigs on a baking sheet. Put the fish fillets skinned side down, on top of the herbs. With a pair of sturdy tweezers, remove the tiny pinbones from the fillets, pressing the surface of the flesh with your fingers to locate the bones. Scatter the remaining herb sprigs over the fish. Cover the fish with plastic wrap, molding the wrap around the fish to keep it moist, and gently press the herbs into the flesh. Place the fish in the refrigerator and chill for at least 1 hour and up to 4 hours.

3   While the fish is chilling, arrange the garlic halves, cut sides up, on a piece of heavy aluminum foil large enough to enclose them. Drizzle with 2 teaspoons water and 2 teaspoons olive oil. Sprinkle with salt. Encase the garlic halves in the foil and seal tightly. Roast until the cloves are buttery soft, about 40 minutes. (To check, open the foil and pierce a clove with a sharp, thin-bladed knife.) Remove the garlic from the oven and set aside to cool. (See Note.)

4   Raise the oven temperature to 450°F.

5   Remove the fish from the refrigerator and let come to room temperature, about 15 minutes.

6   Remove the tough stems from the kale leaves by cutting a narrow V into each leaf. (Do this in advance if freezing the kale.) Cut the kale leaves into quarters. Squeeze the cloves from the garlic halves into a small bowl.

7   Remove the plastic wrap from the fish. Remove the herbs from above and below the fillets and set aside. Rub 1 teaspoon olive oil into each side of the fillets and season both sides with salt. (If using a 1½-pound fillet, rub with 2 tablespoons oil.) Spread all of the herbs on the baking sheet and place the fillets on the herb bed in a single layer. Roast until just opaque in the center, 10 to 15 minutes, depending on the thickness of the fillets (pry apart the flesh on 1 fillet to check for doneness).

8   In a heavy-bottomed 4-quart pot, heat 2 tablespoons olive oil over medium-high heat until hot but not smoking. Add the garlic cloves and cook, stirring, until lightly browned, about 1 minute. Add the kale, 1 cup water, and season with salt to taste. Cook the kale, turning it occasionally with tongs, until the water is almost evaporated, about 5 minutes, then cover the pot and cook for another 5 minutes. Add the cooked beans, a few tablespoons of the bean-cooking liquid, and the butter or olive oil, if desired. Stir gently to combine.

(continued)

9   If serving individual portions, divide the kale mixture among four plates, mounding it in the center. Top each mound with a fish fillet. Drizzle the fish with 1 teaspoon olive oil, a squirt of lemon juice, and a sprinkling of chives and parsley. If using a whole fish fillet, gently lift it onto a platter using two wide spatulas and drizzle with 3 to 4 teaspoons olive oil, several squirts of lemon juice, and a sprinkling of herbs. Pass the kale and beans in a bowl alongside the fish.

NOTE: Step 3 on page 95 is a good, basic recipe for making roasted garlic. For roasted garlic puree, squeeze the cloves out of their skins and mash them with a fork. Roasted garlic puree can be covered and refrigerated for 3 days or frozen for up to 2 months.

Wine

The herb and garlic notes in this dish call for a medium-bodied Italian white such as the Vernaccia di San Gimignano from Tuscany's Ca' del Vispo. Another possibility would be a clean, flavorful Soave from the Veneto, such as Gini Soave Classico.

Berry Clafouti with Crème Fraîche

SERVES 6

The first time I ever had clafouti—a custardy, pancake-style dessert—was in France when I was working with Alain Chapel, who made his with the traditional cherries. I love clafouti with all kinds of fruit; they are delicious with sautéed apples or pears and simply amazing with sautéed quince (page 225).

In the summer, I see clafouti as the perfect platform for celebrating the flavors of all kinds of seasonal berries. My favorites are included in this recipe. They are:

Blueberries. Being a Jersey boy, I insist that my blueberries be as sweet as sugar and from New Jersey. There are three weeks in late June and early July when Jersey blueberries are perfect, and during those three weeks, I honestly believe there's nothing better in the world . . . unless you can find wild blueberries, which—I have to admit—are even better.

Strawberries. Most people think strawberries should be huge, but I think small ones have more intense flavor. Local strawberries appear in June, and if you can find a farmer who produces the Tristar variety, like my friend Rick Bishop (profiled on page 99), jump on them.

Blackberries. Blackberries are strong and in season from mid-August until early September and really should be eaten only at that time. The variety you might get from, say, Chile at other times of the year can be tough and not nearly sweet enough. When blackberries are at their peak, they're my favorites for their firmness and sweetness, which causes them to really explode when you bite into them.

Raspberries. Raspberries actually have two seasons: the first is from June to early July, and the second is from mid-August to late September. All berries are very perishable, but these go more quickly than the rest, so use them as soon as you buy them.

(continued)

2 eggs

⅓ cup sugar

½ vanilla bean, split lengthwise, soft seeds scraped out and reserved

3 tablespoons flour

Pinch of salt

⅓ cup plus 3 tablespoons crème fraîche

⅓ cup milk

Vegetable oil spray

1½ pints mixed berries (hulled and quartered strawberries, blueberries, raspberries, and/or blackberries)

1½ teaspoons confectioners' sugar

1 Preheat the oven to 400°F.

2 In a medium bowl, whisk together the eggs and sugar until frothy. Add the vanilla bean scrapings, flour, and salt, and whisk to combine.

3 In a separate bowl, whisk together ⅓ cup of the crème fraîche with the milk, then whisk that mixture into the batter.

4 Spray a 10-inch nonstick, ovenproof skillet with vegetable oil spray. Pour one-third of the batter into the pan. Bake until just set, about 5 minutes, then remove from the oven. Top with 1 pint of the mixed berries and pour the remaining two-thirds of the batter over the berries. Return the skillet to the oven and bake until the batter has puffed up around the berries and turned golden brown, 20 to 25 minutes.

5 Remove the skillet from the oven and let the clafouti cool for 10 minutes, then slide a thin knife or spatula around the inside edge of the pan to loosen the claflouti. Place a large flat plate upside down over the pan and invert the clafouti onto the plate. Invert again onto another plate, so that the berries are on top. Set aside.

6 In a small bowl, whisk together the remaining 3 tablespoons crème fraîche and the confectioners' sugar. Cut the clafouti into wedges and serve garnished with the remaining ½ pint berries and drizzled with crème fraîche.

Wine

A sure, not-too-sweet bet with berry flavors is the moscato grape from northern Italy made by the monks from Abbazia di Novacella in the Alto Adige region. Or go with a low-alcohol, fruity, sparkling wine like moscato d'Asti.

RICK BISHOP

MOUNTAIN SWEET BERRY FARM
ROSCOE, NEW YORK

The name of their farm says it all. Rick Bishop and his wife, Nicole, grow Tristar strawberries, which develop a remarkable sweetness during the cool Catskill nights on their mountain property. To oversimplify, the cold air concentrates the berries' natural sugars into the fruit. It also makes the berries bigger: for every 10 degrees the median temperature drops, each berry takes on two grams of weight.

Today, the farm is run by Nicole. Rick has taken a job with Sullivan County, helping local farmers secure grants and loans, and assisting them with business planning. In addition to the Tristar strawberry—so named for its uncommonly long growing cycle, which makes it the star of three seasons—the Bishops forage for another of my favorite fruits: thirteen subspecies of wild blueberries that dot the mountainside come mid-July.

Crazy for Corn

Chilled Corn Puree with Red Pepper Caviar and Cilantro

Boiled Lobster with a Corn Salad and Grilled New Potatoes

Fresh Corn Doughnuts with Nectarine Dipping Sauce

Corn on the cob is one of the most summery ingredients. When you think of corn, it's impossible to picture a formal occasion. Instead, you get images of picnics, barbecues, poolside parties, and so on.

I couldn't resist putting a corn menu in this chapter. It includes Chilled Corn Puree with Red Pepper Caviar and Cilantro (page 101), Boiled Lobster with a Corn Salad and Grilled New Potatoes (page 103), and Fresh Corn Doughnuts with Nectarine Dipping Sauce (page 106). These recipes may not be as easy to make as corn on the cob, but they're just as much fun and might give you some ideas for what to serve for a Saturday-night dinner party when you want to include corn but can't get away with something that casual.

There are two primary types of corn: white and yellow. White is the sweetest, but it must be eaten as soon as possible after it's been picked, or else its sugars begin turning into starch. When shopping at the supermarket, yellow corn is the safer bet. If you can find it, bi-color corn combines the best of both worlds—the longevity of yellow with the sweetness of white.

Chilled Corn Puree with Red Pepper Caviar and Cilantro

SERVES 4

f you're wondering what red pepper caviar is, it's a red pepper that's been chopped so fine that it resembles pearls of caviar, a play on the classic eggplant caviar I was introduced to in culinary school. As when cooking dried beans, do not salt the corn until the soup is done, or the kernels will seize up and toughen. For extra corn flavor, put the cobs in the soup pot, then fish them out and discard them just before pureeing the soup.

Soup

1 tablespoon olive oil

1 small leek, white and light green parts only, split lengthwise, sliced crosswise, well washed in several changes of cold water, and drained

½ small onion, sliced

1 clove garlic, sliced

1 medium russet potato, peeled and thinly sliced

3 cups corn kernels (cut from 4 or 5 large ears)

2 cups Vegetable Stock (page 344) or water

Salt

Freshly ground black pepper

1   Heat the olive oil in a 2-quart pot set over low heat. Add the leek, onion, and garlic, and cook until tender, about 7 minutes. Add the potato, corn, and stock, bring to a boil over high heat, then lower the heat and let simmer for 15 minutes.

2   Carefully puree the soup in a blender or food processor filled with the metal blade. Season with salt and pepper, let cool, cover, and chill in the refrigerator.

(continued)

Red Pepper Caviar

1 large red bell pepper

1 Prepare the pepper by charring it over an open flame on the stovetop or under the broiler to blacken the skin. Put the pepper in a bowl, cover it with plastic wrap, and let it steam in its own heat for about 15 minutes.

2 Remove the pepper from the bowl and remove the charred skin, stem, and seeds. Finely chop the pepper and set aside.

Cilantro Puree and Assembly

1 cup tightly packed cilantro leaves   Salt

½ cup extra-virgin olive oil

1 Bring a pot of lightly salted water to a boil. Fill a large bowl halfway with ice water.

2 Add the cilantro leaves to the boiling water and blanch for 20 seconds. Drain, then plunge them into the ice water for 1 minute to stop the cooking and preserve their green color. Gather the cilantro together with your hands and squeeze out the liquid.

3 Place the cilantro in a blender or food processor fitted with the metal blade. Add the olive oil and process until finely pureed. Transfer to a bowl, season with salt, and chill in the refrigerator for at least 1 hour.

4 To serve, divide the soup among four chilled bowls. Spoon some of the pepper into the middle of the soup and drizzle with cilantro puree.

Wine

Pour a light dry chardonnay with enough buttery notes to match the corn flavor, such as the Pellegrini chardonnay from the North Fork of Long Island.

Boiled Lobster with a Corn Salad and Grilled New Potatoes

SERVES 4

an you get any more all-American than this lobster cookout? My favorite thing here is the potatoes, which are wrapped in foil and baked right on the grill, where the high heat concentrates their flavor by drawing out their moisture. To prepare the entire dish on the grill, boil the water for the lobster in a pot set atop the grate.

Corn Salad

4 medium ears corn, in husk

2 beefsteak tomatoes

2 red bell peppers, roasted, peeled, and cut into ½-inch dice (see page 102)

2 tablespoons freshly squeezed lime juice

2 tablespoons freshly squeezed lemon juice

¼ cup white wine vinegar

½ cup extra-virgin olive oil

2 tablespoons chopped flat-leaf parsley

Salt

Freshly ground black pepper

1   Preheat the grill, letting it get as hot as possible. Place the corn on the grill and cook until blackened on one side, about 2 minutes. Rotate and blacken all sides, about 6 minutes total cooking time. Remove the corn from the grill and set aside to cool.

2   Place the whole tomatoes on the grill and cook until the skin begins to blacken and crack, about 1½ minutes. Turn and repeat on the other side, about 3 minutes total cooking time. Remove the tomatoes from the grill.

3   Shuck the corn and cut the kernels from the cob. Peel, seed, and cut the tomatoes into ½-inch dice.

4   Place the corn, tomatoes, peppers, lime juice, lemon juice, vinegar, olive oil, and parsley in a bowl. Season with salt and pepper and toss. Let the mixture marinate for 30 minutes, then taste and adjust seasoning if necessary. Meanwhile, cook the potatoes.

(continued)

Potatoes

1½ pounds small new potatoes (e.g., red bliss, creamer, All Blue), scrubbed clean

3 tablespoons cold butter, cut into chunks

2 sprigs thyme

Salt

1   On a piece of aluminum foil large enough to hold all the potatoes in a single layer, arrange the potatoes. Scatter the butter, thyme, and 3 tablespoons water over the potatoes, and season with salt. Wrap the potatoes in the foil and then wrap them again with another piece of foil, sealing the edges well.

2   Place the potatoes on the hot grill, cover the grill, and cook the potatoes for 10 minutes. Turn the package over and cook the potatoes for an additional 10 minutes. Remove the package from the grill and let it cool enough to handle the foil, about 10 minutes; the potatoes will finish cooking during this time.

Lobster and Assembly

⅔ cup white vinegar

⅔ cup salt

4 lobsters, 1½ pounds each

1   In a lobster pot or stockpot, bring 2 gallons of water to a rolling boil over high heat. Add the vinegar and salt. Let the water return to a rolling boil, then carefully slide the lobsters into the water. Lower the heat to medium and cook, uncovered. Watch the water carefully and do not let the water come to a boil again, the water should bubble occasionally but not simmer. Cook the lobsters for 8 to 10 minutes, then drain. When cool enough to handle, crack the claws but leave the rest of the lobster intact.

2   To serve, present the lobsters, potatoes, and corn salad in separate bowls at the table and let your guests serve themselves. Don't forget the bibs and nutcrackers!

Wine

You could stay with the Pellegrini chardonnay (page 102) or move to a richer style to complement the lobster. The chardonnay blend Potato Barn White from Schneider Vineyards, on the North Fork of Long Island, would be a good choice, as would a California chardonnay with the ripe fruit flavors of the Santa Barbara area like Babcock Grand Cuvée.

LOBSTER

Seek out lobsters that are alive and kicking. I generally don't buy lobsters that weigh more than $1\frac{3}{4}$ pounds, because that's a good amount per person, especially when serving a full meal. (You want everyone to have room for the vegetables and dessert, don't you?) The most humane way to cook lobsters is to kill them first by driving a chef's knife right between their eyes, which kills them instantly and will also give you a more tender tail. After killing lobsters, let them sit for 10 minutes.

Fresh Corn Doughnuts with Nectarine Dipping Sauce

MAKES 48 SMALL DOUGHNUTS

Nectarines are one of those things that really make me want to hammer home my message of local, local, local. As with peaches and plums, when you buy them out of season, you just don't get that super-sweet stone-fruit flavor, or the little extras like the juice running down your arm. The optimum way to purchase nectarines is to get some that give a little, which indicates they are ripe, and some hard ones that will ripen over the next few days. The ones that give a little will be very juicy. Oh, and one more thing: *never* refrigerate nectarines.

This is a very easy recipe because I use baking soda instead of the yeast called for in many doughnut formulas. If possible, make the dough a few hours ahead of time and fry the doughnuts right before serving, which will divide the cooking into stages and give the flavors a chance to develop and deepen. The sauce, which balances nectarine, sugar, and buttermilk, is much more than just a condiment; it's an essential part of this dessert.

3 ripe nectarines	¼ cup yellow cornmeal
1¼ cups sugar	½ teaspoon salt
Juice of ½ lemon	½ teaspoon baking powder
1 cup buttermilk	½ teaspoon baking soda
2 medium ears corn, shucked	Generous pinch of nutmeg, freshly grated if possible
1 egg	
4 tablespoons (½ stick) butter, melted	1 teaspoon vanilla extract
½ cup whole wheat flour	Vegetable oil for frying
1½ cups all-purpose flour, plus more for dusting work surface	½ teaspoon ground cinnamon

1   Make the sauce. Peel, pit, and chop the nectarines. Put them in a small nonreactive saucepan with ¼ cup of the sugar and the lemon juice. Cook over medium heat, stirring occasionally. When the nectarines are thick and pulpy, 7 to 8 minutes, remove from the heat and puree until smooth. A handheld immersion blender is the ideal tool for doing

this, but a standing blender or food processor fitted with the metal blade works fine as well. Add ½ cup of the buttermilk and blend for a couple of seconds to combine. Cover and refrigerate until ready to serve.

2   Bring a pot of salted water to a boil. Add the corn and boil until tender, about 10 minutes. Drain and set aside to cool. When cool enough to handle, one ear at a time, hold the corn upright on a cutting board. Cut into the middle of the corn kernels and slice down the entire length of the cob. Slice again to remove the other half of the kernels. Continue with the entire ear. Discard the cob and reserve the cut corn and any liquid. (You should have ¾ cup of cut kernels.) One ear of corn may be enough; if not, repeat the slicing and chopping with the other ear.

3   Lightly beat the egg in a medium bowl. Add the remaining ½ cup buttermilk, ½ cup of the sugar, and the melted butter, and stir to combine. Combine the whole wheat flour, all-purpose flour, cornmeal, salt, baking powder, baking soda, and nutmeg in a large bowl. Whisk together the dry ingredients to remove any lumps and evenly incorporate the leavenings. Add the liquid ingredients to the dry and mix until just combined. Add the corn kernels and their liquid and the vanilla. Cover the bowl with plastic wrap and chill until firm, about 1 hour.

4   Roll the dough out on a floured surface into a rectangle about 4 by 6 inches and ¼ inch thick. Using a knife or rolling cutter, cut the dough into ½-inch squares.

5   Pour oil into a large, heavy-bottomed pot to a depth of 3 inches. Heat over medium-high heat to 365°F. Line a plate or tray with paper towels. Fry a few doughnuts at a time. Turn each doughnut when it rises to the top of the oil and turn again after 1 minute. Fry the doughnuts until golden then remove with a slotted spoon and drain on the paper towels. When all the doughnuts are fried, combine the remaining ½ cup sugar and the cinnamon in a bowl.

6   Toss the warm doughnuts in the cinnamon sugar. Serve with the nectarine dipping sauce alongside.

Wine

A fantastic and rare late-harvest chardonnay from Wölffer Estate Vineyards and Stables, in New York State, on Long Island's South Fork, has the sweet buttery notes to round out the corn and nectarine flavors in this dish. A sweet white from the Loire Valley, such as a Coteaux du Layon, would also do the trick.

Grilling, Italian Style

Charred Creminis with
Baby Spinach, Pecorino,
and Balsamic Vinegar

Grilled Dry-Aged Rib-Eye
Steak with a Red Onion
Cipollata and Herbed
White Beans

Honey-Grilled Figs with
Sweetened Ricotta

This is a simple menu featuring a salad, a steak, and a grilled fruit dessert. But Italian ingredients such as cremini mushrooms, pecorino cheese, balsamic vinegar, and ricotta cheese elevate it above the everyday, at least for those of us who live in America.

Over the past few years, I've become a big fan and casual student of Italian cuisine. I first began learning about it when I took a consulting gig for a Mediterranean restaurant and bought a stack of cookbooks to educate myself. I was drawn to the big flavors, simple techniques, and reliance on the best raw ingredients that define Italian cooking. In my reading, I also learned that Italians have a strong connection to the seasons, not just in food but in all aspects of life. As you probably can guess by now, this struck a chord with me as well.

Italian cooking most closely resembles American cooking in the summer, when they both rely heavily on the grill, which is where all three dishes here— Charred Creminis with Baby Spinach, Pecorino, and Balsamic Vinegar (page 109); Grilled Dry-Aged Rib-Eye Steak with a Red Onion Cipollata and Herbed White Beans (page 111); and Honey-Grilled Figs with Sweetened Ricotta (page 115)— are cooked.

Charred Creminis with Baby Spinach, Pecorino, and Balsamic Vinegar

SERVES 4

Cremini mushrooms are available year-round, but grilling gives them the taste of summer. Choose creminis that have the caps closed so that the white membrane on the underside completely seals the "fuzzy" part. Trim the bottoms of the stems before using them. Fun fact: As cremini mushrooms get older they get bigger, open up, and become portobello mushrooms.

This is one of my favorite dishes for illustrating culinary balance: there are the earthy mushrooms, their charred flavor offset by sherry vinegar in the dressing and sweet balsamic vinegar drizzled over the top, complemented by the clean crunch of fresh, slightly wilted spinach. There's really no area of taste or texture that this salad doesn't have covered.

Sherry Vinaigrette

1 tablespoon sherry vinegar

1 teaspoon chopped shallot

Salt

3 tablespoons extra-virgin olive oil

Put the vinegar and shallot in a bowl, season with salt, and whisk in the olive oil. Set aside.

(continued)

Cremini Mushrooms

2 cloves garlic, thinly sliced

1 teaspoon crushed red pepper flakes

½ cup plus 2 tablespoons extra-virgin olive oil

1 pound cremini mushrooms, washed and ends of stems trimmed (see page 19)

½ pound baby spinach

Salt

Freshly ground black pepper

¼ cup balsamic vinegar

2 tablespoons chopped chives

2 ounces pecorino cheese, shaved with a vegetable peeler

1   In a bowl, stir together the garlic, red pepper flakes, and ½ cup of the olive oil. Add the mushrooms, toss gently, and let marinate for 1 hour at room temperature.

2   Preheat the grill, letting it get as hot as possible.

3   Remove the cremini mushrooms from the marinade and thread them on 8-inch skewers. Place the skewers on the grill and char the mushrooms over the flame with the top open for 3 to 4 minutes, depending on their size. Rotate the skewers and grill for 3 to 4 more minutes. The creminis should have nice grill marks but still maintain their shape and texture.

4   In a bowl, dress the baby spinach with the vinaigrette, season with salt and pepper, and mound in the center of four plates. Remove the creminis from the skewers and place them around the spinach on each plate. Drizzle the mushrooms with the balsamic vinegar, drizzling a little around the edge of each plate as well. Then drizzle with the remaining 2 tablespoons olive oil, also drizzling some around the plate. Sprinkle each serving with chives and top with a few slices of shaved pecorino.

Wine

You have to go with something Italian here. Go with the cherry flavors of a Sicilian red, a Cerasuolo di Vittoria from the Valle dell'Acate winery, which will be able to stand up to the balsamic vinegar. Something fresh and fruity would go nicely as well, such as a young light dolcetto from Italy's Piedmont region.

Grilled Dry-Aged Rib-Eye Steak with a Red Onion Cipollata and Herbed White Beans

SERVES 4

This is my answer to a Florentine beefsteak, the famously thick, grilled rib-eye steak traditionally drizzled with olive oil after cooking. I dress mine with oil before grilling and match it with a red onion *cipollata,* a Sicilian version of onions braised with wine, and another Italian favorite, white beans, which I make the basis for a creamy-tasting but creamless puree that incorporates the beans' cooking liquid.

Cipollata

2 tablespoons butter

4 medium red onions, thinly sliced

Salt

1 cup fruity red wine

¼ cup red wine vinegar

Melt the butter in a medium pot set over low heat. Add the onions, sprinkle with a little salt, cover, and cook until very soft, about 45 minutes. Add the wine and vinegar, and cook over medium heat until almost all of the liquid has evaporated, about 45 minutes. Remove the pot from the heat and keep covered and warm, or cool, cover, and refrigerate for up to 4 days.

(continued)

Herbed White Beans

1 cup dried Great Northern beans

4 cups Vegetable Stock (page 344) or
2 cups Vegetable Stock plus 2 cups water

Salt

1 tablespoon thyme leaves

1 tablespoon oregano leaves

2 tablespoons chopped flat-leaf parsley

¼ cup extra-virgin olive oil

1 Soak the beans overnight in cold water to cover by 2 inches. Drain.

2 Put the beans and stock in a pot. Bring the liquid to an active simmer over medium heat (the surface of the stock should be bubbling gently), uncovered. Do not let the liquid boil, or the bean skins will separate from the beans and the beans won't cook evenly. Resist the urge to stir, which will break the beans into pieces. If the liquid reduces enough to expose any beans to the air, add some hot water to the pot. When the beans are just tender (cooking time can vary from 30 minutes to 1½ hours depending on how dry the beans are), remove the pot from the heat. Always test more than one bean, as they do not always cook evenly. Add salt to taste, set aside, and let cool in their liquid to absorb even more of the flavorful stock.

3 When cool, transfer ½ cup beans and ¼ cup bean-cooking liquid to a blender and puree until smooth.

4 Chop the thyme and oregano together with 1 teaspoon salt, then transfer to a bowl along with the parsley and olive oil. Stir together. When ready to serve, warm the beans in the puree and stir in the herb oil.

NOTE: When making this dish, the beans can be reheated in a pot set right on the grill, or reheated indoors and kept, covered, by the grill while you cook the steaks.

Steaks and Assembly

4 cloves garlic, roughly chopped

Salt

¼ cup olive oil

Freshly ground black pepper

4 dry-aged rib-eye steaks,
10 to 12 ounces each

1   In a small bowl, stir together the garlic and olive oil. Drizzle this marinade over the steaks and massage it into the meat. Let sit for at least 1 hour.

2   Prepare the grill, letting it get as hot as possible.

3   Remove the garlic pieces from the steaks and season the steaks with salt and pepper. Place the steaks on the grill and sear them for 2 to 3 minutes, then turn 90 degrees to make crosshatch marks and cook for an additional 2 minutes. Turn the steaks over and repeat. After 5 minutes per side, the steak should be rare to medium rare. If medium to well done is desired, leave the steaks on the cooler part of the grill for a few extra minutes to cook further without burning them. Season the steaks with salt and pepper.

4   Serve the meal family style, with the steaks on a platter and the onions and beans on the side.

Wine

A full-bodied cabernet, merlot, or red blend with cabernet franc would be well suited for grilled meat. Try a Bordeaux-style blend from Washington State, such as the L'Ecole No. 41 Pepper Bridge Apogee from the Pepper Bridge Winery, in Walla Walla, Washington.

STEAK

I believe it's worth the extra dollars to buy aged steak because aging draws out the moisture, which results in more flavorful beef. There's been a lot of debate over whether to season meat before or after cooking it. I do both: the initial seasoning peaks the flavor, and the final seasoning offers a bit of contrast in the eating. All steaks should be cooked over high heat, to seal in those priceless juices.

NIMAN RANCH

You might have seen the name Niman Ranch on restaurant menus. A lot of chefs, myself included, have begun including it alongside the listing for pork and beef dishes made with the meat produced by Bill Niman at his northern California company. It's our way of giving credit to a group of people who have done a ton of work to ensure superior quality.

Bill produces some of the best meat I've ever tasted. He does it by, as he says, "adhering to a strict code of husbandry principles." He makes sure that livestock are treated humanely, fed natural feed, and are never treated with growth hormones or sub-therapeutic antibiotics. They are "raised with care, naturally."

Bill works with a small network of family farms so he can monitor the quality of the meat from the field to the kitchen. He also employs his own butchers to be sure that the meat is properly portioned, often to the specifications of individual chefs. The meat is shipped directly from Niman Ranch to chefs like me, or home cooks like you via their Web site (see Mail Order Sources, page 345).

Honey-Grilled Figs
with Sweetened Ricotta

Figs are one of the fruits I look forward to most each summer; they're so sweet and so easily enjoyed, even right off the tree. As much as I enjoy them raw, they're even more interesting grilled; their flavor becomes richer and more complex. This is a wonderful, simple dessert that you can have ready to go before cooking the rest of this, or any, meal. Be sure to clean your grill of any stuck-on steak bits before cooking the figs.

½ cup plus 1 tablespoon flower honey, ideally lavender, linden, or orange blossom

1 tablespoon red wine vinegar

3 sprigs fresh mint

20 small Mission figs

2 tablespoons cream

½ cup good, fresh ricotta (see page 116)

6 to 8 mint leaves sliced into 1 tablespoon thin ribbons

Freshly ground black pepper

1 Soak four 10-inch wooden skewers or beech twigs in warm water for 30 minutes.

2 Combine ½ cup of the honey and the vinegar in a small saucepan. Thoroughly crush the mint sprigs in your hands and add them to the honey mixture. Trim the hard stems from the figs and put the fruit in a bowl or baking dish. Bring the honey mixture to a simmer over medium heat. Pour it evenly over the figs. Let sit at room temperature for 1 hour, turning occasionally.

3 Whip the cream until stiff in a medium mixing bowl. Add the remaining 1 tablespoon honey and begin folding in the ricotta, and sprinkling in the mint leaves. Don't overmix. Transfer the ricotta to a serving dish and refrigerate until serving time.

4 Preheat the grill, letting it get as hot as possible.

5 Thread the figs onto the skewers or twigs. Grill for 1 to 1½ minutes per side to form golden-brown, not black, grill marks, brushing them with the honey mixture as they cook.

6 Serve the warm figs with any remaining honey mixture, pepper, and a few large spoonfuls of ricotta.

(continued)

A well-made *vin santo,* such as Poggio Salvi, is a classic pairing with this dessert.

RICOTTA

If you cannot get fresh ricotta (I use Old Chatham Sheepherding Ricotta), use farmer cheese, or drain commercial ricotta in a cheesecloth-lined strainer over a bowl in the refrigerator for at least 2 hours. Discard the liquid and use the drained cheese.

Veg Out:
A Summer Picnic

Black Olive and Goat
Cheese Sandwiches

Beet and Tomato
Salad with Dill

Chilled Ratatouille

Cassis Butter Tartlets

I'm not a vegetarian. But there are those sweltering summer days when even a bona fide carnivore like myself finds that eating something light is the only way to go.

This picnic menu makes up for the absence of animal protein with vibrant flavors. There are many exciting contrasts here, such as the salty olives and creamy cheese in Black Olive and Goat Cheese Sandwiches (page 118), or the buttery, flaky pastry and astringent fruit in the Cassis Butter Tartlets (page 122).

This menu also features two of my favorite summer dishes, the Beet and Tomato Salad with Dill (page 119) and the Chilled Ratatouille (page 120). On hot summer days, I can't get enough of either of them.

Wine

As with the spring picnic (pages 73–80), Beth recommends one wine to carry the day, again looking to rosé, which is versatile with bright fresh berry fruit that makes it tasty and fun for a picnic. In the summer, she recommends one with Provençal influences, like the Bandol rosé from Domaine de Pibarnon in Provence. Get the most recent vintage available.

Black Olive and
Goat Cheese Sandwiches

SERVES 8

I can't think of a better sandwich to take along to the beach, enjoy next to the pool, or keep on hand in the fridge than these wraps. The combination of olives, goat cheese, frisée, and red pepper reminds me of the Mediterranean Sea, making any summer occasion seem slightly more exotic. Thanks to the durable flour tortillas, which can hold a lot of heft and moisture without soaking through and tearing, these sandwiches can be made ahead of time.

Goat Cheese

1 pound fresh goat cheese

1/4 cup cream

2 tablespoons chopped thyme leaves

Place all of the ingredients in a bowl and stir to combine. Set aside.

Tapenade

1 cup pitted Kalamata olives

2 anchovy fillets

2 teaspoons capers packed in brine, rinsed and drained

1/2 teaspoon smashed garlic (use the edge of a large, wide-bladed knife)

Place all of the ingredients in a food processor fitted with the metal blade and process until finely chopped. Transfer to a bowl and set aside.

Assembly

8 flour tortillas, 10 inches in diameter

2 roasted red bell peppers (see page 102)

2 cups frisée, coarse ends trimmed, curly tips torn into pieces

1   Lay the tortillas in front of you. Spread ¼ cup of the goat cheese over the center portion of each tortilla. Spread 1 generous tablespoon of the tapenade over the goat cheese.

2   Cut each pepper half into 6 strips and lay 3 strips along the center of each tortilla. Top the pepper with some frisée.

3   Fold two sides of the tortilla over the frisée, then roll up the tortilla. Cut each wrap crosswise into 4 pieces and serve from a platter.

Beet and Tomato Salad with Dill

SERVES 8

could eat buckets of this refreshingly tangy salad in the summer, when the combination of beets, tomatoes, red onion, and dill seems heaven-sent. I first made it at home, after the CSA—a New York City food co-op of sorts that I belong to—turned a surplus of tomatoes and beets over to me one August. I hate wasting food, so I came up with this as a way of using them all.

4 large red beets, roasted (see page 28)	Salt
4 large red, ripe beefsteak tomatoes, cut into ½-inch dice	¼ cup red wine vinegar
	¼ cup olive oil
1 small red onion, very thinly sliced	2 tablespoons chopped dill

Peel the roasted beets, cut them into ½-inch dice, and place them in a mixing bowl. Add the tomatoes and onion. Season with salt, and add the vinegar, oil, and dill. Toss gently and let sit for 1 hour, then serve.

Chilled Ratatouille

SERVES 8

Served hot or cold, ratatouille is one of my favorite things in the world: a simple, perfect way to experience the full spectrum of late-summer vegetables such as tomato, eggplant, zucchini, and pepper. It's also an ideal picnic food because it can be enjoyed cold and, like most soups, is even better after a night in the refrigerator gives the flavors a chance to mingle. If you have leftover ratatouille, I recommend serving it with scrambled eggs for an early-morning treat.

Ratatouille Tomato Sauce

¼ cup extra-virgin olive oil

½ small onion, cut into small dice

8 cloves garlic, thinly sliced lengthwise

Two 28-ounce cans whole peeled plum tomatoes, with their juice

Salt

Freshly ground black pepper

1   Heat the olive oil in a sauté pan set over medium-high heat. Add the onion and garlic, and cook over medium-low heat until softened but not browned, about 10 minutes.

2   Add the tomatoes, roughly mash them with a wooden spoon, and let simmer over medium-low heat until the mixture thickens, about 45 minutes.

3   Transfer the mixture to a food processor fitted with the metal blade and process until smooth. Season with salt and pepper and set aside.

Ratatouille

1½ cups olive oil, plus more as needed

2 zucchini, seeds removed, cut into ⅓-inch dice

2 yellow squash, seeds removed, cut into ⅓-inch dice

2 small eggplants, seeds removed, cut into ⅓-inch dice

2 red onions, cut into ⅓-inch dice

2 red bell peppers, stems and seeds removed, cut into ⅓-inch dice

2 yellow bell peppers, stems and seeds removed, cut into ⅓-inch dice

Salt

Freshly ground black pepper

3 sprigs thyme

1 Preheat the oven to 425°F.

2 Do the following for each type of vegetable: Heat ¼ cup of the olive oil in a sauté pan large enough to hold the vegetable pieces in a single layer. Set over high heat. Add the vegetable pieces and cook, tossing occasionally, until they just begin to brown while remaining slightly crunchy, about 2 minutes for the squash, zucchini, and eggplant; 3 minutes for the onion and pepper. Drain in a colander, season with salt and pepper, and transfer each vegetable to an ovenproof casserole as it is cooked.

3 Add the tomato sauce and thyme to the vegetables and stir. Cover and bake until bubbling and the vegetables have finished cooking, about 30 minutes. Let cool to room temperature, then cover and chill in the refrigerator for at least 2 hours before serving.

Cassis Butter Tartlets

SERVES 8

If you love food that gets better over time, then you'll treasure these tartlets. They're good right out of the oven and even better when they're cold. If you can't get fresh black currants, use frozen, or substitute blueberries, huckleberries, or elderberries.

Pastry Shells

2 cups flour, plus more for dusting work surface	10 tablespoons (1 stick plus 2 tablespoons) cold butter, cut into teaspoon-sized pieces
½ teaspoon salt	½ teaspoon cider vinegar
2 teaspoons sugar	3 tablespoons cold milk

1   In the bowl of an electric mixer filled with the paddle attachment, combine the flour, salt, and sugar. Add the butter and mix until large crumbs have formed (small pieces of butter should still be visible). Add the vinegar and sprinkle the milk into the still-turning dough. When the dough has become a crumbly ball, remove it from the mixer and knead a few times with the palm of your hand. Cut the dough into 4 equal pieces and let rest for 15 minutes.

2   Preheat the oven to 375°F.

3   Place eight 4-inch fluted tartlet molds next to your work surface. Cut each piece of dough in half. On a lightly floured surface, roll out each piece to a size slightly larger than the tartlet molds. Place each rolled piece into a mold and press gently into the corners and sides. Using a paring knife, trim flush to the rim. Line each crust with aluminum foil or parchment paper and fill with beans, barley, or pie weights. Bake for 15 minutes. Remove the filled liners and bake for another 10 to 12 minutes, until light golden brown. Remove from the oven and set aside.

Cassis Filling and Assembly

16 tablespoons (2 sticks) butter, softened at room temperature

1 cup sugar

2 tablespoons flour

4 eggs, at room temperature

Grated zest of 1 lemon

Pinch of salt

1 teaspoon cassis, kirsch, or raspberry eau de vie

1 cup fresh black currants, cleaned

1   In the bowl of an electric mixer fitted with the paddle attachment, cream the butter, sugar, and flour until very light and fluffy. Add the eggs one at a time, beating well after each addition. Add the lemon zest, salt, and liqueur. Beat until just combined.

2   Divide the currants among the prebaked shells. Spoon the cassis filling over the currants and jiggle each tartlet to even out the surface. Bake for 20 minutes or until the filling is puffy and light brown. Let cool. Chill briefly before removing from tartlet forms and serving.

Tomato Temptations

Cherry Lane Farms is located in Bridgeton, in my home state of New Jersey, and run by Ray and Sue Dare. They are a loving and lovely couple with true country charm. I consider it a sign of their gentle nature that the deer running around in a pen just outside their house aren't being raised for profit; they're family pets.

Ray grew up in the area, the third generation of a family that farmed about five hundred acres. His parents grew asparagus, potatoes, and tomatoes, all of it sold for processing by big companies. He still remembers two huge tractor trailers pulling up regularly to load all the asparagus bound for New York City. When the prices dropped, they sold the crop to Del Monte.

At age sixteen, Ray bought the family farm from his father. His initial agricultural career was short-lived; he sold the property back to his father, quit farming, and became a commercial pilot. He worked a number of aviation jobs over the next several years, including flying a crop duster. At one point, he even moved as far away as Montana. When he finally returned to New Jersey, he ended up living down the road from his original farm. (This just supports my ever-growing feeling that destiny has a lot to do with the farming trade.)

Ray and Sue met through a friend. They began their joint effort at farming with a pick-your-own strawberry farm. In the spring, they expanded to include asparagus. They didn't grow tomatoes, peppers, squash, or any of the other vegetables I get from them today because people grew those in their own garden, just as my father did. Ah, New Jersey in the summer!

The Dares decided to expand their crops thanks to the Union Square Greenmarket. A neighboring farmer told them that his brother-in-law sold 2,000 quarts of strawberries at the green-market for two dollars a quart. That was all they needed to know. As soon as a slot opened up, they began selling at the Sunday farmers' market at Seventy-seventh Street and Columbus Avenue on Manhattan's Upper West Side. In 1984, they began selling on Thursday at the World Trade Center. They loved the

crowd there, in part because so many New Jerseyans worked at the Trade Center. Ray recalls being absolutely swarmed from 7:00 to 9:00 A.M. Then there would be a long lull until lunchtime. "Then, at twelve noon, the doors would swing open and . . . just get ready."

The biggest change their farm has seen over the years is Sue's taking on restaurant clientele. Ray and Sue learned how to work with chefs like me, and vice versa, to make sure we can always get what we need from them. I do my part by preordering as much as possible by phone or fax, because they could sell out of asparagus by 10:00 A.M. at the Union Square Greenmarket. If I didn't do that, I'd do the next best thing: get there nice and early.

Ray and Sue have developed their business to play to their individual strengths. Sue is a real people person, and Ray is more at home in the fields. "I like walking out and seeing a good crop that you work to grow," he says, though he's quick to add that he's "not crazy about the actual labor." He says it as though he were kidding. But I get the feeling that he's not.

Ray and Sue have been rewarded with quite a bit of attention. Lidia Bastianich, chef-owner of Felidia restaurant, mentions their farm by name on her restaurant menu. I've mentioned them in *New York* magazine. And their farm has been photographed for *The New York Times*.

It's no surprise when Ray tells me that the biggest challenge he faces is the elements. "Hail can wipe you out in a few seconds," he says. So can a frost scare in the spring. They don't really have to worry about hurricanes anymore, so that's a plus. But you still have to admire the optimism and confidence it takes to be a farmer.

Tomato Oil

Drizzling this versatile, easy-to-make condiment over cooked meat, fish, or pasta is a delicious way to bring fresh tomato flavor, not to mention a rosy flash of color, to a dish. It can also be employed as a cooking medium, adding gentle acidity to sautéed vegetables. Or you can make it the basis of a tomato-tinged vinaigrette by whisking together two parts tomato oil, four parts Tomato Stock (page 129), and one part red wine vinegar.

The preparation of this oil leaves you with an irresistible by-product: the pulp that catches in the strainer is highly concentrated and a very satisfying spread on crusty bread.

1 cup plus 1 tablespoon extra-virgin olive oil

2 medium tomatoes, halved vertically, seeded, and roughly chopped

⅛ teaspoon crushed red pepper flakes

1 Combine 1 tablespoon of the olive oil and the tomatoes in a heavy 2-quart saucepan. Cook over low heat until the tomatoes have softened, 2 to 5 minutes. Add the red pepper flakes and let simmer, stirring and mashing slightly with a slotted spoon, until the tomatoes have gently curled skins and resemble tomato paste, about 20 minutes.

2 Stir in the remaining 1 cup olive oil and cook for 2 hours over very low heat. The resulting tomato oil may be used as is, or strained through a fine mesh strainer for a clear oil. The oil keeps, refrigerated, for about a month.

Marinated Cherry Tomatoes

SERVES 4

ere's another tomato recipe for which you'll find endless uses. Spoon these little tomatoes over toasted bread for bruschetta, toss them with hot pasta for a quick meal, or make a tomato salad by topping sliced, lightly salted heirloom tomatoes with them. Or re-create one of JUdson Grill's classic summer salads by tossing them with cooked, cooled wax beans and shards of dry Monterey Jack cheese.

The key to this recipe is letting the tomatoes marinate in the salt for 1 hour, which coaxes out beautiful, subtly nuanced tomato water.

2 pints cherry tomatoes, halved vertically	¾ cup extra-virgin olive oil
1½ teaspoons salt	6 tablespoons red wine vinegar
¼ cup tightly packed fresh oregano leaves	

1   In a small bowl, toss the tomatoes with ½ teaspoon of the salt and let sit for 1 hour to slowly draw out their juices.

2   Make a little mound of the oregano on your cutting board, pour the remaining 1 teaspoon salt on top, and mince very finely. (The salt will help break up the sturdy leaves and cause them to release their oils.) Transfer the paste to a bowl and add ¼ cup of the olive oil and 2 tablespoons of the vinegar. Set aside.

3   When the tomatoes are ready, stir in the remaining ½ cup olive oil and ¼ cup vinegar, and the oregano mixture. Eat this dish the day you make it.

Tomato Stock

This is my tomato stock of choice for cooking vegetables and making vegetable risotto. It also makes a summery vinaigrette (see Tomato Oil, page 127).

2 tablespoons extra-virgin olive oil	2 sprigs oregano
½ cup chopped onion	2 sprigs thyme
4 cloves garlic, thinly sliced	2 medium tomatoes, diced
2 teaspoons black peppercorns	4 cups Vegetable Stock (page 344) or water

1   Combine the olive oil, onion, and garlic in a heavy-bottomed 3-quart saucepan. Cook over medium-low heat, stirring and taking care not to let the mixture brown, until the onions have softened, 3 to 5 minutes.

2   Add the peppercorns, oregano, and thyme, breaking the herbs into bits as you add them. Add the tomatoes and cook for 5 minutes. Add the stock, raise the heat to high, and bring to a boil. Lower the heat and let simmer, stirring occasionally, for 20 minutes.

3   Pour the mixture through a fine-mesh strainer into a container, pressing on the solids to extract as much liquid as possible. Let cool, cover, and refrigerate or freeze until ready to use. The stock will keep, chilled, for 2 weeks, or frozen for 1 month.

Green Tomato Compote

Young, green tomatoes lend themselves to a compote because they're harder than fully matured red tomatoes, which means they can be cooked for a longer time without sacrificing flavor. Their lemony tartness makes them an ideal condiment for the Striped Bass with Shell Beans and Garlic Kale (page 93) or any light fish or meat.

2 tablespoons butter

¼ cup minced onion

3 cloves garlic, peeled

Salt

2 tablespoons white wine vinegar

6 medium green tomatoes, cored, peeled, halved horizontally, seeds removed, and cut into ½-inch dice

1 Place the butter, onion, and garlic in a large, heavy-bottomed saucepan set over medium-low heat. When the butter has melted, add a pinch of salt and cook for 5 minutes. Add the vinegar and cook until it evaporates, about 2½ minutes.

2 Stir in the tomatoes and a pinch of salt, and add enough room-temperature water to just cover the tomatoes. Cook over medium-low heat for 30 to 35 minutes, until the liquid has nearly evaporated and the compote looks slightly translucent.

3 Remove the saucepan from the heat, let the compote cool, transfer to an airtight container, then cover and refrigerate for up to 2 weeks.

Tomato Bread Soup

MAKES 7 CUPS

The classic Italian tomato and bread soup is one of my favorite soups of all time. There are only a handful of ingredients here, but it's deeply flavored and very satisfying. On a recent trip to Italy, I had four different versions of it, one of which was served cold, my preferred way of eating it. This is a composite of those soups, taking the best of each and combining them into one recipe.

3 pounds red plum tomatoes, cored

One 14-ounce can whole peeled plum tomatoes, with their juice

½ cup extra-virgin olive oil, plus more for serving

½ medium onion, minced

3 cloves garlic, minced

Salt

Freshly ground black pepper

4 ounces day-old sourdough bread, crusts removed, cut into ½-inch cubes (about 2 cups cubes)

Basil Ricotta (recipe follows)

Basil Puree (recipe follows)

Grated ricotta salata (see page 144)

1 Fill a large bowl halfway with ice water.

2 Using a small knife, score an X on the bottom of the plum tomatoes. Bring a large pot of water to a rolling boil. Place the tomatoes in the boiling water and boil for 30 seconds to 1 minute, until the scored skin starts to peel away. Transfer the tomatoes to the ice water and let cool for 2 minutes. Peel the skin from the tomatoes.

3 Halve the plum tomatoes horizontally and squeeze the juice and seeds into a strainer. Save the juice; discard the seeds.

4 Place the plum tomatoes in a food processor fitted with the metal blade and pulse to a medium chop. Set aside with the strained juice. Repeat with the canned tomatoes and add them to the plum tomatoes. Set aside.

(continued)

5   Place the olive oil, onion, and garlic into a 4-quart soup pot, season with salt and pepper, and cook over medium heat until tender but not browned, 12 to 15 minutes. Add the tomato mixture, season with salt and pepper, and bring to a simmer. Let simmer for about 1 hour, stirring occasionally.

6   While the soup is cooking, soak the bread in warm water for about 5 minutes. Remove the bread from the water and squeeze it dry in a clean towel. Work the bread into the soup with a whisk and cook an additional 15 minutes. Adjust seasoning.

7   Drizzle the soup with olive oil. Serve hot with Basil Ricotta, or cold with Basil Puree and grated ricotta salata.

Basil Ricotta

1 cup tightly packed basil leaves   Salt

1 cup good, fresh ricotta, drained
(see page 116)

Place the basil leaves in a food processor fitted with the metal blade and pulse to a rough chop. Add the ricotta and process until smooth. Season with salt.

Basil Puree

1 cup tightly packed basil leaves   ½ cup extra-virgin olive oil

1   Bring a pot of lightly salted water to a boil. Fill a large bowl halfway with ice water.

2   Add the basil leaves to the boiling water and blanch for 20 seconds. Drain, then plunge them into the ice water for 1 minute to stop the cooking and preserve their green color. Gather the basil together with your hands and squeeze out the liquid.

3   Place the basil into a food processor fitted with the metal blade. Add the olive oil and process until finely pureed. Season with salt.

Green Tomato Pie

SERVES 8

This pie is a wonderful reminder that, although they are usually used as a vegetable, tomatoes are in fact a fruit. I had my first taste of green tomato pie when my sister Cindy Cascella brought one to my parents' house. I loved it and so did my dad, George, though it took quite a bit of coaxing to get him to try it.

Pie Pastry

2 cups flour, plus more for dusting work surface

Generous pinch of salt

10 tablespoons (1 stick plus 2 tablespoons) cold butter, cut into teaspoon-sized pieces

1 egg yolk

1/3 cup sour cream

1　In the bowl of an electric mixer fitted with the paddle attachment, combine the flour and salt. Add the butter and mix until crumbly (small pieces of butter should be visible). Add the egg yolk and sour cream, and mix just until a dough forms. Wrap in plastic wrap and chill for at least 1 hour in the refrigerator.

2　Cut the dough into 2 equal pieces. On a lightly floured surface, roll 1 piece into an 11-inch circle. Slide a metal spatula underneath the dough to ensure it won't stick. Fold the circle in half and lay it into a 9-inch pie plate. Gently press into the corners and up the sides of the plate. Turn the dough under itself on the edges of the plate. Flour your work surface again and roll the remaining piece of dough into an 11-inch circle.

(continued)

Filling and Assembly

1¼ to 1½ cups plus 2 tablespoons sugar

½ teaspoon ground cinnamon

½ teaspoon freshly grated nutmeg

5 tablespoons flour

2 pounds (about 5 large) green tomatoes, peeled and thinly sliced

2 tablespoons freshly squeezed lemon juice

1 egg

1 In a large mixing bowl, combine 1¼ cups of the sugar, the cinnamon, nutmeg, and flour. Add the tomatoes and lemon juice, and toss to coat. Let sit at room temperature for 45 minutes. Check the sweetness by tasting a coated slice of tomato, not by tasting the sugar mixture alone. Add additional sugar if necessary.

2 Preheat the oven to 400°F.

3 Fill the dough-lined pie plate with the tomato slices and all the juice. Free the rolled dough circle from the work surface, fold it in half, and place on top of the filling. Trim any excess dough and crimp all around the edge of the pie.

4 In a small bowl, beat the egg with 1 tablespoon water.

5 Brush the top crust with the egg wash and sprinkle with the remaining 2 tablespoons sugar. Bake for about 55 minutes, until the pie filling is bubbling around the edges and the crust is brown.

TIM STARK

**ECKERTON HILL FARM
LENHARTSVILLE, PENNSYLVANIA**

I've always considered Tim Stark something of a culinary soul mate. About ten years ago, Tim was an aspiring writer who supported himself by working as a freelance consultant in New York City. Tim began farming as an extension of his love of growing tomatoes in the garden of his own backyard. When he started bringing his homegrown tomatoes and "weird" hot peppers back to New York after the weekend, the word began to get around and chefs like me began buying from him.

In 1996, he and his then girlfriend (now his wife), Jill, began farming between six and seven acres a year from the backyard of the very house he grew up in, which is still owned by his mother. The secret to Tim's success is that he still raises tomatoes the way he did when he was just doing it for himself and his friends. His farm isn't certified organic, but he doesn't use any chemical sprays or fertilizer. He treats all his tomatoes as if he were going to bring them back from a weekend and give them to his friends. What a great way to do business.

Making the Most of Summer Vegetables

Spicy Kohlrabi and Cucumber Ceviche with Muskmelon and Cilantro

Beet Greens Pierogi with Mixed Summer Beets, Brown Butter Sauce, and Ricotta Salata

Napoleon of Corn, Chanterelles, and Shell Beans with Roasted Onions and a Red Currant Compote

Lavender Crêpes with Blueberries

Trust me here: If you really want to appreciate the incredible variety and flavor of summer vegetables, make them the centerpiece of a special-occasion dinner and see how amazed everybody is at how delicious a meat-free meal can be.

This menu throws so many flavors and textures at the palate that some diners might not even notice it's vegetarian. The Spicy Kohlrabi and Cucumber Ceviche with Muskmelon and Cilantro (page 137) adapts a classic way of preparing fish to a vegetarian use. Beet Greens Pierogi with Mixed Summer Beets, Brown Butter Sauce, and Ricotta Salata (page 139) are finished with a rich brown butter sauce. The Napoleon of Corn, Chanterelles, and Shell Beans with Roasted Onions and a Red Currant Compote (page 145) finds a depth of flavor in the variety of vegetables and the combination of roasted onions and sweet currants.

The Lavender Crêpes with Blueberries (page 148) are a nice, light way to conclude this meal, but they would also be at home with a nonvegetarian feast.

Spicy Kohlrabi and Cucumber Ceviche with Muskmelon and Cilantro

SERVES 4

eviche is a Peruvian dish in which the acid in the vinaigrette produces the same changes in the color, texture, and flavor of fish as when fish is cooked. This vegetarian version features many of the fruits, vegetables, and herbs often found in a ceviche, like cucumber, melon, and cilantro.

Kohlrabi, a member of the cabbage family, has an otherworldly appearance, especially when its leaves are intact. It comes in green and purple varieties, and both have a similar taste and texture: crisp and slightly bitter raw, sweet when cooked. Kohlrabi should be hard. If you're lucky enough to get one with its leaves, cook them as I do the kale on page 95 or 186.

1 medium kohlrabi (about ½ pound), peeled, halved, and cut into ⅛-inch half-circle-shaped slices, ideally on a mandoline

½ cup freshly squeezed lemon juice (from about 4 lemons)

½ cup freshly squeezed lime juice (from about 6 limes)

¼ red onion, halved, ends trimmed, and sliced paper-thin, ideally on a mandoline

1 jalapeño pepper, sliced paper-thin, ideally on a mandoline

1 muskmelon or cantaloupe, about 3 pounds

1 cucumber, peeled

½ cup extra-virgin olive oil

2 tablespoons thinly sliced cilantro leaves, plus 8 whole sprigs

2 tablespoons chopped flat-leaf parsley

Salt

1   Place the kohlrabi, lemon and lime juices, onion, and jalapeño in a medium bowl, and stir to combine. Cover the bowl with plastic wrap, pressing the plastic down onto the surface of the mixture to keep air out and make sure the vegetables are submerged in the liquid. Marinate for 2 hours in the refrigerator.

(continued)

2   Halve, seed, and peel the melon, then cut one half into chunks. Place the chunks in a blender and blend until smooth, then pour into a fine-mesh strainer set over a bowl. Press on the puree with a ladle to extract as much liquid as possible. You should have 1½ cups of melon juice. If not, add some water. Cut the remaining half of the melon into quarters, then slice across the quarters to make ⅛-inch slices. Chill the juice and melon slices separately.

3   Halve the cucumber lengthwise, scoop out the seeds, and slice crosswise into ⅛-inch slices. Pour the chilled kohlrabi mixture into a strainer set over a bowl—reserve the marinade—then transfer from the strainer to a separate, larger bowl.

4   In a small bowl, stir together ½ cup of the reserved marinade with the olive oil and chilled melon juice to make a vinaigrette. Add the cucumber, cilantro leaves, and parsley to the kohlrabi, and pour the melon vinaigrette over the vegetables. Stir to combine the ingredients and season with salt to taste.

5   To serve, arrange chilled melon slices in a 3-inch circle in the bottom of four shallow bowls. Use a slotted spoon to top with ceviche, then ladle ⅓ to ½ cup of the melon vinaigrette into the bottom of each bowl. Garnish each serving with 2 cilantro sprigs.

Wine

A white wine with crisp acidity would be the best way to match the can-be-difficult citrus juices and hot pepper in this dish. Go with a wine from the Greek island of Santorini made from the mineral-driven, highly acidic assyrtiko grape, such as Thalassitis (meaning "of the sea") from Gaia Wines. A dry, crisp northern Italian white such as a pinot bianco or tocai would also go well.

TO MAKE A TRUE CEVICHE

Double the quantities used to make the marinade in Step 1, and add 10 halved, peeled shrimp. Cover and let marinate in the refrigerator for 2 hours. Add the kohlrabi and proceed with the recipe.

Beet Greens Pierogi with Mixed Summer Beets, Brown Butter Sauce, and Ricotta Salata

SERVES 4

grew up eating pierogi, Eastern European dumplings that are traditionally filled with potatoes or sauerkraut. I now make them with a wide variety of fillings, most of which are inspired by ravioli. That's how I came to fill pierogi with beet greens, a variation on popular Italian fillings like spinach and kale. Beet greens should be crisp, crunchy, and green. They should snap where they meet the stalk and be nice and juicy. Cook them as you would any wilted or sautéed greens.

The brown butter in this dish is based on one made by Gotham Bar and Grill's Alfred Portale, with whom I worked as sous chef; adding cream and blending it make it silky and extra-rich, and the vinegar gives it a pleasing tang.

Beets

1 bunch baby golden beets with tops, tops trimmed and set aside for filling

1 bunch baby chioggia beets, tops trimmed and set aside for use as filling

2 tablespoons extra-virgin olive oil

Kosher salt

Freshly ground black pepper

2 tablespoons butter

2 tablespoons white wine vinegar

1 Preheat the oven to 450°F.

2 Put each type of beet in a separate baking pan. Drizzle each pan with 1 tablespoon of the olive oil and 2 tablespoons water, and season lightly with salt and pepper. Cover each pan with aluminum foil and roast the beets until they are tender when pierced with a sharp, thin-bladed knife, 25 to 30 minutes. Remove from the oven and set aside to let the beets cool.

(continued)

3 When the beets are cool, peel by rubbing them with a clean, dry kitchen towel; the skins should come right off. Cut into ⅛-inch slices (a mandoline comes in handy here, if you have one). Heat 1 tablespoon of the butter in a large skillet set over high heat. When the butter bubbles, add half of the sliced beets, arranging them in a single layer. When the beets start to brown, after about 2 minutes, add 1 tablespoon of the vinegar and season with salt and pepper. Gently stir and carefully flip the beets with a spatula. Transfer to a warm plate and repeat with the remaining beet slices.

Pierogi Dough

MAKES 14

1½ cups flour, plus more for dusting work surface

2 teaspoons kosher salt

2 eggs

1 Combine the flour and salt in a large bowl. In a separate bowl, beat the eggs with 2 tablespoons water. Form a well in the middle of the flour mixture and pour the eggs into the well. Incorporate the eggs by stirring in the flour mixture from the sides of the well a little at a time.

2 When the dough begins to come together in clumps, transfer it to a clean flat surface and knead for a few minutes until the dough comes together in a smooth ball (don't overwork the dough, or it will develop the gluten in the flour and make the dough tough). Wrap the dough in plastic wrap and let rest for at least 1 hour at room temperature. (Dough may be made 1 day ahead and kept, wrapped in plastic, in the refrigerator.)

Beet-Greens Filling

2 bunches beet greens, about 1¼ pounds (if less than 1¼ pounds; supplement with Swiss chard)

1 heaping tablespoon freshly grated Parmigiano-Reggiano cheese

⅓ cup drained ricotta (see page 116) (if your ricotta is moist, drain it in a cheesecloth-lined sieve for at least 1 hour, until dry and crumbly)

Freshly ground black pepper

Salt

1   Cut the stems from the beet greens at the bottom of the leaves. Wash the greens by swishing them in a bowl of water, letting them sit for a few minutes to settle the dirt, then gently lifting them out (this will also rehydrate the greens should they be a bit wilted; you can try this with lettuces, too).

2   Place a wire cooling rack on a cookie or baking sheet. Bring a large pot of salted water to a boil and blanch the beet greens for 1 minute, then lift them out with a slotted spoon and spread on the rack to simultaneously cool and drain. Put the sheet with the greens in the refrigerator to chill for about 20 minutes. (This fast cooling helps preserve their color and texture.) When the greens are cool, gather them up and squeeze out any liquid. Chop them very finely, then gather them up again, place in a kitchen towel, and wring out more liquid. You should have a heaping ½ cup packed with chopped greens.

3   In a medium mixing bowl, combine the Parmigiano-Reggiano and ricotta until thoroughly blended. Add the squeezed greens and season with pepper and a generous amount of salt. Mash the filling with a wooden spoon to combine. The filling should be moist enough to hold together when pressed. (The filling may be made 1 day ahead and kept, covered, in the refrigerator.)

Brown Butter Sauce

2 tablespoons white wine vinegar	¼ cup cream
4 tablespoons (½ stick) butter	Pinch of kosher salt

1   Place the vinegar in a deep, heatproof bowl.

2   Place the butter and cream in a small, heavy-bottomed saucepan and bring to a boil over medium-high heat. Reduce the heat to medium-low and whisk constantly for about 5 minutes, until the mixture thickens to the consistency of mayonnaise and the milk solids separate out and float on top. Transfer the mixture to a food processor fitted with the metal blade and process for 20 seconds to break up the solids. Return the mixture to the saucepan and cook over medium-low heat, whisking constantly, for about 3 minutes, until its color changes from reddish brown to a deep walnut brown.

3   Add the mixture to the vinegar (it will foam up a bit). Add the salt and swirl the sauce and vinegar around. (You may notice little bits of milk solids in the mixture, but don't worry about them; they're sweet, nutty, and delicious.) Set aside.

(continued)

Assembly

2 tablespoons chopped flat-leaf parsley

One 2-ounce piece of room-temperature ricotta salata, sliced thin with a vegetable peeler (see page 144)

1   To fill the pierogi, divide the dough into 4 pieces and wrap all but one in plastic wrap to keep moist.

2   Sprinkle a work surface with flour. Roll out the unwrapped dough thinly enough to fit through the largest setting of a pasta machine. Feed it through the machine until you attain about 1/16-inch thickness. (If you don't have a pasta machine, use a rolling pin to roll the dough to the desired thickness.) Use a 4-inch ring cutter to cut out circles from the dough sheet. Cover the circles with plastic wrap or a kitchen towel to prevent drying while rolling out the remaining dough. Repeat to form 14 circles. (You're making 2 extra pierogi just in case a couple happen to break.)

3   Place a scant tablespoon of beet-greens filling just to one side of the center of each circle. Working with one pierogi at a time, paint the outer 1/4 inch of the circle with a pastry brush dipped in water. Fold the circle in half over the filling, pressing its edges to seal: start at the top of the pierogi, pressing gently outward around the filling as you do so to push out all the air around the filling—trapped air will make a pierogi swell like a small balloon, and it may burst when cooked. Seal the pierogi by pressing tines of a fork around its edges. Transfer the finished pierogi to a lightly floured baking sheet. Repeat with the remaining circles. Cover the finished pierogi with plastic wrap and set aside.

4   Bring a large pot of salted water to a boil. Carefully add the pierogi, stirring gently to make sure they do not stick to the bottom of the pot. Return to a boil and cook for 7 to 8 minutes, until the dough edge no longer feels stiff when pinched and looks slightly translucent.

5   Using a slotted spoon, transfer the pierogi to kitchen towels to drain. (To make the pierogi several hours ahead of time, transfer them from the boiling water to a bowl of ice water until well chilled, approximately 5 minutes, then drain. Reheat the pierogi in boiling water before proceeding with the recipe. To freeze pierogi, boil them for just 2 minutes, transfer to a bowl of ice water, and drain. Arrange them on a lightly oiled baking sheet and freeze until hard, then lift them from the sheet and transfer to a freezer bag. Pierogi keep, frozen, for 1 month. To cook frozen pierogi, bring a pot of salted water to a boil and add the pierogi. Return to a boil and cook for 2 to 3 minutes, until al dente.)

(continued)

6   Place the pierogi, brown butter, and 1 tablespoon of the parsley in a large skillet, gently stirring (or tossing) once or twice to mingle the flavors. Cook on high heat for about 1 minute, until heated through. Divide the beet slices among four plates (about 18 slices per plate). On each plate, arrange 3 pierogi on top of the beets. Using a spoon, scrape up the sauce from the skillet and dribble a tablespoonful or so over and around the pierogi. Top each serving with a few slices of ricotta salata, and sprinkle with the remaining 1 tablespoon parsley.

Wine

A full-bodied rosé stands up to the complexity of this dish with the earthy beet and beet-green flavors matching the rich brown-butter notes. A cabernet franc–based wine, such as a Chinon rosé from the Loire Valley, has the essential earthy, herbal note necessary to match the beets.

RICOTTA SALATA

It's hard to find fresh ricotta and ricotta salata (salted dried ricotta) at the super-market. Try looking in a good Italian grocery store or a cheese shop, or order them by mail (see Mail-Order Sources, page 345).

Napoleon of Corn, Chanterelles, and Shell Beans with Roasted Onions and a Red Currant Compote

SERVES 4

This dish is a fun take on a napoleon, a layered dessert pastry. The classic is made with puff pastry, but I use corn pancakes in this savory adaptation.

Fresh shell beans are at their peak when the pods begin to feel a bit dry but the shells still retain their bright sheen. Be sure to avoid any that have black blemishes.

Roasted Onions

2 tablespoons butter

1 Vidalia or other sweet onion, cut horizontally into ½-inch rings

Salt

1   Preheat the oven to 400°F. Melt the butter in a heavy-bottomed, ovenproof saucepan set over low heat until just melted. Lay the onion slices in the pan and cover the pan with aluminum foil. Place the pan in the oven and roast for 40 minutes, or until the onions have softened and are lightly browned on the bottom. When the onions are done, remove the pan from the oven. Raise the oven temperature to 450°F.

2   Remove the foil from the pan, add 1 tablespoon water, and season with salt. Toss the onions gently in the pan to form a buttery glaze. Transfer the onions and their glaze to a small bowl and set aside.

(continued)

Red Currant Compote

6 ounces fresh red currants, stemmed and rinsed

1 tablespoon red or white wine vinegar

2 tablespoons sugar

1 Place half of the currants in a small saucepan with the vinegar and sugar. Bring to a simmer over medium heat and let simmer for 2 to 3 minutes.

2 Press the currant mixture through a fine-mesh strainer into a small bowl and discard the pulp in the strainer. Add the remaining currants to the strained liquid, transfer to the same pot, and bring to a simmer. Remove the saucepan from the heat and set aside.

Chanterelles and Corn

2 medium ears corn, in husk

½ pound fresh chanterelles, tough, dirty stem ends and dirty, broken edges of caps trimmed, and large ones cut in half

4 tablespoons (½ stick) butter

Salt

2 cups cooked mixed shell beans (page 94), with ½ cup of their cooking liquid

Freshly ground black pepper

1 tablespoon loosely packed chopped fresh chives, thyme, and/or oregano

1 Grill the corn in its husk on a gas grill or in a ridged grill pan, turning the corn as it cooks until it's blackened on all sides, or broil it under the boiler until blackened on all sides. Remove the corn from the heat and set aside to cool. When the corn is cool enough to handle, remove the husk, cut the kernels off the cobs, and set aside.

2 Preheat a heavy-bottomed, 12-inch sauté pan over medium-high heat. Melt 2 tablespoons of the butter in the pan, add the chanterelles, and season with salt. Cook, tossing occasionally, until the mushrooms begin to release their liquid and are tender but not browned, 3 to 5 minutes. Add the corn, mixed beans and their liquid, and the remaining 2 tablespoons butter. Toss over low to medium heat to warm the beans and melt the butter, with the liquid forming a glaze. Season the mixture with salt, pepper, and the herbs. Set aside.

Corn Blini and Assembly

¾ cup corn kernels (cut from
2 medium ears)

1 egg

1 tablespoon sour cream

⅔ cup milk

6 tablespoons yellow corn flour
(finely ground cornmeal)

6 tablespoons flour

½ teaspoon baking powder

1 teaspoon salt

1 tablespoon chopped chives

3 tablespoons butter

1   Bring a small pot of water to a boil over high heat. Add the corn to the pot and cook
    for 1 minute, or until the water returns to a boil. Drain the corn, turn it out onto a
    cutting board, and finely chop it. Mash the corn with the side of large, wide knife to
    release its starch.

2   In a small bowl, whisk together the egg, sour cream, and milk. In another small bowl,
    stir together the corn flour, flour, baking powder, and salt. Add the flour mixture to
    the egg mixture and stir in the corn kernels and chives.

3   Heat a large, heavy-bottomed, ovenproof sauté pan over medium heat and melt 1 table-
    spoon of the butter. When the butter is bubbling, spoon in 2 tablespoons of the batter to
    form a blini 3 inches in diameter. Cook two or three at a time but do not crowd the pan.
    When the blini edges begin to turn brown, 30 to 45 seconds, pop the pan into the oven
    and cook until done on the surface, 2 to 3 minutes. Remove the pan from the oven, turn
    the blini over, and cook for 1 more minute over medium heat on the stovetop. Transfer
    the blini to a plate and set aside. Repeat with the remaining batter, melting another table-
    spoon of butter in the pan before starting each batch, until the batter is finished.

4   To serve, using a slotted spoon, put a spoonful of chanterelle mixture in the center of
    each of four plates. Top with a blini and 2 or 3 separated onion rings. Top the rings with
    another spoonful of chanterelles, a second blini, a smaller spoonful of chanterelles,
    several onion rings, and ½ teaspoon of currant compote, drizzling another ½ teaspoon
    of compote around the edge of the plate. Finish by drizzling some liquid from the
    chanterelle mixture around and on top of the napoleon.

Wine

A round, full white with earthy notes would pair well with the corn and chanterelles. Try a
white Rhône blend, such as Maison Chapoutier's Crozes-Hermitage Blanc "Les Meysonniers."

Lavender Crêpes with Blueberries

SERVES 6

avender, an herb generally employed to make perfume, has a distinct and arresting aroma that, when used in cooking, gives a dish an enchanting, almost magical, air. You can buy it dried in spice jars, or fresh from greenmarkets. In this recipe, it's the perfect match for blueberries. You can adapt this dish to use strawberries or raspberries and the lavender would still be delicious. The sautéed berries themselves can be used as a great, quick topping for vanilla ice cream.

Filling

1½ cups milk

2 teaspoons dried lavender blossoms, or one 3-inch sprig fresh lavender

⅓ cup plus 1 tablespoon sugar

4 egg yolks

3 tablespoons cornstarch

2 tablespoons butter

1 Place the milk and lavender in a heavy-bottomed saucepan. Bring the milk to a boil, then remove from the heat. Add the sugar and stir until it has dissolved. Steep for 30 minutes to infuse the milk with the lavender.

2 Fill a large bowl halfway with ice water. In a mixing bowl, whisk the egg yolks and cornstarch until they form a smooth paste. Add a large ladleful of the lavender milk to the yolk mixture and whisk until smooth. Pour the yolk mixture into the remaining lavender milk, whisking continuously. Cook over medium heat, stirring constantly, until the mixture comes to a boil. (If the mixture begins to lump, remove from the heat immediately and whisk vigorously until smooth. Lower the heat and continue cooking until the mixture again comes to a boil.) Immediately pour the mixture into a bowl, stir in the butter, and place the bowl over the ice water bath, stirring occasionally to release the heat and help the mixture cool to room temperature as quickly as possible. Cover with plastic wrap and refrigerate.

(continued)

Crêpes

2 eggs

¼ cup milk

½ cup seltzer or club soda

1 tablespoon sugar

2 tablespoons melted butter

¼ teaspoon salt

½ cup flour

1   In a medium mixing bowl, lightly beat the eggs. Whisk in the milk, seltzer, sugar, melted butter, and salt. Add the flour and whisk until the mixture is free of lumps and has reached a pourable consistency.

2   Set a dinner plate next to the stove. Warm a 12-inch sauté pan over low heat. Coat the pan with a thin layer of the batter (¼ cup is plenty per crêpe), shaking and tilting the pan as you pour. Try to form an even layer, as the crêpes cook too quickly to patch any "holes."

3   As soon as the crêpe sits up and smells buttery, lift one edge with a spatula or your fingers and transfer it to the dinner plate. (There is no need to flip and cook the other side.) Aim to have blond, uncolored crêpes. There is enough batter for 8 crêpes, so you may choose the best-looking and thinnest for the dessert. Continue cooking the crêpes, stacking them on the plate when done. Wrap with plastic wrap and set aside.

Blueberries and Assembly

⅓ cup sugar

Juice of 2 lemons

3 tablespoons butter

1 pint blueberries

Confectioners' sugar

1 Preheat the oven to 350°F. Line 6 muffin cups with cupcake or muffin papers.

2 Remove the filling from the refrigerator. It will be quite solid. Whisk until loose and creamy. Carefully lift the top crêpe from the pile, then replace it on the stack. Spoon 3 tablespoons of filling into the center and gather the crêpe around the filling, pinching at the top to seal. Gently lift the "purse" and place it in a lined muffin cup. Continue with the remaining crêpes, releasing each from the pile before filling. There will be enough filling for 6 "purses."

3 Bake for 15 minutes. The crêpes should be toasty brown at the gathered edges and the filling warm.

4 While the crêpes are baking, cook the blueberries: In a small pot, combine the sugar and lemon juice. Bring to a rolling boil and add the butter. Add the blueberries and toss to coat. Cook just until the berries are juicy and warmed through.

5 To serve, unmold the crêpes, place 1 on each of six plates, dust with confectioners' sugar, and top with the sauce.

Wine

The floral notes in the crêpes and the fresh blueberry flavors would go best with a floral muscat from the village of Beaumes-de-Venise in the southern Côtes-du-Rhône. Try one from Domaine Fenouillet.

Make-Ahead Menu

Summer Minestrone
with Basil

Plum Streusel Cake

If you've ever wished that you could use up every vegetable at the market at the height of summer, here's your chance. The minestrone that follows is a deliberately generous recipe that makes a ton of soup; you can freeze any remaining soup in batches. I recommend serving this with thick slices of sourdough toast covered with Parmigiano-Reggiano cheese (see page 154). It doesn't get any yummier than that.

The one vegetable here that might be unfamiliar to some readers is okra. When cooked, okra releases a uniquely viscous starch that naturally thickens soups, and it's also terrific in corn chowder. The easiest way to check okra for freshness is that its pointy tip should snap rather than bend, and it should be green with no black spots, which indicates too much time on the vine.

Plums and streusel are two of my favorite things in the world. The cake here rounds out their flavors with the tangy addition of quark, a fresh, unripened cheese that's produced by a process similar to that used for cottage cheese. Unlike cottage cheese, quark is smooth and creamy, without those little curds. I often use it as a condiment, the same way you'd use crème fraîche.

Summer Minestrone with Basil

SERVES 6 TO 8 (MAKES ABOUT 4 QUARTS)

2 tablespoons pine nuts

1 cup fava beans (from about 2 pounds pods)

³/₄ cup extra-virgin olive oil

¹/₂ medium onion, minced

2 cloves garlic, minced

1 carrot, halved lengthwise and cut into ¹/₈-inch slices

1 celery stalk, peeled and cut on the diagonal into ¹/₈-inch slices

1 white turnip, peeled, quartered, and cut into ¹/₈-inch slices

1 leek, white part only, sliced into ¹/₈-inch rounds, well washed in several changes of cold water, and drained

1 large bunch basil, stems separated from leaves (about 1¹/₂ cups leaves), and both washed stems tied in a bundle with kitchen string

10 cups Vegetable Stock (page 344) or water

One 1 by 4-inch piece Parmigiano-Reggiano cheese rind

2 tablespoons freshly grated Parmigiano-Reggiano cheese, plus more for serving

Salt

Freshly ground black pepper

1 medium Idaho potato, peeled and cut into ¹/₄-inch dice

6 okra pods, cut crosswise into ¹/₄-inch slices

10 wax beans or green string beans, stems removed and halved crosswise

Corn kernels cut from 1 ear corn

1 medium zucchini, halved lengthwise, seeds removed, and cut into ¹/₈-inch slices

1 cup cooked mixed shell beans (page 94) or cooked cranberry beans

1 bunch green Swiss chard (about 12 ounces with stems, 6 ounces without stems), tough stems cut out, leaves julienned

Sourdough toasts, optional (see page 154)

1   Put the pine nuts in a sauté pan set over medium heat and toast, tossing every 30 seconds, for about 2 minutes, until lightly browned. Set aside.

2   Bring a pot of lightly salted water to a boil. Fill a large bowl halfway with ice water.

3   Add the fava beans to the boiling water and blanch for 30 seconds. Drain, then plunge them into the ice water for 2 minutes to stop the cooking and preserve their color.

(continued)

Remove the beans and peel them (if you peel from the smooth end, you can usually push the beans out easily). Set aside.

4   In an 8-quart pot, heat ¼ cup of the olive oil over medium-low heat until hot but not smoking. Add the onion and garlic and cook until softened but not browned, about 5 minutes. Add the carrot, celery, and turnip; cook for 5 minutes, stirring occasionally. Stir in the leek and cook for 3 minutes. Add the basil stems, stock, and cheese rind. Bring the stock to a boil over high heat, then lower the heat and let simmer for 20 minutes.

5   While the soup is cooking, make the pesto: Bring a pot of lightly salted water to a boil. Fill a large bowl halfway with ice water. Add the basil leaves to the boiling water and blanch for 20 seconds. Drain, then plunge them into the ice water for 2 minutes to stop the cooking and preserve their green color. Gather the basil together with your hands and squeeze out the liquid. Place the basil in a blender or food processor fitted with a metal blade and add the remaining ½ cup olive oil, the grated cheese, and pine nuts. Process until smooth. Season with salt and pepper.

6   Returning your attention to the soup, add the potato and okra and simmer for 5 minutes. Add the wax or string beans and simmer for 5 minutes. Add the corn, zucchini, cooked shell beans, favas, and Swiss chard, and bring to a boil. Remove the pot from the heat. Use tongs to pick out and discard the basil stems and rind. Season with salt and pepper.

7   If using the sourdough toasts, place them into warm bowls. Spoon the soup over them and swirl a spoonful of pesto into each bowl. Serve with extra grated Parmigiano-Reggiano on the side.

Wine
The bright, herbal flavors of summer vegetables are a classic pairing with wines that hail from the home of pesto, Italy's Ligurian coast. Try the latest vintage of A Maccia's Pigato. Since a crisp, herbal white is called for with this dish, you could also try an Oregon pinot gris.

TO MAKE SOURDOUGH TOASTS
Preheat the oven to 450°F. Place 3-inch squares of sourdough bread on a cookie sheet. Drizzle them with olive oil and grated Parmigiano-Reggiano cheese. Bake in the oven until golden brown.

Plum Streusel Cake

SERVES 8

10 tablespoons (1 stick plus 2 table-spoons) butter

¾ cup sugar

1 teaspoon vanilla extract

Grated zest of 1 lime

1½ cups plus 2 tablespoons flour

1½ cups mixed varieties of diced plums (about 1 pound), pits removed

Juice of ½ lime

⅛ teaspoon salt

1 egg

¼ teaspoon pumpkin pie spice

⅛ teaspoon baking soda

¼ teaspoon baking powder

⅓ cup quark, or ricotta cheese

1   Make the crumbs by putting 4 tablespoons of the butter, ¼ cup of the sugar, ½ teaspoon of the vanilla, the lime zest, and ¾ cup plus 2 tablespoons of the flour into the bowl of an electric mixer fitted with the paddle attachment. Paddle at low speed until the crumbs are pea-sized. Set aside.

2   In a bowl, toss the plums with the lime juice. Set aside.

3   Preheat the oven to 350°F.

4   In a bowl, cream the remaining 6 tablespoons butter and ½ cup sugar until light. Add the salt, the remaining ½ teaspoon vanilla, and the egg. Beat until well integrated, scraping down the bowl if necessary.

5   Place the pumpkin pie spice, baking soda, baking powder, and remaining ¾ cup flour in a small bowl and whisk to combine. On low speed, incorporate half of the dry ingredients into the creamed mixture. Add the quark, mixing until just combined. Add the remaining dry ingredients and mix until smooth.

6   Line the bottom of an 8-inch round pan with a circle of parchment paper. Spread the cake batter evenly into the lined pan. Top with the plums and sprinkle with the crumbs. Bake for about 50 minutes, until a knife inserted into the center comes out clean. Cool and remove from the pan. Peel away the paper and place on a serving dish. Slice and serve.

Wine

This cake would pair with a wide variety of sweet wines. A special treat would be Mount Horrocks Cordon Cut Late Harvest Riesling from South Australia's Clare Valley.

Preserving and Pickling

My first introduction to preserving and pickling came from my grandmother, who did quite a bit of it. I love pickling for its nostalgic value, and also for the way it lets you save time in a bottle. Here are some of my favorite pickling recipes. For instructions on sterilizing jars and processing the pickles, I refer you to the experts at www.homecanning.com

Bread-and-Butter Pickles

n school, I was the kid who asked all the other kids for the pickles off their hamburgers. I still love pickles, and when we make these at the restaurant, I eat them like candy. The secret ingredient is the celery seed, which is what imparts that bread-and-butter-pickle flavor.

4 pounds Kirby cucumbers, scrubbed, tips removed, and cut into ¼-inch slices

2 onions, halved lengthwise, ends trimmed, and thinly sliced lengthwise

1 cup kosher salt

5 cups sugar

5 cups cider vinegar

3 teaspoons celery seeds

3 teaspoons mustard seeds

3 teaspoons turmeric

1 In a large bowl, stir together the cucumbers, onions, and salt, and add water to cover. Cover the bowl with plastic wrap and let sit overnight in the refrigerator.

2 The next day, drain the cucumbers and onions, and squeeze out as much of the remaining moisture as possible by hand; they don't need to be completely dry. Divide the cucumbers and onions among three sterilized 1-quart jars (or six 1-pint jars).

3 In a 2-quart saucepan, bring the sugar, vinegar, and spices to a boil over medium-high heat. Carefully pour the hot liquid over the vegetables in the jars. Fill to ¼ inch from the top with liquid. With a long thin spatula, gently stir the contents to release any trapped air bubbles. Seal the jars and process for 10 minutes. Let them cool to room temperature, then refrigerate. Pickles keep, chilled, for several months.

Pickled Beets

MAKES 2½ QUARTS

This is essentially the recipe for bread-and-butter pickles adapted for beets. It's a superior alternative to store-bought pickled beets.

4 pounds red beets, washed and trimmed, 1 inch of stem left intact to hold while slicing

2 tablespoons vegetable oil

1 teaspoon freshly ground black pepper

2 onions, halved lengthwise, ends trimmed, and thinly sliced lengthwise

2½ cups sugar

2½ cups cider vinegar

¼ cup kosher salt

1½ teaspoons celery seeds

1½ teaspoons mustard seeds

1   Preheat the oven to 450°F. Put the beets in a large baking pan. Drizzle them with the oil and ¼ cup water, and sprinkle with the pepper. Cover the pan with aluminum foil and roast the beets until they are tender when pierced with a sharp, thin-bladed knife, 45 minutes to 1 hour. Remove the pan from the oven and let the beets cool.

2   When the beets are cool, peel by rubbing them with a clean, dry dish towel; the skins should come right off. Cut them into ¼-inch slices. Divide the beet slices among three sterilized 1-quart jars.

3   Place the onions in a 2-quart pot. Add the sugar, vinegar, salt, celery seeds, and mustard seeds, and bring the mixture to a boil over medium-high heat. Carefully pour the hot liquid and onions over the beets in the jars. Fill to ¼ inch from the top with liquid. With a long thin spatula, gently stir the contents to release any trapped air bubbles. Seal the jars and process for 10 minutes. Let them cool to room temperature, then refrigerate. Pickles keep, chilled, for several months.

Dill Pickles

This recipe is a delicious way to use Kirby cucumbers, which are abundant in the summer.

1½ cups white vinegar

1 teaspoon mustard seeds

1 teaspoon coriander seeds

1 teaspoon black peppercorns

1 teaspoon celery seeds

¼ teaspoon crushed red pepper flakes

10 cloves garlic

3 small jalapeño peppers

¼ cup kosher salt

3 pounds Kirby cucumbers, scrubbed, tips removed, and cut into quarters lengthwise

6 sprigs dill

3 sprigs thyme

1 Combine the vinegar, mustard seeds, coriander seeds, peppercorns, celery seeds, red pepper flakes, garlic, jalapeño peppers, and 4½ cups water in a 2-quart pot. Bring the liquid to a boil over medium-high heat. Add the salt, lower the heat, and let simmer until it dissolves. Remove from the heat, let cool, and chill in the refrigerator.

2 Divide the cucumber quarters, dill, and thyme among three sterilized 1-quart jars (visit www.homecanning.com). When the liquid from the saucepan is cold, divide it among the jars. Seal the jars and let marinate in the refrigerator for at least 2 days. Pickles keep, chilled, for several months.

Cippoline-Rosemary Pickles

MAKES 3 QUARTS

This recipe uses vegetables that are plentiful in the late summer. Feel free to replace the cippoline with pearl onions.

1½ cups white vinegar

1 teaspoon mustard seeds

1 teaspoon coriander seeds

1 teaspoon black peppercorns

1 teaspoon celery seeds

¼ teaspoon crushed red pepper flakes

10 cloves garlic

¼ cup kosher salt

4 pounds cippoline onions, peeled, washed, roots trimmed, and larger ones halved through the root end

6 sprigs rosemary

1   Combine the vinegar, mustard seeds, coriander seeds, black peppercorns, celery seeds, red pepper flakes, garlic, and 4½ cups water in a 3-quart pot. Bring the liquid to a boil over medium-high heat. Add the salt, lower the heat, and let simmer until it dissolves. Add the onions to the liquid and let simmer for 5 more minutes.

2   Divide the onions and rosemary among three sterilized 1-quart jars. Carefully pour the hot liquid over the vegetables in the jars. Fill to ¼ inch from the top with liquid. With a long thin spatula, gently stir the contents to release any trapped air bubbles. Seal the jars and process for 10 minutes. Let them cool to room temperature, then refrigerate for at least 2 days. Pickles keep, chilled, for several months.

Chowchow

A chowchow is a relish-like mixture of diced vegetables including corn and cucumbers; it's traditionally served with tangy fried foods and barbecue. A great chowchow has a good balance of pepper, sugar, and vinegar. It even balances the often overwhelming flavor of bell peppers.

3 small cucumbers, peeled, seeded, and cut into ½-inch dice

Corn kernels cut from 5 ears corn

3 medium red bell peppers, seeded and cut into ½-inch dice

3 medium yellow bell peppers, seeded and cut into ½-inch dice

3 small red onions, cut into ½-inch dice

4 stalks celery, peeled and cut into ½-inch dice

4 whole cloves

4½ cups cider vinegar

1 cup sugar

⅓ cup kosher salt

1 In a large mixing bowl, stir together the cucumbers, corn, red peppers, yellow peppers, onions, and celery. Divide among four sterilized 1-quart jars (or eight 1-pint jars). (For helpful advice, visit www.homecanning.com)

2 In a 2-quart saucepan, bring the cloves, vinegar, and sugar to a simmer over high heat. Add the salt and let simmer until it dissolves. Carefully pour the hot liquid over the vegetables in the jars. Fill to ¼ inch from the top with liquid. With a long, thin spatula, gently stir the contents to release any trapped air bubbles. Seal the jars and process for 10 minutes. Let them cool to room temperature, then refrigerate for at least 2 days. Chowchow will keep, chilled, for several months.

Peach and Red Pepper Chutney

MAKES 1½ QUARTS

This lip-smacking tart-and-sweet chutney, tinged with just a bit of heat, is a delicious condiment for Foie Gras Terrine (page 182), and is also a perfect match with roasted and grilled meats.

5 slightly underripe peaches, skin on, cut into ½-inch dice

1 red bell pepper, cut into ¼-inch dice

1 red onion, cut into ¼-inch dice

¾ cup packed light brown sugar

1 cup cider vinegar

2 teaspoons black mustard seeds

1 tablespoon salt

1 Combine all of the ingredients in a heavy-bottomed 3-quart saucepan. Cook, stirring occasionally, over medium-low heat until syrupy, about 1 hour.

2 Divide the chutney among three sterilized 1-pint jars, filling them to ¼ inch from the top (visit www.homecanning.com). With a long, thin spatula, gently stir the contents to release any trapped air bubbles. Seal the jars and process for 10 minutes. Let them cool to room temperature, then refrigerate. This chutney will keep, chilled, for about 1 month.

Dishes for
All Seasons

Despite my loyalty to cooking by the seasons, there's a small batch of dishes that never come off my restaurant menu. You'll find them there year-round for two good reasons: (1) my customers love them, and (2) so do I. In fact, there are customers who came into JUdson Grill regularly for years just to order one of them over and over again. And that's fine with me. You should cook to please others, and if people want to eat the same meal every time they visit me, it's my pleasure to make it for them.

When I sat down to write this book, I realized there's a perfectly good reason why people love these dishes all year long: For the most part, they know no season. For example, the Romaine Salad with Bacon and Garlic Croutons (page 180), Peekytoe Crab Cocktail with Sevruga Caviar, Avocado, Scallion, and a Lemon Verbena Vinaigrette (page 189), Breaded Veal with Lemon Linguine and Broccoli (page 193), or the dish affectionately known to my inner circle as *The* Chicken (page 177) depend on crops, catches, and livestock that are plentiful throughout the year. So you could serve them at any time and still be seasonally correct.

Some of these dishes don't have any vegetable garnish, like the Foie Gras Terrine (page 182), Bone Marrow Flan (page 198), and Tuna Tartare (page 200), so serving them whenever you like doesn't violate any rules of seasonality. Then there are the dishes that are appropriate to any season, like the Smoked Trout, Seasonal Blini, and Cream (page 173) and the Market Vegetable Salad with Creamy Lemon Vinaigrette (page 191), because I tweak them periodically, adjusting their composition to include vegetables of the moment.

There are, I must admit, a few dishes here that bend the rules a bit, like the Potato-Crusted Crab Cakes with Spicy Coleslaw and Shell Bean–Avocado Salad (page 168), or the Chickpea Soup with Rosemary Croutons and Black Kale (page 186). Strictly speaking, those are summer dishes, but I just can't get through the three seasons between summers without them.

So, here are my personal-favorite recipes, and the ones most adored by my customers. I hope you enjoy them all year round as well.

Potato-Crusted Crab Cakes with Spicy Coleslaw and Shell Bean–Avocado Salad

Smoked Trout, Seasonal Blini, and Cream

The Chicken

Romaine Salad with Bacon and Garlic Croutons

Foie Gras Terrine

Chickpea Soup with Rosemary Croutons and Black Kale

Peekytoe Crab Cocktail with Sevruga Caviar, Avocado, Scallion, and a Lemon Verbena Vinaigrette

Market Vegetable Salad with Creamy Lemon Vinaigrette

Breaded Veal with Lemon Linguine and Broccoli

Pan-fried Trout with Baby Spinach, Bacon, and Balsamic Vinegar

Bone Marrow Flan

Tuna Tartare

Potato-Crusted Crab Cakes with Spicy Coleslaw and Shell Bean–Avocado Salad

SERVES 8 AS AN APPETIZER OR 4 AS A MAIN COURSE

ike many universally beloved classics, crab cakes are rarely reexamined. As I say in the Bill-osophies section of the book, I firmly believe that if it ain't broke, don't fix it. But there are ways of improving or embellishing something that work just fine, and I think these crab cakes do just that. They begin with a fish mousse to which crabmeat is added before the patties are crusted with grated potato and pan-fried. The mousse is made with cream, but the overall character of these cakes is lighter than traditional crab cakes coated with egg and bread crumbs.

These decadent discs are balanced by the accompaniments of a jalapeño-spiced coleslaw and a cooling shell-bean-and-avocado salad with a lively citrus dressing.

Bean-Avocado Salad

2 cups cooked mixed shell beans (page 94)

½ avocado, halved, pitted, peeled, and cut into medium dice

Juice of ½ lemon

Juice of ½ lime

1 tablespoon white wine vinegar

3 tablespoons extra-virgin olive oil

1 tablespoon chopped cilantro leaves

Salt

Freshly ground black pepper

Place all of the ingredients in a mixing bowl and toss well. Season to taste with salt and pepper. Set aside for at least 1 hour, or refrigerate overnight if desired.

(continued)

Potato-Crusted Crab Cakes and Assembly

½ pound white-fleshed fish (e.g., cod or pike), cut into small pieces

½ teaspoon salt

½ teaspoon freshly ground white pepper

¾ cup cream

1 pound lump crabmeat, picked through to remove any bits of shell

1 tablespoon Dijon mustard

1½ teaspoons Worcestershire sauce

1½ teaspoons Tabasco

2 medium Idaho potatoes

½ lemon

8 tablespoons (1 stick) butter, melted

Flour for dredging

1 cup vegetable oil

Spicy Coleslaw (page 338)

1 Place the fish, salt, and pepper in a food processor fitted with the metal blade and pulse to roughly chop the fish. Scrape down the sides of the bowl. With the machine running, slowly pour in the cream to make a fish mousse. Transfer the mousse to a bowl and fold in the crabmeat, mustard, Worcestershire sauce, and Tabasco. Set aside.

2 Line a baking sheet with waxed paper. Using a large spoon, divide the crab mixture into 8 mounds on the baking sheet. Put the sheet in the refrigerator while you prepare the potatoes.

3 Peel and coarsely grate the potatoes. Place them in a strainer and rinse under cold water until the water runs clear. Drain any excess water from the potatoes, squeeze them as dry as possible with your hands, and put them in a bowl. Squeeze the lemon over the potatoes, catching any seeds, add the butter, and toss.

4 Remove the crab cakes from the refrigerator. Place some of the grated potato in the palm of your hand and put a crab cake on the potato. Gently press some more potato onto the top of the crab cake, then pat some potato around the sides. Don't worry if it looks as if the potato won't stay put; the flour will help bind it. Repeat with the remaining cakes, returning them to the baking sheet, and chill in the refrigerator for 1 hour or up to 8 hours. (Cover the sheet with plastic wrap if chilling for more than 1 hour.)

5   When ready to proceed, spread some flour out on a plate. Pat the cakes on all sides in the flour, pressing gently to ensure that the flour adheres. In a pan large enough to accommodate 4 cakes, heat ½ cup of the oil over medium-high heat. When the oil is hot but not smoking, gently place 4 cakes in the pan without crowding and fry on each side until nicely browned, about 4 minutes per side. Transfer to a paper towel–lined plate to drain. Heat the remaining ½ cup oil and repeat with the remaining 4 crab cakes.

6   To serve as a main course, pile some bean-avocado salad on each of four warm dinner plates. Mound some coleslaw alongside and lean 2 crab cakes on the coleslaw. To serve as an appetizer, use the same presentation, but divide the components among eight plates, placing 1 crab cake on each serving.

Wine

The spicy notes in this dish need a fruity wine with balanced acidity. Try a unique wine made from a blend of local grapes from the northern Basque region of Spain, Txakoli, produced by Bodega Txomin Etxaniz. The nearby region of Galicia also offers a lovely, fresh albariño.

Smoked Trout, Seasonal Blini, and Cream

SERVES 4 AS AN APPETIZER

I f there's such a thing as New York comfort food, smoked fish may be it. And I guess I've finally become a New Yorker because, when I'm in a certain mood, craving something simple and homey, smoked trout hits me just right. I've found that a great many New Yorkers share my affection for this delicacy, and they're delighted to spot it on the menu. So I try to include it on my menu, accompanied by seasonal blini.

My blini don't follow the Russian formula; they're more like American pancakes with a seasonal vegetable folded in. They have a nice, silky texture even though they're made without yeast. I strongly recommend that you make them fresh rather than cooking them in advance; they're never as good as when they've just come out of the pan.

I hot-smoke trout to rare, which gives it a beguiling flavor that tastes more like smoked sushi than smoky fish.

Here are four variations, one for each season.

Spring: Potato-Chive Blini and Sweet Onion Sour Cream

Smoked Trout

2 whole trout, filleted, skin on, pinbones removed	2 tablespoons freshly squeezed lemon juice
Salt	6 tablespoons olive oil
Freshly ground black pepper	

1 Start 10 to 15 coals in a charcoal grill and bring them to a temperature of 150°F to 170°F.

2 Generously season the trout with salt and pepper and lay them, skin side down, on a wire rack. When the coals are ready, spread them out in a single layer in the middle of the grill. Prepare the rack at the highest setting, farthest from the coals, and have two bricks ready

to place on the rack in order to get the trout even farther from the heat. Sprinkle 1 cup of wood chips—preferably apple or alder wood—over the coals. Blow on the coals or use a bellows to encourage the wood to smoke. Set the rack with the trout on top of the bricks and cover the grill. Adjust the airflow so the coals have enough air to burn but as much smoke as possible stays inside. Smoke the trout until just opaque, 10 to 15 minutes.

3   Remove the trout from the grill and let cool. They can be wrapped in plastic wrap and refrigerated for up to 4 days.

4   To use in the recipes, remove the skin and break the trout into large chunks. Put the lemon juice in a bowl and whisk in the oil; gently stir in the trout. Season to taste with salt and pepper and mix gently but thoroughly.

Potato-Chive Blini

1 medium Idaho potato, peeled and cut into medium chunks	1 teaspoon sugar
1 egg	1 teaspoon salt
²/₃ cup milk	½ teaspoon baking powder
1 tablespoon sour cream	2 tablespoons chopped chives
³/₄ cup flour	2 tablespoons butter

1   Preheat the oven to 450°F.

2   Bring a small pot of lightly salted water to a boil over high heat. Add the potato and cook until tender, about 20 minutes. Drain, then place the potato in a pan set over medium heat. Cook, stirring, until the pieces are dry, about 3 minutes. Pass them through a ricer (see page 8) or food mill, or press through a wire sieve. You should have 1 cup of riced potato. Discard any extra and let the 1 cup cool completely.

3   In a small bowl, whisk together the egg, milk, and sour cream. Put the flour, sugar, salt, and baking powder in another small bowl and mix to combine. Stir the egg mixture into the flour mixture. Add the potato and chives, and mix well.

4   Melt 1 tablespoon of the butter in an ovenproof sauté pan set over medium heat. When the butter is bubbling, pour in ⅓ cup of the batter to form a blini 4 inches in diameter. You can cook 2 at a time, but do not crowd the pan. When the blini's edges begin to turn brown, 30 seconds to 1 minute, transfer the pan to the oven until the surface is cooked,

4 to 5 minutes. Remove the pan from the oven, turn the blini over, and cook 1 to 2 more minutes over medium heat on the stovetop, until lightly browned. If the blini gets too dark, lower the heat on the stovetop. Transfer the blini to a wire rack and repeat with the remaining butter and batter.

Sweet Onion Sour Cream and Assembly

1 tablespoon butter	2 tablespoons sour cream
¼ cup minced Vidalia or other sweet onion	1½ teaspoons freshly squeezed lemon juice
Salt	2 smoked trout, broken into large chunks

1 Melt the butter in a sauté pan set over low heat. Add the onion, sprinkle with salt, cover, and slowly cook until tender but not browned, about 10 minutes. Let cool, add the sour cream and lemon juice, and stir to combine.

2 To serve, place a blini on each of four plates, spread a tablespoon of the sour cream on each blini, and pile the trout on top.

Summer: Corn-Chive Blini and Scallion Sour Cream

Corn-Chive Blini

Replace the potato with ¾ cup corn kernels (cut from about 2 medium ears). In Step 2, bring a small pan of water to a boil, add the corn, and cook until the water returns to a boil, about 1 minute. Drain the corn and chop finely, then mash with the side of a chef's knife to release the starch. Proceed with the rest of the recipe, omitting the sugar. Use ¼ cup plus 2 tablespoons flour, 1 tablespoon chives, and 2 tablespoons butter. Add ¼ cup plus 2 tablespoons yellow corn flour (finely ground cornmeal) along with the all-purpose flour in Step 3.

Scallion Sour Cream and Assembly

Omit the onion and add 1 tablespoon sliced scallion, white and light green parts only.

Fall: Celery Root Blini
and Apple Sour Cream

Celery Root Blini

Replace the potato with 1 small celery root, cooking it in boiling, salted water for about 12 minutes. Proceed with the rest of the recipe, omitting the chives.

Apple Sour Cream

Omit the butter and onion and add ¼ cup peeled, finely grated green apple with any juice released from grating.

Winter: Buckwheat-Potato Blini
and Black Radish Sour Cream

Buckwheat-Potato Blini

Omit the chives, reduce the amount of flour to ¼ cup plus 2 tablespoons flour, and add ¼ cup plus 2 tablespoons buckwheat flour along with the all-purpose flour in Step 3.

Black Radish Sour Cream

Replace the onion with ½ teaspoon chopped shallot and add ¼ cup finely grated black radish with any juice released from grating.

Wine

Since the most dominant flavor in all of the variations here is the trout itself, a classic pairing would be an Austrian grüner veltliner. The white pepper notes and subtle fruit are made to order for smoked fish or meats. Try the Bründlmayer Grüner Veltliner from the Kamptaler Terrassen vineyard.

The Chicken

SERVES 4

Restaurant staffs refer to themselves as a family, and you could say that this dish is a family favorite. Longtime associates of mine refer to it simply as "*the* chicken" because it never changes and we all love it for its unique take on comfort flavors. The mushroom sauce makes it a little special, like a taste of Thanksgiving.

The first incarnation of this dish was at Ansonia restaurant, where I introduced a roast chicken with mushrooms and barley. The owner wanted a simple roast chicken with roast potatoes and other classic accompaniments, so I combined the existing dish with the one he had in mind. It then became a favorite for a number of longtime JUdson Grill regulars who went out of their way to come in just to eat it. (This means you, Mr. Martinez and Mr. Finley.)

The key to the chicken is that it cooks on one side only, letting the skin get crispy, crispy, crispy, but keeping the bird succulent and moist, a contrast you can intensify by basting the meat occasionally.

8 tablespoons (1 stick) butter

1/2 pound mixed wild mushrooms, such as shiitake, cremini, and oyster, stem ends trimmed, cut into 1/4-inch slices

2 tablespoons dry white wine

1 cup Brown Chicken Stock (page 343)

Salt

Freshly ground black pepper

1 1/2 pounds Swiss chard (about 2 bunches), thick stems removed by cutting a "V" into the leaves, large leaves cut into quarters

1/2 cup canola or vegetable oil, plus more for frying potatoes

4 large red bliss potatoes, skin on, scrubbed, blemishes removed, and cut into 3/4-inch dice

2 chickens, 2 1/2 to 3 pounds each, quartered

2 teaspoons chopped rosemary

2 teaspoons chopped thyme leaves

2 teaspoons chopped flat-leaf parsley

(continued)

1   Melt 2 tablespoons of the butter in a large sauté pan set over high heat and continue to cook until the butter begins to brown, about 3 minutes. Add the mushrooms to the pan in a single layer, lower the heat to medium, and sauté until golden brown, about 5 minutes. Add the wine, raise the heat to high, and reduce until almost dry, about 1 minute. Add the stock, bring to a boil, then lower the heat and let simmer for 12 minutes to develop the flavor. Season with salt and pepper, then set the pan aside, covered, to keep the mushrooms warm.

2   Place 2 tablespoons of the butter and 1 cup water in a small pot and bring to a boil over high heat. Add the Swiss chard, season with salt and pepper, cover, and wilt the chard for about 5 minutes, turning it after a couple of minutes, until tender. Drain, taste, and adjust seasoning. Set aside the hot pot, covered, to keep the chard warm.

3   Preheat the oven to 450°F.

4   Pour oil into a large sauté pan to a depth of 1 inch and set the pan over high heat. When the oil is smoking hot, carefully add the potatoes in a single layer and fry them for 4 to 5 minutes, stirring occasionally, until lightly browned. Remove with a slotted spoon and set on a paper towel–lined plate to drain. Season with salt and pepper and set aside.

5   Generously season the chicken pieces with salt and pepper.

6   Pour ¼ cup of the oil into a wide, deep, ovenproof sauté pan large enough to hold the 4 chicken legs, and set the pan over high heat, letting it get very hot. Add the legs to the pan, skin side down, and brown until the skin is a light golden color, about 3 minutes.

7   Drain the oil from the pan and add 2 tablespoons of the butter. Cook for 3 minutes, until the butter is browned and the chicken skin is golden brown. Transfer the pan to the oven and roast until the juices run clear when the chicken is pierced at the bone with a sharp, thin-bladed knife, 16 to 20 minutes. Remove the pan from the oven, transfer the legs to a plate, and cover them with aluminum foil to keep them warm. Drain off and discard the fat from the pan and use the same pan for Step 8.

8   Repeat Steps 6 and 7 with the breasts, roasting them in the oven for 12 to 15 minutes. Remove rib and breast bones from each chicken breast after cooking.

9   While the chicken breasts are in the oven, continue making the potatoes: Melt the remaining 2 tablespoons butter in an ovenproof pan set over high heat and cook until bubbling and beginning to brown. Add the potatoes and toss to coat. When the butter begins to sizzle, transfer the pan to the oven and roast until browned and crisp, about 8 minutes. Remove the pan from the oven, season the potatoes well with salt and pepper, and toss with the rosemary, thyme, and parsley.

10 Gently reheat the mushrooms and chard over low heat.

11 To serve, divide the potatoes and chard among four warm dinner plates. Place a chicken leg and a breast on each plate, and top with mushrooms and sauce.

Wine

A sangiovese-based red from the lesser-known region of Umbria, Italy, would be fitting. Try the Arnaldo Caprai Poggio Belvedere or their Rosso di Sagrantino. In a pinch, a simple Chianti Classico, also made from the sangiovese grape, would do.

Romaine Salad with Bacon and Garlic Croutons

SERVES 4

Artisanal cheese makers are every bit as devoted as the farmers profiled in this book. I'm a big supporter of American cheeses. This adaptation of a Caesar salad, using an eggless dressing, is one of my favorite ways of using Vella dry Monterey Jack, a cheese with a Parmesan-like crystalline texture but a distinctly American tang. The recipe gives you the option of using Parmigiano-Reggiano, but if you can find the Vella, please use it.

¼ cup red wine vinegar

½ cup canola oil

¼ cup plus 2 tablespoons extra-virgin olive oil

¼ cup cream

4 ounces Parmigiano-Reggiano or dry Jack cheese, half grated (about ¾ cup), half shaved

Salt

Freshly ground black pepper

1 ficelle, cut into 24 ¼-inch rounds (or a baguette, halved lengthwise, then cut into rounds)

1 clove garlic

8 slices bacon, cut into 1-inch squares

4 hearts romaine lettuce (about 1½ pounds), washed and ends trimmed

1 Preheat the oven to 350°F.

2 Pour the vinegar into a food processor fitted with the metal blade. With the machine running, slowly add ¼ cup of the canola oil, ¼ cup of the olive oil, and the cream. Stop the motor, add the grated cheese, then pulse until emulsified. Taste, season with salt and pepper, and set aside.

3 Place the ficelle rounds on a baking sheet, drizzle with the remaining 2 tablespoons olive oil, and season with salt and pepper. Toast in the oven until completely dry, about 15 minutes. Remove from the oven and let cool enough to handle, then rub each crouton with the garlic clove.

4   Place the bacon in a small pot, cover with cold water, and bring to a boil over high heat. Drain and pat dry with paper towels. Place the bacon and the remaining $\frac{1}{4}$ cup canola oil in a frying pan set over medium-high heat. Cook for about 10 minutes, until crisp. (Be careful: the hot oil may splatter a bit.) Drain and set aside on a paper towel.

5   Place the romaine in a large mixing bowl and dress with about a cup of the vinegar dressing. Wash your hands well and use them to mix the salad; this is the best way to make sure the leaves are thoroughly coated.

6   To serve, divide the romaine among four plates, mounding it in the center of each plate. Arrange 6 croutons around the romaine, sprinkle with bacon, and top with the shaved cheese. Drizzle some of the remaining dressing over the croutons and around the edge of the plate.

Wine

The 2002 grüner veltliner from Geyerhof, in Austria, has a slight white pepper spice and a smoky flavor that perfectly complement the bacon and garlic in this salad.

Foie Gras Terrine

SERVES 6

When reviewing recipes with young cooks in my kitchen, I always ask them, "Are you writing this down," because I want to be sure that they are following the recipes to the letter. Like many home cooks, line cooks are always looking for ways to be creative with a chef's recipe. I don't let my line cooks do this, especially with a dish like this. You, on the other hand, paid good money for this book and aren't cooking for my customers, so I think you should feel free to tweak away at any of the recipes. But not with this one, because terrines have to be made just so. The most important consideration is not to let the internal temperature fall outside the 95°F to 100°F range. If overcooked, it will become grainy. If undercooked, it's just plain bad.

Another chef taught me the crucial technique of hand-pressing—rather than simply weighting the terrine. This makes the terrine creamier and forces out any air bubbles.

¼ cup Sauternes	Pinch of freshly ground white pepper
1 pound 2 ounces foie gras, deveined (see page 185)	Pinch of sugar
1 teaspoon salt	

1 Line a 9 by 12-inch pan with plastic wrap and drizzle 2 tablespoons of the Sauternes over it. Put the foie gras in the pan and drizzle with the remaining 2 tablespoons Sauternes. Season with the salt, pepper, and sugar. Cover with plastic wrap and let marinate overnight in the refrigerator.

2 Preheat the oven to 275°F.

3 Remove the pan from the refrigerator and leave it out at room temperature for 45 minutes.

4 Pack the foie gras into a half-liter mold, placing the smaller half on the bottom, smooth side down, and the larger half on top, smooth side up. Press well to make sure there are no air pockets. Don't worry if the foie gras doesn't fit perfectly and bulges about ¼ inch over the top.

(continued)

5   Wrap the entire mold with plastic wrap three times over. Bring a pot of water to a boil. Put the mold in a deep baking pan, then pour the hot water around the terrine mold until it comes halfway up the sides of the mold. Transfer the pan to the oven and cook for 20 to 30 minutes, until the internal temperature of the foie gras reaches 95° to 100°F, *never letting it exceed this temperature.* Check after 10 minutes by gently poking a small hole in the plastic with the tip of a sharp knife and inserting an instant-read thermometer through the hole.

6   Place the mold in a clean, dry baking pan and carefully remove the plastic wrap. Spoon off and reserve as much of the fat from the top of the terrine as possible.

7   Cut a piece of cardboard about ¼ inch smaller than the inside top of the terrine. Thoroughly wrap the cardboard in plastic wrap. Using the cardboard, gently press air bubbles out of the foie gras, beginning in one corner of the terrine and working your way around. Air bubbles, blood, and fat will rise to the surface. Don't worry if some of the foie gras pops out of a corner; just push it back in. Do this until all air bubbles seem pressed out, about 5 minutes, and then continue for another 5 minutes because there are usually some more hiding in there.

8   The reserved fat will separate, with the clear fat rising to the top and the blood settling to the bottom. Pour some of this clear fat over the foie gras so it is completely covered, leaving no part of the foie gras exposed to the air.

9   Refrigerate the foie gras for 24 to 48 hours before serving. It will keep for 2 weeks in the refrigerator.

10   To serve, unmold the terrine and slice into individual portions.

Wine

Sauternes is the classic pairing with foie gras, but there are other, more affordable options, such as sweet wines from the tiny villages of Ste.-Croix-du-Mont and Loupiac, or even the more well known Barsac, where the individual wines are named for the villages where they are produced.

DEVEINING FOIE GRAS

Take the foie gras out of the refrigerator and let it warm to room temperature for about an hour. Lay a towel on a cutting board to prevent the foie gras from slipping. Split the lobe in half lengthwise along the seam. Place the larger of the two lobes on the cutting board with the concave side up, the smooth side down, running north–south, the flat end toward you and the larger end away from you. Work gently, keeping the foie gras as whole as possible. If it gets too soft and begins to break apart, return it to the refrigerator for a few minutes.

About one-third of the way down in the middle you will see the exposed end of the vein that connects the two halves of the foie gras. Using the dull side of a paring knife, cut up the vein to the top of the foie gras, exposing it. Gently remove the vein by sliding a knife under it to hold down the foie gras and open up a hole to get your finger under it. Run your finger under the vein to remove it. Trace the same vein down the length of the foie gras, butterflying out to the side the layer of foie gras above the vein, exposing the vein. Remove the vein.

There is an upside-down Y-shaped vein under the one just removed. Start at the top and find the end of the Y. Again work down the vein, using the dull side of a paring knife to butterfly open the foie just down to the vein. When you get to the point where the Y splits, work down the left half, opening the foie out to the left, and then repeat with the right side. When the entire Y is exposed, gently remove the vein from the top down. If it sticks at any point, gently loosen around it with a paring knife. If it breaks, remove the broken part separately. Fold the foie back together and set aside.

Place the smaller half of the foie gras on the cutting board with the concave side up, the smooth side down, this time running east–west, the fatter end to the left and the flatter end to the right. The veins in this half are smaller and more fragile, so work carefully. Press on the foie, flattening it and opening up the middle, to expose the veins. If there is a lot of fat, clean it out. Starting at the middle where the connecting vein is, open up the foie toward you. Open up the top away from you. Gently remove the vein from the middle down.

There is again a Y-shaped vein, this time branching from one point on your left into two on the right. Butterfly open the foie to expose the vein and remove it. Fold the foie back together.

Chickpea Soup with Rosemary Croutons and Black Kale

MAKES 6 CUPS

I fell in love with chickpeas while learning about Italian cooking. This soup may not be strictly Italian, but it's certainly Italian in its soul, my take on *pasta e fagioli* (pasta and bean soup) that's rounded out with two ingredients closely associated with Tuscan food, rosemary and kale.

Rosemary Croutons

3 or 4 slices sourdough bread, crusts removed, cut into ½-inch cubes (about ¾ cup cubes)

1 tablespoon chopped rosemary

2 tablespoons extra-virgin olive oil

Salt

1   Preheat the oven to 300°F.

2   Place the bread cubes on a cookie sheet in a single layer. Toast in the oven until the bread is completely dried but not browned, about 20 minutes.

3   In a bowl large enough to hold the croutons, stir together the rosemary and olive oil, and season the mixture with salt.

4   When the croutons are crisp, remove them from the oven, transfer them to the bowl with the rosemary oil, and toss well. Set aside.

Black Kale

2 tablespoons butter

1 bunch black Tuscan kale (about 10 ounces)

Salt

Freshly ground black pepper

Put the butter and 1 cup water in a large pot and bring to a boil. Add the kale, cover, and wilt for 12 to 15 minutes, until tender. Season with salt and pepper. Let cool, squeeze in a towel to dry as much as possible, and roughly chop. Set aside.

Chickpeas, Soup, and Assembly

½ pound (about 1 cup) dried chickpeas

⅓ cup dried pennette (small penne) pasta

½ cup extra-virgin olive oil

¼ small yellow onion, minced

1 clove garlic, minced

One 14-ounce can whole peeled plum tomatoes, juice drained, squeezed by hand in a strainer, and roughly chopped

8 cups Chicken Stock (page 343)

¾ cup diced celery (chickpea-sized dice)

¾ cup diced carrot

Salt

¾ cup diced leek

1   Soak the chickpeas overnight in cold water to cover by 1 inch. Drain and set aside.

2   Bring a small pot of salted water to a boil. Add the pennette and cook until al dente, about 8 minutes. Drain and set aside.

3   Heat ¼ cup of the olive oil in a pot set over low heat. Add the onion and garlic, and cook for about 7 minutes, until tender. Add the tomatoes and cook for 5 minutes. Add the chickpeas and stock, and cook until the chickpeas are tender, about 30 minutes.

4   In another pot, heat the remaining ¼ cup olive oil over medium-high heat. Add the celery, carrot, and a few pinches of salt, and cook over medium heat, covered, for about 5 minutes, until half cooked but still crunchy. Add the leek and cook for about 4 more minutes, until tender.

5   Puree half of the chickpea mixture in a blender. Put the puree, the vegetable mixture, and the remaining chickpea mixture into a pot set over high heat. Bring to a boil, lower the heat, and let simmer for 10 minutes. Add the kale, return to a simmer, and season with salt. You want the soup to be creamy but not porridge-like. If it is too thick, thin with a little stock or water.

6   To serve, divide the pasta among four bowls. Ladle some soup over the pasta in each bowl and garnish with the rosemary croutons.

Wine

A pinot blanc or the Pinot Auxerrois Vieilles Vignes from Albert Mann of Alsace, France, would do well with this hearty dish.

Peekytoe Crab Cocktail with Sevruga Caviar, Avocado, Scallion, and a Lemon Verbena Vinaigrette

SERVES 4

When I worked at Ansonia restaurant, the father of one of the owners would often return from trips to California with Dungeness crab claws in tow. He often asked me to make up a simple crab cocktail, which I did. But it got to the point where I couldn't resist trying to impress him by taking the crab in a slightly more decadent direction. My plan backfired: he and his family were upset that I deprived them of the pleasure of cracking the claws themselves, but the dish became a hit with my customers. This recipe calls for peekytoe crab, but if you can get Dungeness, go ahead and use that.

2 cups grapeseed oil

1 bunch fresh lemon verbena (1 cup loosely packed dried lemon verbena leaves can be substituted)

Grated zest of 1 lemon

1 egg yolk (see Note)

6 tablespoons warm Chicken Stock (page 343)

¼ cup plus 1 tablespoon freshly squeezed lemon juice

Salt

Freshly ground black pepper

3 tablespoons extra-virgin olive oil

1 avocado, peeled, halved, pitted, halves cut in half lengthwise

2 ounces baby greens or chopped mesclun

½ pound peekytoe crabmeat

2 scallions, white and light green parts thinly sliced on the diagonal, green parts thinly sliced and set aside separately

2 teaspoons chopped flat-leaf parsley

1 ounce sevruga caviar

1   Make a lemon verbena oil by putting the grapeseed oil, lemon verbena, and lemon zest in a pot and warming them over medium heat. Remove the pot from the heat and let the oil infuse for 3 hours at room temperature. Strain the oil and set aside.

(continued)

2   Put the egg yolk, stock, and ¼ cup of the lemon juice in a food processor fitted with the metal blade. Season with salt and pepper. Process on low speed, adding the lemon verbena oil in a thin stream to make an emulsified dressing. Taste and adjust seasoning. This makes more vinaigrette than you need. Use it to make the same recipe again, or use it in place of the dressing in the Market Vegetable Salad (page 191).

3   Make a basic vinaigrette by putting the remaining 1 tablespoon lemon juice in a small bowl and seasoning it with salt and pepper. Slowly drizzle in the olive oil while continuing to whisk. Taste, adjust seasoning, and set aside.

4   Lay the avocado quarters flat with the pitted side up. Trim the center portion to level the upward-facing side of each quarter. Turn the slices over and slice three-quarters of the way down from the wide end almost to the narrow bottom of each quarter. This will enable you to spread each slice out into a fan. Do this, then set the fans aside.

5   In a small bowl, dress the baby greens with some of the basic vinaigrette. Season with salt and pepper. Divide among four large martini glasses.

6   Put the crabmeat in another bowl. Add the white and light green parts of the scallions, the parsley, and ⅓ cup of the lemon verbena vinaigrette. Season with salt and pepper.

7   To serve, spoon some crabmeat over the greens in each glass. Top with some caviar. Drizzle the avocado fans with some of the basic vinaigrette, season them with salt and pepper, and place an avocado fan in each martini glass. Garnish with the sliced green scallion tops and serve with a cocktail fork.

Wine

A very crisp, elegant white would blend with all these flavors. The caviar would be especially well paired with a sparkling wine like the Lenoble Blanc de Blanc from Champagne, France.

NOTE: Eating raw eggs carries the risk of salmonella. Foods containing raw eggs should not be eaten by the very young, the very old, pregnant women, or anyone with a compromised immune system.

Market Vegetable Salad with Creamy Lemon Vinaigrette

SERVES 6 AS AN APPETIZER OR 4 AS A MAIN COURSE

This salad recipe is flexible and is designed to let you use the freshest, most appealing vegetables from your garden, local farm stand, or supermarket on any day of the year. It's a chopped salad in spirit, but some of the vegetables are lightly cooked rather than raw. This dish will change seasonally and gradually. As spring turns to summer, omit the asparagus and peas, adding cherry tomatoes on the side. Toward late summer, add corn, zucchini, and wax beans, moving on in the fall and winter to celery root, red and savoy cabbage, and Belgian endive. If you have a mandoline, use it to slice the vegetables as thinly as possible.

1 tablespoon freshly squeezed lemon juice

1 teaspoon red wine vinegar

1 teaspoon Dijon mustard

Salt

Freshly ground black pepper

6 tablespoons extra-virgin olive oil

6 cups mixed seasonal vegetables

- fava beans, blanched and shelled
- fresh peas, shelled and blanched
- carrots, thinly sliced
- radishes, thinly sliced
- beets, roasted (see page 28), peeled, quartered, and thinly sliced
- zucchini, thinly sliced
- sugar snap peas, strings removed, cut on the diagonal into 3 pieces, and blanched
- asparagus, cut into 1/2-inch segments and blanched
- wax beans, cut into 1/2-inch segments and blanched
- kohlrabi, peeled and thinly sliced

Creamy Lemon Vinaigrette (recipe follows)

2 tablespoons mixed chopped herbs such as chives, parsley, basil, and/or chervil

1 cucumber, sliced paper thin

1 small bulb fennel, cleaned and sliced paper thin

1 1/2 ounces mesclun greens

(continued)

1   Make a basic vinaigrette by whisking together the lemon juice, vinegar, and mustard in a small bowl. Season with salt and pepper. Continue to whisk while slowly drizzling in the olive oil. Taste, adjust seasoning, and set aside.

2   Dress the mixed vegetables with ¾ cup of the Creamy Lemon Vinaigrette. Add the chopped herbs, season with salt and pepper, and toss well to separate the vegetables.

3   To serve, overlap the cucumber slices in a ring in the center of each plate. Tightly pack the vegetables into a ring mold on top of the cucumbers, or into a cup measure, and invert onto the cucumbers. In a small bowl, dress the fennel with 3 tablespoons of the basic vinaigrette and stack the slices on top of the mixed vegetables. In a small bowl, dress the mesclun with the rest of the basic vinaigrette, season with salt and pepper, and pile on top of the fennel on each plate.

Wine

Select a very clean, light white, like an herbal Orvieto from Salviano in the Italian region of Umbria, to go with this salad any time of year. A well-made pinot grigio is another alternative.

NOTE: Eating raw eggs carries the risk of salmonella. Foods containing raw eggs should not be eaten by the very young, the very old, pregnant women, or anyone with a compromised immune system.

Creamy Lemon Vinaigrette

1 egg yolk, at room temperature
(see Note above)

¼ cup freshly squeezed lemon juice

Salt

Freshly ground black pepper

¾ cup extra-virgin olive oil

¼ cup cream

In a medium bowl, whisk together the egg yolk and lemon juice. Season with salt and pepper. Continue to whisk while slowly drizzling in the olive oil, then the cream, to form an emulsified dressing. Taste and adjust seasoning.

Breaded Veal with Lemon Linguine and Broccoli

SERVES 4

n restaurants, I make this dish with veal from Duane Merrill (see page 195). I've always loved my mother's breaded pork chops, and I've also been a longtime fan of veal Milanese, which is traditionally served with a lemon wedge. When I made lemon linguine as an accompaniment to this veal at home one night, I knew that it was bound for my restaurant menu. I like to think that my fondness for each component shows every time this dish comes out of the kitchen.

Veal

8 slices brioche bread, crusts removed, cut into ½-inch cubes (or enough to render about 2 cups fresh bread crumbs)

3 eggs

Salt

Freshly ground black pepper

1 pound veal cutlets, pounded thin into scaloppine

1 cup flour

Olive oil for frying

1 Place the bread cubes in a food processor fitted with the metal blade and process to form crumbs. Set aside.

2 Lightly beat the eggs in a bowl, stir in 2 tablespoons water, and season with salt and pepper.

3 Dredge the veal in the flour, then in the eggs, then in the bread crumbs.

4 Pour olive oil into a large skillet to a depth of ½ inch and set over high heat. Add the veal in batches and fry until golden brown, 45 seconds to 1 minute per side. Change the oil and wipe the pan as soon as any lingering bread crumbs begin to burn.

(continued)

Broccoli

2 tablespoons extra-virgin olive oil

¼ cup sliced onion

1 clove garlic, sliced

½ teaspoon crushed red pepper flakes

2 heads broccoli, cut into 2-inch florets

¼ cup Vegetable Stock (page 344) or water

1 tablespoon butter

Salt

Warm the olive oil in a sauté pan set over medium heat. Add the onion and garlic and sauté until softened but not browned, about 7 minutes. Add the red pepper flakes and broccoli and cook for 1 minute. Add the stock, butter, and a pinch of salt, cover, and cook until the liquid is reduced and the broccoli is crisp-tender, about 8 minutes.

Linguine and Assembly

6 ounces dry linguine

Juice and zest of 2 lemons (about 6 tablespoons juice)

¼ cup extra-virgin olive oil

½ teaspoon crushed red pepper flakes

⅓ cup freshly grated Parmigiano-Reggiano cheese

1 tablespoon chopped flat-leaf parsley

Salt

Freshly ground black pepper

1   Bring a pot of salted water to a boil over high heat. Add the linguine and cook until al dente, about 7 minutes. Drain, reserving about ½ cup of the pasta water.

2   Put the linguine, lemon juice, lemon zest, olive oil, red pepper flakes, and 2 tablespoons pasta water in a sauté pan set over high heat. Cook until warmed through, about 7 minutes, then remove from the heat. Toss in the cheese and parsley, and season with salt and pepper.

3   To serve, divide the linguine among four plates, using a pair of tongs to twirl it into a mound. Put the broccoli next to the linguine and top with the breaded veal.

Wine

A full-flavored grüner veltliner from Austria, like the Nigl Privat from the Kremstal region, would stand up to the veal yet have the acidity to blend with the lemony notes.

DUANE MERRILL

HILLDALE FARMS
HAMDEN, NEW YORK

This Catskill Mountains farmer, based in the upper watershed of Delaware County, is one of my favorite people. And I guess he likes me, too, because we have our own nicknames for each other, even though they aren't particularly clever. I call him Mr. M. He calls me Mr. T.

Mr. M raises pasture-fed veal just for me. The benefit of pasture-fed veal is that the calf is still "on its mother" out in the pasture, so the animal receives all of its nutrition from natural sources, though there is some feed mixed into its diet. Think of this as the equivalent of free-range veal. After seven months, they are ready to be sold.

Mr. M used to grow vegetables but found it too labor intensive. All he does now is beef. When you talk to him, it's clear that he's proud of how he raises his veal. "This is different than what everyone perceives as force-fed," he says. "These animals aren't confined to a barn and are not on a low-iron diet," the method some farmers use to keep veal anemic and therefore lean and white. He has experimented with various natural diets, feeding the veal high-quality hay and grain to give them more energy. Today he uses balage, which is hay with a high moisture content that ferments and forms lactic acid. All of these factors improve the life of the veal and, ultimately, the flavor of their meat.

Pan-fried Trout with Baby Spinach, Bacon, and Balsamic Vinegar

SERVES 4

You've heard of the "ladies who lunch"? Well, many of the businesswomen who lunched at JUdson Grill enjoyed this relatively healthful dish as often as twice a week. If you're looking for an even lighter version, omit the bacon and start the dish with a few tablespoons of olive oil.

½ pound slab bacon, cut into ¼-inch dice (see page 197), or 8 slices strip bacon, cut into ¼-inch slices

½ cup olive oil

Salt

Freshly ground black pepper

¼ cup balsamic vinegar

¼ cup pine nuts

2 tablespoons canola oil

4 trout, 8 to 10 ounces each, butterflied, bones and head removed (see Mail Order Sources, page 345)

½ pound baby spinach

1 Preheat the oven to 450°F.

2 If using strip bacon, skip this step. Put the diced bacon in a pot of lightly salted cold water and bring to a boil over high heat. Drain, and dry on a paper towel.

3 In a medium frying pan, cover bacon with the olive oil and cook over high heat until crisp, about 10 minutes. Be careful, as it may splatter. Drain, reserving the oil. Season the bacon with salt and pepper and set aside.

4 Mix the reserved olive oil with the balsamic vinegar, season with salt and pepper, stir in the bacon, and set aside.

5 Place the pine nuts in a sauté pan set over medium heat and toast, tossing every 30 seconds, for about 2 minutes, until lightly browned. Set aside.

6   Warm the canola oil in a large sauté pan set over high heat. Season the trout with salt and pepper and add them to the pan, skin side down, 1 or 2 at a time depending on the size of the pan—do not crowd the pan. Cook for about 1 minute, until the skin starts to brown, then transfer them to a cookie sheet. Repeat with the remaining trout, placing them on the cookie sheet without crowding.

7   Place the trout in the oven and roast for 2 to 3 minutes, until the flesh is just barely opaque.

8   The vinaigrette should still be warm, but if not, put it in a pot and warm over low heat.

9   To serve, place 1 trout in the center of each of four warm dinner plates. In a bowl, combine the spinach and pine nuts, toss with ½ cup of the warm vinaigrette, and season with salt and pepper. Pile the spinach onto the middle of the trout and drizzle some vinaigrette around the edge of the plate.

Wine

The smoky bacon notes and the spinach work well with a light rosé. Try the rosé from the Wölffer Estate Vineyards and Stables, in New York State, on Long Island's South Fork, made from a blend of merlot and chardonnay. A dry rosé from the Loire Valley region of France would also work.

SCORING SLAB BACON

To cut ¼-inch dice from slab bacon, keep the rind intact and cut a ¼-inch crosshatch pattern in the meat all the way down to, but not through, the rind. Then cut off the rind, and the bacon will fall in perfect dice.

Bone Marrow Flan

SERVES 8

If you like beef, you owe it to yourself to try bone marrow, the most perfect expression of the true essence of beef flavor. I'm so fond of marrow that when I was asked to prepare a dish for the tasting party following the annual James Beard Foundation Awards, I served these marrow bones filled with a red wine flan. What else do you need to know? It's pure, creamy, beefy yumminess.

Red Wine Flan

2 large shallots, minced	1½ cups cream
1 cup dry red wine	Salt
2 eggs	Freshly ground black pepper

1 Place the shallots and wine in a saucepan and reduce over medium-high heat until almost all of the wine has evaporated, 8 to 10 minutes. Remove from the heat and let cool.

2 Place the eggs and cream in a blender or food processor fitted with the metal blade and pulse until just blended. Whisk in the cooled shallots. Season with salt and pepper, strain through a fine-mesh strainer, and set aside.

Bone Marrow and Assembly

Kosher salt	Milk to fill a pot for cooking
Eight 2-inch marrow bones, both ends cut and exposed (ask your butcher to cut them)	

1 In a deep pan, pour a layer of kosher salt to a depth of ¼ inch. Place all the marrow bones in the pan with a cut side in the salt. Fill the pan with salt, covering the bones. Cover with plastic wrap and refrigerate overnight to draw out the blood and moisture from the bones.

(continued)

2   While the marrow is cold, brush off the salt and push the marrow out of the bone with your thumb or the bottom of a small knife. If it does not come out easily, force it out with an implement.

3   Once the marrow is out, place the marrow in ice water and refrigerate for 3 hours or overnight, to remove the blood.

4   Place the bones in a pot and cover with water. Bring to a boil and cook for 2 hours, or until all the fat and meat on the outside of the bones can be easily scraped away. Remove the bones from the water, let cool, and scrape clean.

5   Preheat the oven to 300°F.

6   Wrap the bottom hole and half the length of each bone in plastic wrap, then do the same with aluminum foil. Fill the bones with the flan mixture, filling each bone halfway. Place the bones in a shallow pan in a hot water bath. Cover the pan with plastic wrap, then foil, and cook in the oven for about 45 minutes, until the flan is firm.

7   Cut the marrow into ½-inch slices. Bring a pot of milk to a simmer. Put all the slices into the pot and poach until they are soft yet still hold their shape, 4 to 5 minutes. Remove the slices with a slotted spoon and season lightly with kosher salt.

8   Remove the plastic and foil wraps from the flan-filled bones, and carefully place each on a separate plate. Top each with a slice of the poached marrow.

Tuna Tartare

SERVES 4

Ever since I tasted André Soltner's salmon tartare at Lutèce, I wanted to have a seafood tartare on my menu. The version owes a nod to Gotham Bar and Grill's Alfred Portale, who showed me the taste and texture benefits that came from carefully dicing—rather than grinding—raw fish. The result offers the sublime quality of sushi but with more conventional Western touches.

This dish must be made only with the freshest fish. If you can't get fresh, sushi-grade tuna, don't make this.

1 pound sushi-grade tuna, cut into ⅓-inch cubes	¼ cucumber, peeled and sliced into 1-inch strips
1 teaspoon minced shallot	2 radishes, julienned into 1-inch strips, ideally on a mandoline
1 teaspoon finely sliced chives	
2 tablespoons plus 1 teaspoon freshly squeezed lime juice	1 teaspoon freshly squeezed lemon juice
	2 teaspoons extra-virgin olive oil
2 tablespoons mayonnaise	1 cup baby greens
Salt	4 chives, cut into 1-inch lengths
Freshly ground black pepper	4 pieces sourdough bread, ½ inch thick, toasted

1 In a bowl, mix together the tuna, shallot, chives, 2 tablespoons of the lime juice, and the mayonnaise, and season with salt and pepper. Set aside.

2 Toss the cucumber and radish with the remaining 1 teaspoon lime juice, the lemon juice, and the olive oil.

3 Divide the baby greens among four chilled salad plates. Mold the tuna onto the greens using a 3-inch ring mold, or simply mound the tuna on top of the greens. Garnish with the cucumber and radish mixture, top with the chive batons, and serve with the sourdough toast on the side.

Wine

The bright tart citrus notes go well with a Southern Hemisphere riesling, such as one from Australia. Try the tangy, tropical riesling from Lengs & Cooter, from the Clare Valley Watervale region. Its lime rind accents would go great with this dish.

Fall

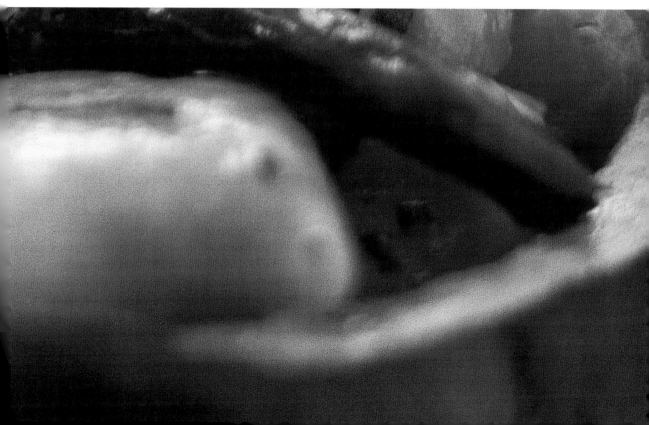

pring transforms into summer gradually, one seamlessly becoming the other, and the same is true of the turning of autumn into winter. But there's no mistaking the onset of fall. The first cold day comes along, with its early sunset, a gray heaviness in the air, and the sudden need to break a heavy coat out of storage, and you can literally feel it in your bones that a profound change is taking place.

It's the same way with the foods of the season. Once that first frost has occurred, the delicate, quick-cooking tomatoes, peas, and zucchini of late summer give way to hearty fall squash, earthy mushrooms, and root vegetables that, thanks to some divine plan, are exactly what we want to eat in the days ahead.

Fall casts such a long shadow that it even influences the cooking equipment we use. If you own a grill, it's used less for the rest of the year as you move your whole life indoors and start doing much of your cooking in the oven with a slower, more gentle heat, producing braises and stews brimming with rich, deep flavors.

The spirit of the fall holidays seems to infuse the entire season. I find myself socializing a lot more as we anticipate the holidays, often with friends hanging out in the kitchen, celebrating the spirit of this festive season and anticipating the meal ahead.

A Squash Sampler

Roasted Acorn Squash
with Hazelnuts and a
Ham and Parsley Salad

Buttercup Squash
Gnocchi with Sage
and Black Trumpet
Mushrooms

Pumpkin Pancakes with
Candied Walnuts and
Orange-Maple Syrup

You can't talk about fall or winter cooking without including the orange-fleshed squashes such as butternut, buttercup, and Hubbard that come into season each October. These substantial vegetables bear no resemblance to the summer varieties, which have green or yellow skins and decidedly more juicy flesh. The flavors of cold-weather squashes get along great with maple syrup, brown sugar, and the spices we associate with fall, such as cinnamon, allspice, and nutmeg. Because they store very well, they're available right through to the end of winter, making them a constant and defining presence for half the year.

Squashes are as at home in savory dishes as they are in sweet, which makes an all-squash menu the perfect way to kick off a chapter of autumn recipes. This one opens with a Roasted Acorn Squash with Hazelnuts and a Ham and Parsley Salad (page 207), followed by Buttercup Squash Gnocchi with Sage and Black Trumpet Mushrooms (page 209).

The dessert is Pumpkin Pancakes with Candied Walnuts and Orange-Maple Syrup (page 214). While pumpkin is not *technically* a squash, it's part of the same family of gourds, and so close in flavor to squash that I think it works in the menu.

Roasted Acorn Squash with Hazelnuts and a Ham and Parsley Salad

SERVES 4

Acorn squash has a distinct round shape and deep vertical ridges that make peeling it all but impossible. It's one of the reasons you often see soups or purees made from acorn squash served in a bowl fashioned from the hollowed-out rind. This recipe plays on that tradition by cutting the squash into wedges and using two of them to form an oval container for the salad on each plate.

The salad that accompanies the squash here demands the best possible ingredients. Make a point of specifying Black Forest ham at the deli counter, and find the freshest, most robust flat-leaf parsley available. It stands in for lettuces rather than playing its traditional role as an herb garnish.

4 tablespoons (½ stick) butter	1 tablespoon sherry vinegar
1 acorn squash (2 pounds), stem removed, halved lengthwise, seeds removed, and each half cut lengthwise into 4 wedges	2 tablespoons hazelnut oil (walnut oil can be substituted)
	Salt
1 tablespoon Grade B maple syrup (see page 208)	Freshly ground black pepper
	2 cups flat-leaf parsley, washed and patted dry with paper towels
1 teaspoon coriander seeds, cracked with a mortar and pestle or the bottom of a heavy pan	½ cup diced Black Forest ham (about a 4-ounce piece)
½ cup peeled hazelnuts, roughly chopped	

1 Preheat the oven to 450°F.

2 In a wide, deep-sided, ovenproof sauté pan, melt the butter over high heat until bubbly but not brown. Add the squash and shake the pan around to lightly brown the wedges all over, 2 minutes. Place the pan in the oven and roast the squash for 5 minutes. Remove

the pan from the oven and turn the squash over. Return the squash to the oven and roast until tender, 8 to 12 minutes.

3   Remove the pan from the oven, drizzle the syrup over the squash, and sprinkle the squash with the coriander. Return the pan to the oven for 1 minute. Remove the pan from the oven and use tongs or a large spoon to transfer the squash to a plate. Set aside.

4   Spread the hazelnuts out on a cookie sheet. Place the sheet in the oven and toast until the nuts are lightly browned, 3 to 5 minutes. Remove the sheet from the oven and set aside.

5   Whisk the vinegar and oil together in a small bowl and season with salt and pepper. Place the parsley, hazelnuts, and ham in another bowl and gently stir. Drizzle the vinaigrette over the ham salad and toss.

6   To serve, arrange 2 wedges of the squash on their sides to create an oval in the center of each of four plates. Spoon some salad into the center of each oval.

Wine

A pinot gris from Oregon would match well with the golden squash flavors in this dish. Try the Chehalam Pinot Gris from the Willamette Valley in the latest vintage.

MAPLE SYRUP

If you've eaten only industrially produced maple syrup, then you don't know how nuanced this condiment can be. Try one of the slightly more expensive varieties, especially if you can find maple syrup at a farm stand. Grade A maple syrup is the very best, and should be used straight, as when you're pouring it right over pancakes or waffles. For cooking, when the syrup will be concentrated by the heat and combined with other ingredients, Grade B can be just as good, and in fact has a more pronounced maple flavor.

Buttercup Squash Gnocchi with Sage and Black Trumpet Mushrooms

SERVES 4

Gnocchi, a cross between pasta and dumplings, are made from mashed potatoes and flour, and have a fullness of flavor and texture that could never be achieved with flour alone. Even in Italian restaurants, great gnocchi are all too rare, which is too bad, because they really aren't that difficult to make. In fact, the key to great gnocchi is doing as little work as possible; as soon as you've shaped them, *stop!* Overworking the dough is the culprit of 95 percent of all the leaden gnocchi out there.

These gnocchi are made with buttercup squash (a drier-than-average variety) and accompanied with sage and black trumpet mushrooms, elegant little fungi that are rich in flavor and, like the squash, available from the end of summer to the end of the year. If you can't find them, substitute creminis.

Buttercup squash, with its green skin and flat top and bottom, is easy to spot in the market. It has more water content than potato, so after roasting it's important to squeeze out most, but not all, of its liquid. You want the squash to resemble mashed potatoes, with just enough moisture to hold little clumps of it together.

If it's easy for you to obtain the gourds this recipe calls for—buttercup and butternut squash and baby pumpkin—by all means use them, because it doesn't take any extra effort to cook with the variety. However, if you can't put your hands on all three, you can make the entire dish with buttercup squash and skip using the baby pumpkin for presentation.

This is a truly beautiful dish. The dark, almost black, mushrooms look quite dramatic against the squash, and their flavors and textures are a perfect marriage.

(continued)

Buttercup Squash Gnocchi

1 large buttercup squash
(2 to 3 pounds)

Salt

1 egg

1½ cups flour, plus more for dusting
work surface

¼ cup freshly grated Parmigiano-
Reggiano cheese

1   Preheat the oven to 450°F.

2   Cut the squash in half lengthwise and scoop out the seeds. Salt the flesh and place the squash halves skin side down in a shallow baking pan. Pour ½ inch of water around the squash and cover the sheet with aluminum foil. Place the pan in the oven and then bake the squash until tender, about 45 minutes. (A sharp, thin-bladed knife should pierce easily to the center of a piece.) Remove the pan from the oven, set aside, and let cool.

3   When the squash is cool enough to handle, scoop the flesh out into a cheesecloth- or paper towel–lined strainer in batches, squeezing out most of the excess moisture (see headnote), then placing the flesh in a bowl. (You can also put it in a large, lined strainer and weight it down for 20 minutes with a heavy pan or a few cans of food wrapped in a clean plastic bag.) Measure out 2 cups of squeezed squash and pass it through a food mill or ricer (page 8) into a large bowl. Discard any extra squash.

4   Beat the egg in a small bowl with a whisk and add it to the squash, then stir in the flour, cheese, and 1 teaspoon salt with a wooden spoon until the dough just comes together. Form the dough into a ball, wrap it in plastic wrap, and place it in the freezer for 30 minutes.

5   Place the dough on a well-floured work surface and divide it into 8 equal pieces. Roll out 1 piece into a rope about ½ inch thick, working from the middle out and applying even pressure. (If the rope won't roll, wipe any excess flour from the work surface and roll using just enough flour to keep the dough from sticking.) Cut the dough into segments about ¾ inch long. Using the edge of a large, wide-bladed knife or a flat spatula, transfer the gnocchi to a well-floured baking sheet. Repeat with the remaining dough, then place the sheet in the freezer until the gnocchi harden, about 1 hour. These can be made in advance and frozen (see page 212).

Assembly

4 baby pumpkins

Salt

Freshly ground black pepper

¼ cup pine nuts

8 tablespoons (1 stick) butter

1 small butternut or buttercup squash
(about 2 pounds), peeled, halved
lengthwise, seeded, and cut into ¼-inch
dice (about 3 cups dice)

½ pound black trumpet mushrooms
or wild mushrooms such as cremini or
shiitake, cleaned and cut into ⅛-inch
slices

4 sage leaves, cut into thin strips

1 tablespoon chopped flat-leaf parsley

1 Preheat the oven to 450°F.

2 Remove the tops of the pumpkins by cutting a circle into the top of each pumpkin at an angle with a paring knife. Scoop out the pulp and seeds with a spoon. Put the pumpkins and tops in a pan. Pour ½ inch of water around them, season with salt and pepper, and cover with aluminum foil. Bake until tender, 20 to 25 minutes. Let cool enough to touch, then cut a little "window," about 2 inches square, into one side of each pumpkin, starting from the top.

3 Spread the pine nuts out on a cookie sheet and toast in the oven until lightly browned, about 5 minutes.

4 Heat a large sauté pan over high heat until very hot, then add 2 tablespoons of the butter. When the butter has melted and begins to brown, add the squash. Sauté until golden and tender, about 6 minutes. Transfer the squash to a plate and set aside.

5 Set the same pan over high heat and add 2 tablespoons of the butter. When the butter has melted and begins to brown, add the mushrooms and sauté until golden brown, about 5 minutes. Set aside.

6 Bring a 12-quart pot of lightly salted water to a vigorous boil over high heat. Add the gnocchi and cook until they all float to the top, then cook for 1 minute more. While the gnocchi are cooking, prepare to finish the dish (Step 7).

7 Place the remaining 4 tablespoons butter in a large sauté pan. Add the cooked squash and mushrooms, the sage, and the pine nuts, and set aside. Put the pumpkins and tops on a cookie sheet and reheat briefly in the oven.

(continued)

8   Use a heatproof measuring cup to scoop up ½ cup of the gnocchi's cooking liquid and add it to the pan with the squash and mushrooms. Bring the mixture to a boil over high heat, stirring to emulsify the liquids, until a creamy sauce has formed, 2 to 3 minutes. Use a slotted spoon to transfer the gnocchi from their pot to the pan with the squash and mushrooms. Add the parsley, toss, and season to taste with salt and pepper.

9   To serve, place 1 pumpkin on each of four warm dinner plates. Spoon the gnocchi into the pumpkins and out the "windows," replace the tops on the pumpkins, and serve immediately.

Wine

A Rhône Valley viognier would be a great pairing with this dish. A Château de Saint-Cosme Condrieu would be a fine choice, as would a 2002 viognier from Domaine Alan Paret.

FREEZING GNOCCHI

To freeze gnocchi, let them harden on a flour-dusted cookie sheet as described in the recipe. Transfer the frozen gnocchi into large Ziploc-type plastic bags, squeeze out any excess air, and keep in the freezer until ready to use. There is no need to thaw frozen gnocchi before cooking them; simply add 1 minute or 2 minutes to their cooking time.

JAN GREER AND MICHAEL KOKAS

UPSTATE FARMS
TIVOLI, NEW YORK

The husband-and-wife team of Jan Greer and Mike Kokas grow a wide variety of vegetables at their farm in upstate New York. Some of my favorites are their baby beets and carrots, and autumn vegetables like big candy-stripe beets and squash. They also grow about twelve types of lettuce and twelve varieties of baby greens, all of them superior.

Jan and Mike have been quiet heroes of a sort to me for their initiative and sense of community: not only do they farm, but they have organized a cooperative with a few dozen farms, some of them local and all of them small, family-run operations. Their simple mission is to promote "small family farms and in-season, locally produced products."

As an extension of their cooperative, Jan and Mike have opened a store in Hudson, New York, the Hudson River Farm Market, where they sell locally grown fruits and vegetables and locally produced meats and cheeses. It's on Fourth Street, just off the antique-store-packed Warren Street in "downtown" Hudson. If you ever find yourself there, drop in and take home a delicious souvenir.

Pumpkin Pancakes with Candied Walnuts and Orange-Maple Syrup

SERVES 4

've always served pancakes as part of savory dishes, such as pea pancakes in the spring and a corn "napoleon" in the summer. Here, they're made with pumpkin and adorned with sweet and sticky accompaniments—candied walnuts and a buttery orange-maple topping. This is a fun dessert to serve; the little pancakes are stacked atop one another so each serving looks like a short stack you might order at a pancake house.

Candied Walnuts

1 egg white

1 cup chopped walnuts

¼ teaspoon finely grated orange zest

¼ cup sugar

1 Preheat the oven to 350°F. Line a baking sheet with parchment paper.

2 In a medium bowl, whisk the egg white until foamy. Add the orange zest and toss the walnut pieces into the egg white mixture. Sprinkle in the sugar, mixing as you go.

3 Turn the nuts out onto the lined baking sheet and spread them out into a single layer. Bake for 8 minutes, then stir the nuts around to ensure both an even toasting and an even sugar coating. Return the sheet to the oven and bake for another 5 to 6 minutes. The nuts should be toasted, but the sugar should not be caramelized. Remove the sheet from the oven.

4 Lay a fresh sheet of parchment paper on the counter. Remove the nuts from the baking sheet, scraping if necessary, and leave them on the parchment to cool. Stir occasionally to separate them. These can be made up to 5 days in advance and stored in an airtight container at room temperature.

Orange-Maple Syrup

1 cup Grade A maple syrup
(see page 208)

4 tablespoons (½ stick) butter

Juice of ½ orange

Put the syrup, butter, and juice in a small pot and warm over medium heat. Stir together and set aside. This can be made up to 24 hours in advance and kept, covered, in the refrigerator.

(continued)

Pumpkin Pancakes

³/₄ cup flour

1 teaspoon baking powder

Generous pinch of salt

1¹/₂ teaspoons pumpkin pie spice

1 whole egg plus 1 egg yolk

2 tablespoons Grade A maple syrup

1 cup milk

1¹/₂ cups canned pumpkin or roasted pumpkin (page 211, Steps 1 and 2)

4 tablespoons (¹/₂ stick) butter

Vanilla ice cream, optional

1   Preheat the oven to 250°F.

2   In a medium mixing bowl, whisk together the flour, baking power, salt, and pumpkin pie spice. In a small bowl, whisk together the egg and yolk with the maple syrup, then whisk in the milk. Pour the liquid mixture over the dry ingredients, add the pumpkin, and stir to combine. Set an ovenproof plate or a parchment-lined baking sheet in the oven.

3   Heat a wide nonstick pan over medium-low heat. Add 1 tablespoon of the butter. As soon as the butter melts and begins to foam, ladle in four 3-inch pancakes. For perfect circles, you can use pancake rings, but lightly swirling the batter with the underside of the ladle will work just as well. Cook the pancakes for 4 minutes, flip them, and cook for another minute or so. Transfer the pancakes to the plate in the oven to keep them warm, stacking the batch in a neat little pile. Repeat with the remaining butter and batter.

4   To serve, place a stack of pancakes in the center of each of four plates. Top with warm syrup and generously sprinkle with nuts. If you like, add a scoop of vanilla ice cream to each serving.

Wine

The caramel and maple notes need a dessert wine with those same flavors, such as a sticky from Australia's Rutherglen region, known for their fantastic and good-value sweet muscats. Try Campbell's Rutherglen Muscat.

Fresh Ideas and Undiscovered Treasures

Chilled Shrimp with an Autumn Slaw

Salmon with Braised Cauliflower, Lemon Brown Butter, and a Pine Nut–Currant Crust

Quince-Pomegranate Cheesecake Parfait

This is a relatively light fall menu—a shrimp and coleslaw appetizer followed by a salmon dish and finished with a granité-topped parfait. But it'll more than satisfy your palate, because each course brings its own distinct medley of fall flavors to the table.

I designed this menu to demonstrate some new ways of using familiar fall ingredients. The Chilled Shrimp with an Autumn Slaw (page 218) includes the apple in an original seasonal context, and the Salmon with Braised Cauliflower, Lemon Brown Butter, and a Pine Nut–Currant Crust (page 221) roasts cauliflower to make it a more powerful presence than usual.

I've also included some less popular fall ingredients that are worth discovering and using frequently, such as the root vegetable kohlrabi and the two fruits in the Quince-Pomegranate Cheesecake Parfait (page 224). All three are sources of different flavors and textures, work well in a variety of cooking styles, and are ingredients that I use as much as the favorite offerings of the season.

Chilled Shrimp
with an Autumn Slaw

here's cabbage in this light, crunchy coleslaw, but its resemblance to traditional recipes pretty much ends there. The cabbage is balanced by equal quantities of tart green apple and grated kohlrabi, a member of the cabbage family with a sweet flavor and juiciness that make it a logical pairing with apple. You might not know this vegetable, but I love it: it has floppy, dark green leaves that almost seem out of proportion, an exquisitely slender stalk, and a small bulb, both of which are very pale. There's also a purple variety that you could use in this recipe as well.

This slaw isn't tossed with mayonnaise; it calls for a vinaigrette of lemon juice, grapeseed oil, and apple cider.

Autumn Coleslaw

2 cups green cabbage, cut into thin ribbons

1½ teaspoons salt

1 cup peeled, grated green apple

1 cup grated kohlrabi (see page 219)

¼ cup grapeseed or other vegetable oil

2 tablespoons freshly squeezed lemon juice

2 tablespoons apple cider

1½ teaspoons ground coriander

Freshly ground black pepper

Place the cabbage in a bowl, sprinkle with the salt, and let sit for 1 hour. Squeeze out the excess liquid with your hands, wipe out the bowl, and return the cabbage to the bowl. Add the remaining ingredients, toss, and let marinate for 1 hour while you prepare the shrimp. (This slaw can be made up to 2 days in advance and kept in an airtight container in the refrigerator.)

Poached Shrimp and Assembly

⅓ cup white wine vinegar

⅓ cup salt

16 to 20 jumbo shrimp, heads removed

1   In a large pot, bring 4 quarts water to a rolling boil over high heat. Add the vinegar and salt. When the water returns to a rolling boil, add the shrimp, lower the heat, and poach for 2 minutes. Remove the pot from the heat and let sit until the water cools to room temperature. Remove the shrimp with a slotted spoon, place them in a bowl, cover, and chill in the refrigerator until cold.

2   Peel the shrimp, leaving the last joint and tail intact. Devein by cutting along the back, removing the dark vein.

3   To serve, mound some of the slaw in the center of each of four dinner plates. Arrange the shrimp around the slaw.

Wine

A light, fresh sparkling wine would do nicely with this dish. Try a prosecco from the Veneto region in Italy, such as the latest vintage of Bisol Crede Prosecco.

GRATING KOHLRABI

Kohlrabi must be peeled before it can be grated. Because it has a thick skin, a vegetable peeler may not do the trick; use a paring knife. If you are not skilled at turning a vegetable in one hand while holding the knife in the other, use a larger knife to cut off the skin and form the kohlrabi into a naked square. You may waste a bit of the root, but it's a small price to pay for your safety.

Salmon with Braised Cauliflower, Lemon Brown Butter, and a Pine Nut–Currant Crust

SERVES 4

his salmon dish was inspired by the flavors and textures of *pasta alla palina,* a traditional Sicilian pasta dish made with bread crumbs, cauliflower, pine nuts, currants, and anchovies. I'd serve this with the roasted potatoes on page 178 to soak up the juices.

The thing that drew me to this recipe was the cabbage-like flavor of cauliflower, which I've always enjoyed pureed and in soups, and even steamed with cheese sauce when I was a kid. Roasting or braising cauliflower is the best way to maximize its flavor, but you can use it just about any way you'd use broccoli: steamed, blanched, or sautéed. When shopping for cauliflower, there's an easy way to test its freshness: if you rub its florets and they break easily, it's getting old and should be passed over.

Crust

1 tablespoon pine nuts

1 tablespoon dried currants, soaked in warm water for 1 hour and drained

½ anchovy fillet, rinsed, patted dry, and chopped

2 tablespoons butter

2 tablespoons minced onion

1 teaspoon minced garlic

1 tablespoon dry white wine

¼ cup dried bread crumbs

Salt

Freshly ground black pepper

1 Preheat the oven to 450°F.

2 Spread the pine nuts out on a cookie sheet and toast in the oven until lightly browned, about 5 minutes. Remove the sheet from the oven and let the pine nuts cool to room temperature.

3 Place the currants, pine nuts, and anchovy in a food processor fitted with the metal blade and process until coarsely chopped.

(continued)

4 Melt 1 tablespoon of the butter in a sauté pan set over low heat. Add the onion and garlic, and sauté until tender, about 5 minutes. Add the wine and reduce until dry, 2 to 3 minutes.

5 Place the remaining 1 tablespoon butter in a sauté pan set over high heat and cook until melted and brown. Add the bread crumbs, season with salt and pepper, and sauté until golden brown, working quickly so the crumbs remain crisp. Add the currant mixture and onion and garlic, season with salt and pepper, toss, and set aside.

Cauliflower

2 tablespoons butter	½ cup Vegetable Stock (page 344)
1 small head cauliflower, cut into 2-inch-long florets, then halved lengthwise	

Melt the butter in a large sauté pan set over medium-high heat. Add the cauliflower florets, cut side down, and sauté until well browned, about 5 minutes. Turn and cook until the other side is lightly browned, about 2 minutes. Add the stock, cover, and let simmer over low heat until the florets are almost tender, about 5 minutes. Remove the lid, raise the heat to high, bring the liquid to a boil, and let boil until reduced and thickened, about 2 minutes. Remove the pan from the heat and set aside.

Salmon

8 sprigs rosemary	4 skinless salmon fillets, 6 to 7 ounces each, ideally cut from the head end
8 sprigs thyme	
8 sprigs flat-leaf parsley	Extra-virgin olive oil
	Salt

1 Arrange half the rosemary, thyme, and parsley sprigs on a baking sheet. Put the fish fillets, skinned side down, on top of the herbs. Scatter the remaining herb sprigs over the fish. Cover the fish with plastic wrap, molding the wrap around the fish to keep it moist, and gently press the herbs into the flesh. Place the fish in the refrigerator and chill for at least 1 hour and up to 4 hours.

2 Preheat the oven to 450°F.

3 Remove the fish from the refrigerator and let come to room temperature, about 15 minutes. Remove the plastic wrap from the fish. Remove the herbs from above

and below the fillets and set aside. Rub 1 teaspoon olive oil into each side of the fillets and season both sides with salt.

4   Spread all of the herbs on the baking sheet and place the fillets on the herb bed in a single layer. Roast until just opaque in the center, 10 to 15 minutes, depending on the thickness of the fillets (pry apart the flesh on 1 fillet to check for doneness).

5   Brush the top of the salmon (not the skinned side) with olive oil and sprinkle with the crust.

Brown Butter and Assembly

1 tablespoon freshly squeezed lemon juice	¼ cup cream
	Salt
4 tablespoons (½ stick) butter	Freshly ground black pepper

1   Place the lemon juice in a deep, heatproof bowl.

2   Place the butter and cream in a small heavy-bottomed saucepan and bring to a boil over medium-high heat. Reduce the heat to medium-low and whisk constantly for about 5 minutes, until the mixture thickens to the consistency of mayonnaise and the milk solids separate out and float on top. Transfer the mixture to a food processor fitted with the metal blade and process for 20 seconds to break up the solids. Return the mixture to the saucepan and cook over medium-low heat, whisking constantly, for about 3 minutes, until its color changes from reddish brown to a deep walnut brown.

3   Add the mixture to the lemon juice (it will foam up a bit). Swirl the sauce and lemon around, and season with salt and pepper. (You may notice little bits of milk solids in the mixture, but don't worry about them; they're sweet, nutty, and delicious.) Set aside.

4   To serve, divide the cauliflower among four warm dinner plates. Top with the salmon. Drizzle with brown butter and pass any remaining brown butter on the side.

Wine

A rich, ripe Alsatian white would stand up to the flavors in this dish. Try a pinot blanc or the Pinot Auxerrois Vieille Vignes from Albert Mann, a producer from Alsace, France.

Quince-Pomegranate
Cheesecake Parfait

SERVES 4

'm told that the quince was once very popular in American home cooking. If that's true, I'd love to know how it fell out of favor, because I find this fruit irresistible. (In fact, quinces are the most irresistible fruit in history; one was actually the love apple with which Eve tempted Adam.) Most home cooks I know have never used them and would be hard-pressed to explain exactly what a quince is.

Well, it's one of the most appealing of all autumn fruits, with a flavor reminiscent of both apples and pears but with one important distinction: quinces must be cooked to be eaten. Most people poach quinces, because they're quite resilient and hold their shape very well, but this recipe calls for them to be grated and sautéed.

Quinces go through a spectrum of color during their lifespan. It's best to buy them when they're yellow; if you get them when they're fuzzy green, they may take too long to ripen.

This dish also features one of the most beautiful of all fruits, pomegranates, which have a short season; they're available only from October to December. They are as suitable to a dessert as they are to game and other savory pairings. These juicy little jewels are a mess to deal with but worth the trouble. That said, if you don't have time to make the granité, simply pick out the seeds and layer the pomegranates in the parfait. Do *not* leave them out; their flavor cuts the creaminess of the cheese.

This dessert can be made up to four days in advance.

Pomegranate Granité

3 pomegranates   2 tablespoons sugar

1   With a sharp knife, remove the top and bottom of the pomegranates. Pull apart each fruit and, breaking through the pith as you go, remove all of the seeds.

2   Put the seeds and sugar into a food processor fitted with the metal blade and process until little to no pulp remains on the seeds. Strain through a fine-mesh strainer, place in a shallow dish, and freeze until solid.

Sautéed Quince

1 English Breakfast tea bag

4 medium quinces

2 tablespoons butter

1/3 cup sugar

1/2 vanilla bean, split lengthwise, soft seeds scraped out and reserved

1/4 teaspoon ground ginger

1   Bring 1 cup water to a boil in a small pot set over high heat. Remove the pot from the heat and lower the tea bag into the water. Let steep for at least 5 minutes. Reserve 3 tablespoons of the tea and drink or discard the rest.

2   Peel and coarsely grate the quinces: you should have 3 cups packed quince.

3   Heat the butter in a sauté pan set over medium heat until melted and foamy. Add the quince and turn it with a wooden spoon. Add the sugar, 3 tablespoons brewed tea, 1/2 cup water, the vanilla bean scrapings, and the ginger, and let simmer until the quince is very tender, about 35 minutes. Remove the pan from the heat and set aside.

(continued)

Cheesecake

3 ounces cream cheese

4 ounces goat cheese

1/4 cup plus 1 tablespoon sugar

Juice of 1/2 lemon

1/2 cup cream

4 graham crackers

1 Cream the cream cheese and goat cheese with the sugar until very light. Add the lemon juice and beat until fluffy.

2 In another bowl, softly whip the cream. Don't overwhip it, or it will break into butter lumps as you add the cheese mixture.

3 With a whisk, fold a small portion of the cheese mixture into the whipped cream, gently shaking off the mixture clinging to the inner part of the whisk as you fold. Fold in the remaining cheese mixture in the same manner.

4 Crumble the graham crackers into bite-size pieces. Divide the pieces among four parfait glasses. Divide half of the cheesecake filling among the glasses and top with the shredded quince. Layer the remaining cheesecake filling over the quince. Cover with plastic wrap and chill in the refrigerator until very cold and firm, at least 1 hour.

5 With a tablespoon, scrape across the pomegranate ice. Continue scraping until all of the ice is a light, spoonable granité.

6 To serve, top the parfaits with the pomegranate granité and serve immediately.

Wine

The celebrated Austrian sweet wines from the Burgenland region would work well. Try the Alois Kracher Cuvée Beerenauslese.

Hearty Fall Food

Cabbage and Potato Soup
with Kielbasa and Sweet
Hungarian Paprika

Fresh Bacon with Organic
Grits and Escarole

Hungarian Apple Pie
with Caramel Sauce

The term *comfort food* gets tossed around a lot these days. Usually, it's interpreted to mean all-American (often guilty) pleasures like meat loaf, fried chicken, and apple pie.

I think comfort food means different things to different people. To me, it's dishes that make me feel warm. In the cold-weather months, I lean toward the ones that remind me of my childhood, with echoes of the Hungarian classics I grew up on, or indulgences I discovered as an adult in the food profession that make me feel special when they land in front of me in a restaurant or in my own home.

This menu would comfort me on the coldest, windiest day of the year. The Cabbage and Potato Soup with Kielbasa and Sweet Hungarian Paprika (page 228) is based on one of my favorite of my mother's recipes. Fresh Bacon with Organic Grits and Escarole (page 230) is a truly decadent treatment of pork belly, a delicacy I've come to appreciate in New York restaurants. And the dessert, Hungarian Apple Pie with Caramel Sauce (page 234), is a blend of American and Hungarian comfort foods that never fails to cheer me up.

Cabbage and Potato Soup with Kielbasa and Sweet Hungarian Paprika

MAKES 7 CUPS

The food of my ancestral home might not get the same attention or respect as that of France or Italy, but in my heart, and in my stomach, Hungary will always hold a special place. Two of my favorite ingredients are Hungarian paprika and kielbasa.

Hungarian paprika is naturally spicy, but there's a sweet version that's made by removing the pepper's seeds before it's dried and ground. I often use the sweet variety, which is easier to find, adding some cayenne to replace some of the heat, as I do here.

Then there's the kielbasa. Ahhh, kielbasa! This sausage was a constant presence throughout my childhood. We ate it grilled in the summertime and topped with sauerkraut (page 335) in the winter. We devoured it at every holiday except Thanksgiving and Christmas, saving the best for the last day of the year, eating roasted pork with kielbasa on New Year's Eve, a tradition I still observe today.

There are two kinds of kielbasa—smoked and unsmoked. You can tell them apart by sight because smoking turns the kielbasa red. (I don't really count the mass-produced version; there's sugar added to please the palates of as many people as possible.) I get my kielbasa from a Polish butcher shop near my parents' home, and I suggest you buy homemade kielbasa, ordering it by mail if necessary (see Mail-Order Sources, page 345). You can use either smoked or unsmoked kielbasa in this recipe, though I think smoked is best.

This is my version of the hearty, thick potato and lima bean soup my mother made for us when I was growing up, but it's really a way to get all my favorite childhood flavors— especially that paprika and kielbasa—into one bowl.

¼ cup canola or other vegetable oil

1 stalk celery, peeled and cut into ⅓-inch dice (see Note)

½ onion, thinly sliced

6 medium leeks, quartered, cut into ⅓-inch dice, well washed in several changes of cold water, and drained

Salt

4 cups Chicken Stock (page 343) or water

1 pound Yukon gold potatoes, peeled and cut into ⅓-inch dice

½ pound high-quality kielbasa (see headnote), quartered and cut into ½-inch dice

3 cups white cabbage, cut into thin ribbons

2 tablespoons sweet Hungarian paprika

1 teaspoon cayenne pepper

2 tablespoons chopped flat-leaf parsley

1 Warm 2 tablespoons of the oil in a large pot set over medium-low heat. Add the celery, onion, half the leeks, and a pinch of salt. Cover and cook until tender but not browned, about 12 minutes. Add the stock and half the potatoes, raise the heat to high, and bring to a boil. Lower the heat and let simmer until the potatoes are tender, about 10 minutes. Transfer to a food processor fitted with the metal blade, process until pureed, and set aside.

2 Place the remaining 2 tablespoons oil and the kielbasa in a separate pot set over medium heat. Cook until the kielbasa has rendered enough fat to coat the bottom of the pot and has turned a light golden brown, about 7 minutes. Lower the heat to medium-low, add the cabbage and a pinch of salt, cover, and cook, stirring occasionally, for 12 minutes. Add the remaining leeks and potatoes, and cook, covered, stirring occasionally, for 12 minutes. Add the paprika and cayenne, and cook, covered, for 3 minutes more. Add the pureed vegetables and bring to a boil. Lower the heat and let simmer for 2 minutes. (This soup can be cooled, covered, and refrigerated for up to 1 week or frozen for up to 2 months. Let come to room temperature before gently reheating over medium heat.)

3 To serve, stir in the chopped parsley and ladle the soup into individual bowls.

Wine

The smoky notes in this soup would do well with the subtle flavors of a white Rhône-style wine. Try the Cuvée Blanc from Tablas Creek, a New World version of Châteauneuf-du-Pape blanc.

NOTE: It might seem a bit affected to peel celery, but there are times when it's absolutely essential. Because this soup is pureed but not strained, peeling the celery is the only way to eliminate the fibrous outer portion of the vegetable's stalk and guarantee a pleasing mouthfeel.

Fresh Bacon with
Organic Grits and Escarole

SERVES 4

resh bacon is the fabulously fatty part of a pig also known as pork belly, which braising turns into a luxurious, melt-in-your-mouth delicacy. It's not the kind of thing you'd eat every day, but I make a point of enjoying it occasionally, especially in the winter.

Something as rich as fresh bacon calls for a strong accompaniment, a perfect job for escarole. You've probably seen this bitter, leafy green in soups, a logical use for it because it can be cooked almost endlessly without sacrificing its texture or flavor. It's also a dependable fall vegetable because it survives the cold in the field better than almost any other green. When purchasing escarole, look for bunches with no brown spots on the leaves, and no wilting. When you hold the bunch from the bottom as you would a bouquet of flowers, it should stand straight up.

As for grits, I have to direct you to my favorite producer: Anson Mills (see page 233). I'm not related to the owner and they're not friends of mine. They haven't even paid me for this plug. They just produce the best grits I've ever tasted; they're freshly milled, then frozen to preserve freshness, resulting in a fresh corn flavor unlike any other grits you've ever had.

Fresh Bacon

2 tablespoons canola or other vegetable oil	4 cups milk
	Salt
4 squares fresh bacon, 6 ounces each (available from butchers and by mail order, see page 345)	Freshly ground black pepper
	4 cups Chicken Stock (page 343)

1   Put the oil in a 3- or 4-quart pot set over high heat. When the oil is almost smoking, add 2 pieces of the bacon and brown on all sides, about 3 minutes per side. Transfer the bacon to a plate. Repeat with the other 2 pieces of bacon. After all of the bacon is cooked, pour off and discard the grease from the pot.

2   Pour the milk into the pot and bring to a boil over high heat. Return the bacon to the pot, lower the heat, and cook at a low simmer until tender, about 2 hours. Periodically check on the liquid to make sure it is at a low simmer, adjusting the heat as necessary to maintain it. The pork is done when it begins to break apart when a sharp, thin-bladed knife is applied to it with very little pressure.

3   Remove the bacon to a plate, season with salt and pepper, and cover with a damp towel or paper towel, to let cool without drying out.

4   Raise the heat to medium-high and reduce the milk until all that remains are the milk solids. (They will resemble brown scrambled eggs.) Whisk the solids until they turn a deep caramel color, about 5 minutes. Add the stock and let simmer rapidly over medium heat for about 20 minutes. Strain. You should have about 1½ cups of liquid; if there's more, pour it back into the pot and bring to a boil over high heat until it is reduced to the proper amount. Conversely, if there's not enough liquid, add water to reach 1½ cups. (You can make the bacon up to 3 days in advance and store it in the liquid in an airtight container in the refrigerator. Let come to room temperature before reheating.)

5   Warm the bacon in the liquid over low heat. Taste and adjust seasoning with salt and pepper.

Grits

½ cup Anson Mills organic yellow corn grits

2¾ to 3 cups milk

1   In the lower pot of a double boiler, bring a few cups water to a boil. Put 1¼ cups of the milk in the upper pot of the double boiler and bring to a simmer over medium-high heat. Stir in the grits and let return to a simmer. Place the upper pot on top of the simmering water. Cook the grits on the double boiler, stirring only occasionally. Add the remaining milk in two ½-cup additions followed by ¼-cup additions, adding the next addition only when the previous one has been absorbed. Cook until the grits are creamy, 1 to 1½ hours.

2   Cover with plastic wrap and keep at room temperature until ready to serve.

(continued)

Braised Escarole

1 bunch escarole (about 1½ pounds) (kale or Swiss chard can be substituted)

2 tablespoons extra-virgin olive oil

¼ medium sweet onion, thinly sliced

1 clove garlic, thinly sliced

Salt

½ cup Chicken Stock (page 343), Vegetable Stock (page 344), or water

1   Cut the escarole into 1-inch pieces and wash in cold water.

2   Place the olive oil, onion, garlic, and a pinch of salt into a large pan and set over medium heat. Cook the vegetables, covered, stirring occasionally, until tender, about 7 minutes. Add the escarole and stock and cook, covered, until tender, 12 to 15 minutes. Season with salt and set aside.

Bread Crumbs and Assembly

¼ cup dried bread crumbs

1½ teaspoons chopped rosemary

1½ teaspoons chopped flat-leaf parsley

⅛ teaspoon salt

1   Toss all of the ingredients together in a small bowl and set aside.

2   Place the bacon in its liquid in a pot and warm over low heat.

3   To serve, mound some grits in the center of each of four plates and make a well in the center of the mounds. Put some escarole in the center of each mound. Put the bread crumbs in a bowl and use tongs to roll each piece of bacon in the bread crumbs. Place a piece of bacon atop the escarole on each plate and spoon some sauce onto the grits and onto the plate.

Wine

An earthy chardonnay would blend well with the rich bacon and grits, or a white Burgundy like the Château Fuissé Saint-Véran from the Côte Chalonnaise region in France.

TED BLEW

OAK GROVE PLANTATION AND HIGH HOPE HOGS
PITTSTOWN, NEW JERSEY

Ask Ted Blew what he specializes in and he'll tell you, with a defiant grin, "everything." Which is largely true: he does raise and grow hogs, vegetables, and grains on not one but two farms in Pittstown, New Jersey. Oak Grove Plantation grows and sells produce; High Hope Hogs raises hogs and turns them into a full range of sensational products, from boneless hams, pork tenderloin, and baby back ribs (all of which I used at JUdson Grill) to smoked and cured products like bacon and sausage. Like so many of the farmers profiled in this book, Ted runs an organic farm that isn't certified organic. His hogs are raised with no steroids, no hormones, and no antibiotics. "It takes longer to raise them, but they taste great," he says.

GLEN ROBERTS

ANSON MILLS
CHARLESTON AND COLUMBIA, SOUTH CAROLINA;
CHAPEL HILL, NORTH CAROLINA

Glen Roberts, the founder of Anson Mills, says that his company practices the "lost art of farming." A veteran of the hotel and restaurant business, Roberts started milling on his own in 1998, when he couldn't find the ingredients he needed to create authentic meals for the antiquated properties he restored for a living. Today, Anson Mills produces and sells sixty historic ingredients from twenty-five farms in six states.

That's an impressive list, but I'd love Anson Mills even if all they made were their superior, incredibly fresh-tasting grits. They do this the old-fashioned way, using corn that's as close as possible to its original antecedent, intensely rotating the crops, and doing as much as possible by hand; they even have four farms in their "family" that use only mules.

Hungarian Apple Pie with Caramel Sauce

SERVES 4

This pie is really more of a tart, with a cookie-style crust that's enriched with sour cream.

Like the quince dessert on page 224, it calls for grated rather than sliced fruit. Most apple pie recipes use cubed or sliced apple, but I prefer to grate it for a number of reasons. One is that the fruit surprises most people with a meltingly soft texture. The other is that the filling is more intensely flavored because more of its surface area is exposed to the heat. In the give-credit-where-it's-due department, I should mention that I learned this technique from my former pastry chef, Anne-Michelle Andrews.

For this recipe, I prefer Fuji apples, which are sweeter than most apples, with a firmness that makes them easy to grate. (They're also my daughter's favorite.) For snacking, I like winesaps in the early fall and Mutsu year-round.

Caramel Sauce

½ cup sugar

1 cup cold cream

Put the sugar and ¼ cup water in a small saucepan and bring to a boil over medium-high heat. Continue to cook the sugar until it is a deep mahogany color, about 10 minutes, then reduce the heat to low. From a height (it will bubble furiously), slowly pour in the cream, stir to combine, and pour the caramel sauce into a bowl. Set aside and let cool to room temperature.

Pie Crust

2¾ cups flour, plus more for dusting work surface

½ teaspoon salt

¼ teaspoon baking powder

⅓ cup sugar

1½ sticks plus 1 tablespoon butter, cut into teaspoon-sized pieces

1 whole egg plus 1 egg yolk

3 tablespoons sour cream

Grated zest of ½ lemon

1 teaspoon vanilla extract

1   Place the flour, salt, baking powder, and sugar in the bowl of an electric mixer fitted with the paddle attachment and paddle briefly to combine. Add the butter pieces and mix until crumbly. Add the whole egg, egg yolk, sour cream, lemon zest, and vanilla, and mix until just combined. Pat the dough into a 4 by 8-inch rectangle, wrap with plastic wrap, and chill in the refrigerator for 30 minutes.

2   Place the oven rack toward the bottom third of the oven. Preheat the oven to 350°F.

3   Cut the dough into 2 equal pieces. Lightly flour your work surface and roll a piece into an 11-inch square (see page 236). Lay a 9-inch-square tart pan with a removable bottom next to the work area. Gently fold the crust in half on the diagonal and place it into the pan. Pat the dough into the corners of the pan. Trim the dough flush to the top of the pan's sides.

4   Lay a sheet of waxed or parchment paper on the countertop. Roll the second piece of dough on the paper into a square slightly larger than 9 by 9 inches. Trim to a perfect 9 by 9-inch square.

Apple Filling and Assembly

4 cups packed, finely grated apple (about 7 large, peeled apples)

½ teaspoon ground cinnamon

Juice of 1 large lemon

⅓ cup plus 1 tablespoon sugar

2 teaspoons cornstarch

1 egg

(continued)

1   In a large bowl, mix together the apple, cinnamon, lemon juice, sugar, and cornstarch.

2   Pat the filling evenly into the lined tart pan. Dampen your fingertips with water and run them along the top edge of the crust. Dry your hands. Pick up the paper with your fingertips and turn the top crust over the filling. Press the edges lightly to seal.

3   Beat the egg with 1 tablespoon water and brush the top of the pie with this mixture. Place in the oven and bake until the crust is firm and golden, about 50 minutes.

4   To serve, gently reheat the caramel sauce over low heat. Cut and serve individual slices, topping each slice with some sauce.

Wine
The Malvasia Passito from La Stoppa, a single-vineyard cuvée called Vigna del Volta, from Emilia-Romagna, has the caramel and honey notes to pair with this dessert. A medium-weight, inexpensive Sauternes from France, such as Château Romieu-Lacoste, would also do nicely.

ROLLING A SQUARE

Rolling dough to a square or rectangular shape is a bit different from rolling dough for a pie crust. To begin, use a short, gentle, back-and-forth rolling motion. Turn the dough 90 degrees, and roll in the same manner. As the dough thins, switch to longer, more powerful strokes. To create corners, roll over the dough in an X pattern from one opposite corner to the other.

SUPPORT YOUR LOCAL (ORGANIC) FARMERS

Apples are one of the hardest fruits to produce organically because they're so vulnerable to insects. Ironically, they're also one of the most difficult to market, because organic apples aren't as perfectly pretty as those grown industrially. If you happen across local producers who use low amounts of, or organically acceptable, pesticides to grow their apples, please support them.

My Favorite Fall Vegetables

Baby Fennel Confit

Candy Cane Beet Salad

Spicy Carrots

Sunchoke Puree

Squash Pierogi with Balsamic Vinegar and Walnuts

Alex Paffenroth's family has been farming for three generations. He was originally an onion farmer, but in 1987 a hailstorm—in mid-July, of all times—wiped out his entire crop. It was such a blow that he got out of farming and sold off fourteen of his eighty-six acres.

Would it surprise you to learn that, in time, he found himself running the family's business again?

The first thing that strikes you when you set foot on the land at Paffenroth Gardens in Warwick, New York, is how moist the ground is. You leave impossibly deep footprints as you walk around, as though you had the weight of a dinosaur behind you. This area is called the Drowned Lands, just a hair this side of a swamp, created years ago when the lake that filled its borders was drained off. If there's such a thing as bright black, that's what color the organic muck soil is. It's actually quite beautiful, and even to the layperson's eye, it's clear why vegetables flourish here.

In 1990, Alex began coming to the Union Square Greenmarket on Wednesdays and Saturdays. That's where I met him. He finds his regular trip into the city makes for a long day, but he likes that it gets him away from the farm. When he tells me "I would miss it if I didn't do it," I realize for the thousandth time that cooking and farming have a lot in common. They're both solitary occupations, and it's nice to have a chance to make them social when you can.

Alex and his wife, Linda, have a beautiful tradition that I think of every Thanksgiving: they make a wonderful dinner for their workers, and they all get together in the big barn behind Alex and Linda's house to savor it together. One, big, happy family.

Alex's most popular crops at the Greenmarket are five different colors of carrots, four varieties of beets, and root crops like salsify, parsnips, burdock, parsley root, and sunchokes. He also grows excellent onions, shallots, and garlic.

It takes Alex, Linda, daughter Deanne, and four helpers to make his popular booth at the Greenmarket run right. I love dropping by and visiting with them. Just like Alex, I find that coming to the market myself makes for a long day. I could send others down there in my place, just as he could. But, like him, I'd miss it if I didn't do it.

Baby Fennel Confit

SERVES 4

onfit is a French technique in which poultry or meat is cooked in its own fat. In contemporary American cooking, it has come to mean anything, even fish or vegetables, that are slow-cooked in olive oil until silky-soft and fork-tender. Here, baby fennel is given the confit treatment. It's salted to coax out its pleasing, sweet flavor, then simmered in olive oil with fennel seed added to punch up the anise flavor. As the fennel cooks, the oil infuses the fennel and vice versa. The fennel-flavored oil can be used as a warm vinaigrette for flaky white fish.

24 pieces baby fennel, tops trimmed, larger bulbs halved, and 2 branches reserved

2 tablespoons salt

2 teaspoons ground fennel seed

5 cups olive oil

1   Preheat the oven to 325°F.

2   Mix the fennel and salt in a bowl and let sit for 10 minutes. Remove the fennel, letting any excess water drip off, and transfer it to a 3- to 4-quart casserole. Scatter the fennel seed and pour the olive oil over the fennel and add the branches to the casserole. Set over low heat until the oil begins to bubble gently. Cover the casserole and braise the fennel in the oven until just tender, about 30 minutes.

3   Let the fennel cool in the oil before serving it. If you like, strain the oil and save it for up to 2 weeks. Warm it and spoon over fish as a vinaigrette.

Candy Cane Beet Salad

SERVES 4

love the sweet flavor of candy cane beets, also known as chioggia beets, and I'm always looking for new ways to use them. In this recipe, they're combined with another of Alex's finest offerings, black radish.

¼ cup Basic Vinaigrette (recipe follows)	Freshly ground black pepper
½ cup coarsely grated black radish	1 teaspoon chopped flat-leaf parsley
4 medium candy cane beets, roasted (see page 28) and cooled	1 bunch watercress (about 6 ounces), stems trimmed
Salt	1 tablespoon extra-virgin olive oil

1 In a bowl, mix the vinaigrette with the radish and let sit for 1 hour.

2 Peel and cut the beets into ⅓-inch slices. Arrange the slices in an overlapping circle on four plates. Season with salt and pepper.

3 Toss the radish with the parsley and season with salt and pepper. Spoon the dressed radish over the beets. Drizzle the watercress with the olive oil, season with salt and pepper, and top the radish with it. Serve.

Basic Vinaigrette

1 tablespoon freshly squeezed lemon juice	Salt
1 teaspoon red wine vinegar	Freshly ground black pepper
1 teaspoon Dijon mustard	6 tablespoons extra-virgin olive oil

Whisk together the lemon juice, vinegar, and mustard. Season with salt and pepper. Slowly drizzle in the olive oil while continuing to whisk. Taste and adjust seasoning.

Spicy Carrots

This is my take on a traditional Sicilian vegetable dish. Rather than achieve heat with cayenne or other one-dimensional spices or peppers, the carrots are tossed gently with a carefully stewed pepperoncini mixture.

½ cup extra-virgin olive oil

½ large onion, julienned

6 cloves garlic, julienned

Salt

3 stalks celery, peeled and cut on the diagonal into ¼-inch pieces (1 cup)

8 sun-dried tomatoes, cut into thin strips

8 pepperoncini peppers, seeds removed from 2, cut into thin strips

1½ pounds multicolored carrots

4 tablespoons (½ stick) butter

½ cup Vegetable Stock (page 344)

1   Warm the olive oil in a sauté pan with a lid over medium-low heat. Add the onion, garlic, and a pinch of salt, cover the pan, and cook for 3 minutes. Add the celery and another pinch of salt, cover, and cook for 5 minutes. Add the tomatoes, cover, and soften for 2 minutes. Add the peppers, cover, and cook for 3 to 4 minutes. Remove the pan from the heat and let cool.

2   Cut the carrots into oblique 1-inch segments by cutting on the bias and then rotating the carrot 180 degrees before cutting again, or simply cut into 1-inch pieces.

3   Melt the butter in a large sauté pan set over medium heat. Add the carrots, season with salt, and cook without browning for 6 minutes. Add the stock and cook, uncovered, over medium-high heat until the carrots are al dente and the liquid forms a glaze, about 7 minutes.

4   Add the pepperoncini mixture to the pan, toss, taste, and adjust seasoning.

5   To serve, transfer the carrots to a bowl and present family style in the center of the table.

Sunchoke Puree

SERVES 4 (MAKES 2½ CUPS)

As you can see from the recipe on page 296, I enjoy sunchokes raw. But I also like simmering them in a mixture of olive oil and broth, softening them up so they can be pureed and served as an unusual side dish. The cooking liquid can be saved and used as the base for an equally intriguing vinaigrette for fish (see page 245).

2 tablespoons extra-virgin olive oil

2 shallots, sliced

3 cloves garlic, sliced

1 teaspoon coriander seeds

1 teaspoon black peppercorns

2 sprigs thyme

¾ cup dry white wine

4 cups Chicken Stock (page 343) or Vegetable Stock (page 344)

2 pounds sunchokes, peeled and cut into 1-inch dice

2 tablespoons butter

Salt

Freshly ground black pepper

1   Heat the olive oil in a sauté pan set over medium heat. Add the shallots and garlic and sauté until tender but not browned, 5 to 7 minutes. Add the coriander seeds, peppercorns, thyme, and wine, bring to a boil over high heat, and reduce until dry, about 8 minutes. Add the stock, bring to a boil over high heat, then lower the heat and let simmer for 15 minutes. Strain the mixture, taste, and season with salt and pepper. Return it to the pot and bring to a boil. Add the sunchokes, return the liquid to a boil, then lower the heat and simmer the sunchokes until they are tender when pierced with the tip of a sharp, thin-bladed knife, about 10 minutes.

2   Strain the sunchokes through a fine-mesh strainer set over a bowl, then transfer them to a blender, add the butter, puree, and season with salt and pepper. To serve, transfer to a serving bowl and present at the table.

3   Cool, cover, and refrigerate the cooking liquid until ready to use it in a vinaigrette.

SUNCHOKE VINAIGRETTE

To make enough vinaigrette to serve 4, combine ½ cup of the cooking liquid, 2 tablespoons freshly squeezed lemon juice, and ¼ cup olive oil. Serve over any fish. If you like, add sautéed mushrooms and chopped parsley to it as well.

Squash Pierogi with Balsamic Vinegar and Walnuts

SERVES 4

These autumn dumplings, sautéed in brown butter and finished with a vinegar reduction and toasted walnuts, were a JUdson Grill classic. If you can't find kabocha squash, substitute butternut.

2¼ cups flour, plus more for dusting work surface

1 tablespoon salt

3 eggs

2- to 3-pound kobacha squash

5 tablespoons butter

¼ small onion, minced

1 small clove garlic, minced

3 tablespoons crème fraîche or sour cream

Freshly ground black pepper

2 tablespoons balsamic vinegar

2 tablespoons red wine vinegar

½ cup walnuts, toasted and chopped

2 tablespoons chopped flat-leaf parsley

1   Combine the flour with the salt in a large bowl. In a separate bowl, beat the eggs with 3 tablespoons water. Form a well in the middle of the flour mixture and pour the eggs into the well. Incorporate the eggs by stirring in the flour mixture from the sides of the well a little at a time.

(continued)

2   When the dough begins to come together in clumps, transfer it to a clean flat surface and knead for a few minutes until the dough comes together in a smooth ball (don't overwork the dough, or it will develop the gluten in the flour and make the dough tough). Wrap the dough in plastic wrap and let rest for at least 1 hour at room temperature. (Dough may be made 1 day ahead and kept, wrapped in plastic, in the refrigerator.)

3   When ready to proceed, preheat the oven to 450°F.

4   Cut the squash in half and remove the seeds. Salt the squash and place it skin side down in a shallow baking pan. Cover the bottom of the pan with ½ inch of water. Cover the squash with aluminum foil and bake until tender, about 45 minutes. Remove the pan from the oven, let the squash cool, then scoop the flesh out and set aside. Discard the skin. Pass the squash through a food mill or ricer (page 8) or mash thoroughly with a potato masher.

5   Melt 2 tablespoons of the butter in a medium saucepan set over medium heat. Add the onion and garlic and sauté until tender, about 5 minutes. Add the squash and cook, stirring, until dry. Let cool completely, then stir in the crème fraîche and season with salt and pepper.

6   To fill the pierogi, divide the dough into 4 pieces and wrap all but one in plastic wrap to keep moist.

7   Sprinkle a work surface with flour. Roll out the unwrapped dough thinly enough to fit through the largest setting of a pasta machine. Feed it through the machine until you attain about ¹⁄₁₆ inch-thickness. (If you don't have a pasta machine, use a rolling pin to roll the dough to the desired thickness.) Use a 4-inch ring cutter to cut out circles from the dough sheet. Cover the circles with plastic wrap or a kitchen towel to prevent drying while rolling out the remaining dough. Repeat to form 24 circles. (Makes 2 extra pierogi just in case a couple happen to break.)

8   Place a scant tablespoon of squash filling just to one side of the center of each circle. Working with one pierogi at a time, paint the outer ¼ inch of the circle with a pastry brush dipped in water. Fold the circle in half over the filling, pressing its edges to seal: start at the top of the pierogi, pressing gently outward around the filling as you do so to push out all the air around the filling—trapped air will make a pierogi swell like a small balloon, and it may burst when it's cooked. Seal the pierogi by pressing tines of a fork around its edges. Transfer the finished pierogi to a lightly floured baking sheet. Repeat with the remaining circles. Cover the finished pierogi with plastic wrap and set aside.

9 Bring a large pot of salted water to a boil. Carefully add the pierogi, stirring gently to make sure they do not stick to the bottom of the pot. Return to a boil and cook for 7 to 8 minutes, until the dough edge no longer feels stiff when pinched and looks slightly translucent.

10 Using a slotted spoon, transfer the pierogi to kitchen towels to drain. (To make the pierogi several hours ahead of time, transfer them from the boiling water to a bowl of ice water, then drain. Reheat the pierogi in boiling water before proceeding with the recipe. To freeze pierogi, boil them for just 2 minutes, transfer to a bowl of ice water, and drain. Arrange them on a lightly oiled baking sheet and freeze until hard, then lift them from the sheet and transfer to a freezer bag. Pierogi keep, frozen, for 1 month. To cook frozen pierogi, bring a pot of salted water to a boil and add the pierogi. Return to a boil and cook for 2 to 3 minutes, until al dente.)

11 Place the balsamic and red wine vinegars in a small saucepan set over medium heat. Cook until reduced by half, then set aside.

12 Melt 1½ tablespoons of the butter in each of 2 large sauté pans. Add half of the pierogi to each pan, top side down, and lightly brown to crisp, about 1 minute. Season with salt and pepper, then turn them over and brown quickly on the other side, about 45 seconds.

13 To serve, divide the pierogi among four warm plates using a slotted spoon to keep the butter in the pans. Collect all the browned butter in one of the pans and add the walnuts and parsley. Toss until creamy, then drizzle over the pierogi. Drizzle the vinegar reduction over the pierogi.

A New Look at Old-World Cuisine

Mackerel with Salted
Capers, Red Cippoline
Onions, and an Herb Salad

Black Sea Bass with a
Lobster-Champagne Broth,
Lobster Dumplings, and
Baby White Turnips

Roasted Loin of Veal
with Porcini, Artichokes,
and Roasted Garlic

Huckleberry Strudel
with Indian Pudding

In the fall, cooking for a special occasion makes me think of the more formal food I was taught to prepare in cooking school but which you don't see very much these days. This menu is composed of my loosely interpreted variations on classic dishes.

The first course, Mackerel with Salted Capers, Red Cippoline Onions, and an Herb Salad (page 249), brings to mind such timeless delicacies as smoked salmon and cured sturgeon. The second course, Black Sea Bass with a Lobster-Champagne Broth, Lobster Dumplings, and Baby White Turnips (page 252), echoes venerable lobster preparations like Newburg and Thermidor. The main course, Roasted Loin of Veal with Porcini, Artichokes, and Roasted Garlic (page 256), is in the grand Italian tradition, while the finale, Huckleberry Strudel with Indian Pudding (page 259), is an American twist on a Viennese dessert classic.

This would be a fine menu for the most special evening of your year, when people linger for hours and you use your best china and silverware. Its individual courses could be used to add a touch of class to more ordinary dinners or to serve as small meals in their own right.

Mackerel with Salted Capers, Red Cippoline Onions, and an Herb Salad

SERVES 4

There's a small group of fish that actually taste "fishy," with that sort of briny, oily flavor that practically screams "I came out of the ocean." I prefer not to cook these fish, looking instead for ways to eat them raw and cold, states that let their flavors and textures really shine. Salt-curing mackerel produces a silky flesh and softens the mackerel's aggressive flavor. You can serve it instead of gravlax (cured salmon), and it's great with caviar.

Cured mackerel is rich, so I surround it with contrasting accompaniments: salty capers, sweet cippoline onions, and herbs. The herbs play a dual role here: both their fragrance and taste refresh the palate.

Mackerel

1 cup kosher salt

1 Spanish mackerel fillet, 12 to 16 ounces, or 2 fillets, 8 ounces each

1 shallot, thinly sliced

2 cloves garlic, finely chopped

1 teaspoon cracked black pepper

4 sprigs flat-leaf parsley, roughly chopped

3 tablespoons extra-virgin olive oil

1 Put ⅓ cup of the salt on the bottom of a plastic-wrapped baking sheet. Place the fish, skin side down, on top of the salt and top with the remaining ⅔ cup salt. Cover with plastic wrap and chill in the refrigerator for 5 hours, but no longer.

2 Remove the fish from the baking sheet and rinse off the salt under cold running water. Pat dry with paper towels. Using a pair of needle-nose fish pliers or tweezers, remove the pinbones from the middle of the fillets (see page 251).

(continued)

3 In a bowl, mix together the shallot, garlic, pepper, and parsley. Spread half of this mixture out on a fresh sheet of plastic wrap. Drizzle with 1 tablespoon of the olive oil, then lay the fish on top, skin side down. Top with the remaining mixture and drizzle with the remaining 2 tablespoons olive oil. Wrap tightly in plastic wrap and chill in the refrigerator for at least 4 hours, or up to 4 days.

Cippoline Onions

2 tablespoons extra-virgin olive oil	Kosher salt
2 large or 4 small cippoline onions, unpeeled and halved (large pearl onions can be substituted)	

1 Preheat the oven to 400°F.

2 Put the olive oil in a small ovenproof sauté pan, add the onions, cut side down, and sprinkle with salt. Cook over high heat until the onions begin to sizzle, 2 to 3 minutes. Cover with a lid or aluminum foil and roast in the oven until the onions are tender but not falling apart, about 15 minutes. Remove from the oven and let cool.

3 When the onions are cool enough to handle, remove the skins, cut off the root, and break apart into rings. Set aside.

Assembly

4 teaspoons freshly squeezed lemon juice	1/8 cup flat-leaf parsley
2 tablespoons plus 2 teaspoons extra-virgin olive oil	1/8 cup 1-inch chive batons
Salt	1/8 cup tarragon leaves
1/2 teaspoon crushed red pepper flakes	1/8 cup dill leaves
1 tablespoon minced shallot	1/8 cup chervil leaves (if not available, double the amount of tarragon)
24 to 28 salt-packed capers, or 2 teaspoons nonpareil capers, rinsed and drained	

1   Brush the marinade from the mackerel. Lay the fish flat on a cutting board, skin side down, and remove the skin by cutting parallel to the board just above the skin. Starting at the tail end and holding the knife at a 45-degree angle, cut ⅛-inch slices on the diagonal.

2   Arrange the fish slices, without overlapping them, in a circle covering the center of each of four chilled dinner plates. Cover with plastic wrap and press until flat. In a small bowl, stir together the lemon juice and olive oil. Remove the plastic wrap from the fish, brush the lemon oil onto the mackerel, and lightly season with salt. Sprinkle with the red pepper flakes, shallot, and capers. Place the onions in the middle and top with the parsley, chives, tarragon, dill, and chervil. Serve at once.

Wine

Mediterranean whites would be perfect with this dish, in particular the herbal flavors of a Cantina del Taburno falanghina from the region of Campania, Italy, or a white Bandol from Provence, France.

REMOVING PINBONES FROM FISH

To remove the small pinbones from fish, it's helpful to first get the bones to stand up by brushing your finger across the length of the fillet. On most fish, pinbones are located only in the central area of the body, but on mackerel, they can be found all the way to the tail.

Black Sea Bass with a Lobster-Champagne Broth, Lobster Dumplings, and Baby White Turnips

SERVES 4

assembled this dish out of a yearning for something unabashedly luxurious, the kind of thing you might order in a restaurant or cook at home for a special occasion or for a day when you just feel like spoiling yourself. There are only a handful of raw ingredients that automatically suggest luxury: caviar, foie gras, and lobster, of course. And there's no other wine or spirit that says "special" like Champagne.

While lobster is expensive, this recipe uses the entire creature. The head flavors the broth, while the meat is used in the dumplings. The bittersweet flavor of the turnips makes a subtle but essential contribution.

Broth and Dumplings

1/3 cup white vinegar	2 tablespoons finely chopped carrot
1/3 cup salt	2 tablespoons finely chopped celery
One 1½-pound lobster (see page 105)	1 teaspoon finely chopped shallot
2 tablespoons canola or other vegetable oil	1 clove garlic, finely chopped
	1½ cups Champagne
3 tablespoons finely chopped onion	½ teaspoon black peppercorns
3 tablespoons finely chopped leek, white part only, well washed in several changes of cold water and drained	2 sprigs tarragon
	1½ cups Chicken Stock (page 343)

1   In a large pot, bring 4 quarts of water to a rolling boil over high heat. Add the vinegar and salt. Slide the lobster into the water, lower the heat to medium, and cook, uncovered, for 5 to 6 minutes. Watch the water carefully and do not let it come to a boil again: the water should bubble occasionally but not simmer. Use tongs to remove the lobster from the pot.

Discard the liquid. Break apart the lobster into head, claws, and tail. Shell the tail, knuckles, and claws. Discard the top portion of the claw, from where it separates into pincers. Finely chop the lobster meat.

2   Open up the head by pulling the leg half away from the top half. Scrape away and discard the feathery lungs and insides from the head. Using a large, wide-bladed knife, chop the shell into small pieces.

3   Make the lobster-Champagne broth: Warm the oil in a 3-quart pot set over medium heat. Add the onion, leek, carrot, celery, shallot, and garlic, and gently sauté, covered, until tender but not browned, 5 to 7 minutes. Add the Champagne, peppercorns, and tarragon, raise the heat to high, and bring the liquid to a boil. Add the lobster and the chicken stock, return to a boil, reduce the heat, and let simmer for 20 minutes. Remove the pot from the heat and let rest for 20 minutes. Strain the contents through a fine-mesh strainer lined with cheesecloth, pressing down on the solids with a wooden spoon to extract as much flavorful liquid as possible. Discard the solids and set the liquid aside. You should have about 1¼ cups of broth.

Fish Mousse

2 ounces white-fleshed fish (e.g., cod or pike), cut into small pieces

Pinch of salt

Pinch of freshly ground white pepper

¼ cup cream

1   Place the fish, salt, and pepper in a food processor fitted with the metal blade and pulse to roughly chop the fish. Scrape down the sides of the bowl. With the machine running, slowly pour in the cream to make a fish mousse. Transfer the mousse to a mixing bowl and fold in the chopped lobster meat. Cover with plastic wrap and chill in the refrigerator for 30 minutes.

2   Divide the mousse into 12 equal portions. Work each portion back and forth between 2 tablespoons with a scraping motion to form them into 3-sided ovals (like an egg). As they are formed, set the dumplings aside on a plate.

(continued)

Turnips and Bass

2 tablespoons butter

1 bunch baby turnips (6 to 8 turnips), peeled and quartered, greens cleaned, stems removed, and cut into thick ribbons

Salt

2 tablespoons Vegetable Stock (page 344), Chicken Stock (page 343), or water

¼ cup canola or other vegetable oil

4 black sea bass fillets, skin on, 6 ounces each

Freshly ground black pepper

1 Preheat the oven to 450°F.

2 Melt 1 tablespoon of the butter in a sauté pan over medium-low heat until melted but not browned. Add the turnips and a pinch of salt and sauté until just about tender, 5 to 7 minutes. Add the stock, turnip greens, and remaining 1 tablespoon butter. Toss and cook until the greens have wilted and a glaze has formed, about 2 minutes. Remove the pan from the heat and set aside.

3 Warm the oil in a large ovenproof sauté pan over medium-high heat until almost smoking. Pat the fillets dry with paper towels, season with salt on the skin side, and with both salt and pepper on the flesh side. Place the fillets in the sauté pan, skin side down, and let the fish curl for 30 seconds, then flatten with a spatula. Continue to cook until the edges start to brown, about 1 minute, then place the pan in the oven. Roast the fish until almost cooked through, about 6 minutes. (When looked at from above, the cooked portion will creep toward the middle of the fish.) Remove the pan from the oven, turn the fish over, and let sit for 30 seconds. Transfer the fish to a warm plate and set aside.

Assembly

2 tablespoons butter

1 teaspoon chopped flat-leaf parsley, plus 4 leaves for garnish

1 teaspoon thinly sliced chives, plus four 1-inch batons for garnish

1 teaspoon chopped tarragon, plus 8 leaves for garnish

1 teaspoon chopped chervil, plus 8 leaves for garnish

1   Pour the lobster stock into a pot and bring to a boil over medium heat. Add the dumplings and poach for 3 minutes.

2   Remove the dumplings with a slotted spoon, return the broth to a boil, and whisk in the butter. Add the chopped parsley, chives, tarragon, and chervil, and mix well.

3   Divide the turnips and greens among four bowls and top with the fish. Arrange the dumplings around the turnips. Divide the lobster-Champagne broth among the bowls, and garnish each with 1 parsley leaf, 1 chive baton, 2 tarragon leaves, and 2 chervil leaves. Serve at once.

Wine

The lobster flavors are subtle in this dish, so it's best to choose a sparkling wine or Champagne to match the sauce. Beth recommends a sparkling wine such as the Blanc de Blancs NV Champagne from "small grower" Pierre Gimonnet.

Roasted Loin of Veal with Porcini, Artichokes, and Roasted Garlic

SERVES 4

or my money, there's no more pure, intense, autumn flavor than fresh porcini mushrooms browned in olive oil with garlic. Porcini can be hard to find; unless you have access to a really extraordinary gourmet market, you will probably have to order them. But they're worth the effort. In a pinch, replace them with cremini mushrooms, but do *not* use dried porcini. They have an unpleasant, cardboard texture, though they can be useful as a source of flavor for soups and stews.

The artichokes here might surprise you: when you brown them, their flavor changes, lending this dish an earthy, mineral "acidity" that perfectly complements the porcini.

Try to buy pasture-raised veal, which has a more beefy flavor than the milk-fed variety.

Veal

2 pounds boneless veal loin, cut into 4 portions

Salt

Freshly ground black pepper

¼ cup canola or other vegetable oil

2 tablespoons butter

1 sprig thyme

1 Preheat the oven to 450°F.

2 Season the veal on all sides with salt and pepper. Warm the oil in an ovenproof sauté pan set over high heat, add the veal, and sear for 2 minutes on one side until nicely browned. Flip the veal over and sear for another 2 minutes until nicely browned. Pour off the oil from the pan and add the butter. As soon as the butter is browned and foamy, add the thyme, turn the veal 90 degrees, and place in the oven for 3 minutes. Flip the veal over and cook for 3 minutes more. Let rest.

Artichokes and Porcini

5 tablespoons extra-virgin olive oil

4 large artichoke hearts, 1 inch of the stem left on, each cut into four to five ½-inch slices (see page 258)

Salt

Freshly ground black pepper

½ cup Vegetable Stock (page 344)

4 ounces porcini mushrooms, each cut into four ⅓-inch slices

1 tablespoon roasted garlic puree (see page 96)

½ cup Brown Chicken Stock (page 343)

2 tablespoons butter

Juice of ½ lemon

1 tablespoon chopped flat-leaf parsley

1 Warm 2 tablespoons of the olive oil in a large pan set over medium-high heat. Add the artichokes and cook until golden brown on one side, about 3 minutes. Turn them over and brown for 1 minute more, then season with salt and pepper. Add ¼ cup of the vegetable stock, cover, and let simmer for 2 minutes, then remove the cover and reduce until glazed, about 3 minutes. Meanwhile, fill a bowl with ice and set another bowl on top of it. When the artichokes are done, transfer them to the top bowl and let chill.

2 Repeat Step 1, using the porcini, adding them to the artichokes to chill.

3 Warm the remaining 1 tablespoon olive oil in the same sauté pan set over medium heat. Add the roasted garlic puree and cook until lightly browned, 1 minute. Return the artichokes and porcini to the pan, add the chicken stock, and bring to a boil over high heat. Let boil for 3 minutes. Remove the pan from the heat, and stir in the butter, lemon, and parsley. Taste and adjust seasoning.

(continued)

Potato Puree and Assembly

1 pound Yukon gold potatoes, peeled
and quartered

½ cup cream

8 tablespoons (1 stick) butter, cut into
small pieces

Salt

Freshly ground black pepper

1   Preheat the oven to 450°F.

2   Place the potatoes in a pot and cover with cold water. Salt the water, bring the water to
a boil over high heat, and cook until the potatoes are tender, about 15 minutes. Drain the
potatoes and transfer to a cookie sheet. Bake in the oven until dry, about 5 minutes.

3   Place the cream in a sauté pan and bring to a boil over medium-high heat.

4   Add the butter, whisk for 1 minute, then remove from the heat and finish whisking in
the butter. Pass the potatoes through a food mill or ricer (see page 8), mix in the cream
and butter, and season with salt and pepper.

5   Divide the potato puree among four warm plates. Using a slotted spoon, place the
porcini and artichokes on top of the potatoes. Slice each veal portion into 4 or 5 slices
and fan the veal around the edge, then drizzle with the sauce. Serve at once.

Wine

A medium-bodied sangiovese would pair well with the veal and porcini flavors. Try the
Chianti Classico from a small producer in Tuscany named Casaloste.

TO PREPARE
ARTICHOKE HEARTS

Remove all the leaves down to the soft cone-shaped light yellow leaves. Cut around the
base of these leaves with a paring knife and remove them. Remove the choke with a
spoon or melon baller. Rub the exposed flesh with half a lemon to prevent browning.
Peel the tough skin from the outside of the heart with a vegetable peeler or paring
knife, working around the top and down the stem, rubbing periodically with the
lemon. Reserve the prepared hearts in water acidulated with lemon juice.

Huckleberry Strudel
with Indian Pudding

SERVES 4

f you ever see huckleberries at a farm stand or greenmarket, grab them! They look just
like blueberries, but they come along later in the year and their sweetness is offset by
a touch of tartness. They have considerably more seeds, which makes them pleasingly
crunchy. They're a real treat.

You could purchase frozen strudel dough, but it's much easier than it seems to pull
your own. True, your first attempts won't be as thin as store-bought, but practice will
correct that problem. If you are concerned about failing to pull the dough correctly, double
or even triple the recipe. Keeping the dough warm and moist and using even pressure is
the key to a smooth, thin sheet.

This dessert would work on your Thanksgiving menu. Historically speaking, it would
make perfect sense: Indian pudding was one of the recipes that Native Americans taught
the Pilgrim women to help them make the most use of the abundant corn.

Strudel

1½ cups flour, plus more for dusting
work surface

Pinch of salt

1 tablespoon canola or other vegetable oil

1½ cups cleaned huckleberries

⅔ cup butter cookie or cake crumbs

¼ cup sugar

1 tablespoon freshly squeezed lemon juice

2 tablespoons melted butter

1   Place the flour and salt in a medium bowl. Add the oil and ½ cup plus 1 tablespoon
warm water, mixing with the tips of your fingers. After the oil and water are incorporated, turn the sticky mass out onto a floured surface and knead with the base of your
hands until a sticky, stretchy dough forms. Wrap in plastic and let rest in a warm spot
for at least 2 and no longer than 10 hours.

(continued)

2   Place the huckleberries, cookie crumbs, sugar, and lemon juice in a bowl, and work them together with your fingers. You're using your hands for convenience and also because it's the best way to be sure you don't have any pieces of dry cookie remaining in the mixture. Set the bowl aside.

3   Lay out a kitchen towel or a 12 by 18-inch sheet of waxed paper. Flour the towel or paper lightly. Unwrap the dough and pat it into a square. Lift the square by two corners, letting the dough hang down. Give the dough light shakes; gravity will stretch it for you. Turn 90 degrees and shake again. Continue to turn and shake until you have an 8 by 8-inch square. Lay the dough in the middle of the towel. Pull in opposite directions from underneath the middle of the square, using the undersides of your fingertips. Pull the dough until it is 12 inches long, tugging at the thick spots; turn it 90 degrees and pull the short side to 12 inches long. Switch the position of your fingertips and pull the dough to 18 inches long. If a hole threatens while pulling, relax, place the palm of your hand on top of the thin spot, and gently tug around it. Don't worry if the sheet has a border of thick dough; simply trim it with a sharp paring knife. Brush the sheet with the melted butter. Make a log of filling across the bottom edge of the 12-inch side, about an inch from the bottom of the sheet. Flip the edge of the towel over the filling and roll back to release the dough. Continue to roll the towel, flipping the strudel as you go. Pick up both ends of the towel and gently roll the strudel onto a baking sheet. Brush with butter. Chill in the refrigerator until 20 minutes before serving.

Pudding

1¼ cups milk	2 tablespoons sugar
¼ cup fine cornmeal	1 egg
1 teaspoon grated lemon zest	¼ cup grated Granny Smith or other tart green apple
½ teaspoon vanilla extract	
⅛ teaspoon ground cinnamon	⅓ cup molasses
Generous pinch of salt	2 tablespoons golden raisins

1   Preheat the oven to 350°F. Line four individual aluminum muffin cups with cupcake liners.

2   Combine 1 cup of the milk, the cornmeal, lemon zest, vanilla, cinnamon, and salt in a small saucepan. Bring to a boil over medium heat, then lower the heat and let simmer until the mixture has the consistency of thick oatmeal or grits, about 4 minutes. Remove the pot from the heat and set aside.

3 Lightly beat the egg and sugar in a small bowl. Add the remaining ¼ cup milk, then the grated apple. Mix the warm corn mush into the egg mixture. Blend in the molasses and then stir in the raisins.

4 Divide the mixture among the lined muffin cups. Place the aluminum cups into a shallow baking dish (a 9 by 12-inch pan works well), place the dish in the oven, and fill with water three-quarters of the way up the sides of the muffin cups. Cover the dish tightly with aluminum foil and bake for 45 minutes or until the puddings are set. Remove the baking dish from the oven and leave covered and warm until ready to serve.

Topping

½ cup crème fraîche	1 tablespoon confectioners' sugar
2 tablespoons cream	¼ teaspoon grated lemon zest

Combine the crème fraîche, cream, and confectioners' sugar in a large bowl. Whip until fluffy, then fold in the lemon zest. Chill until ready to serve.

Sauce and Assembly

½ cup cleaned huckleberries	1 teaspoon cornstarch
¼ cup sugar	

1 Place all of the ingredients and ½ cup water in a small saucepan, and bring to a boil over medium heat, then puree in a blender, let cool, and chill in the refrigerator.

2 When ready to serve, preheat the oven to 475° F. Bake the strudel for 8 minutes or until light brown. Slice on an angle into 4 pieces.

3 Put 1 slice of strudel on a plate at the 12 o'clock position. Put some pudding at the 8 o'clock position. Place some topping at 4 o'clock, in between the strudel and the pudding. Spoon some sauce over the corner of the strudel and spoon a shallow pool of sauce around the plate.

Wine

The huckleberry and molasses flavors would do well with the prune and spicy notes of an American late-harvest zinfandel. Presidio and J. Fritz are both recommended California producers.

Thanksgiving

Thanksgiving is, without a doubt, my favorite holiday. I appreciate the fact that it is first and foremost an American holiday that everyone, regardless of religion (or lack thereof), can celebrate. I appreciate that it hasn't been commercialized. And, as a chef and food lover, I love that it's built around a meal.

A lot of people opt to go out for dinner on Thanksgiving these days, which would have been unthinkable when I was a kid. When they come to the restaurant where I'm the chef, I consider it an honor to serve them. But I don't think of Thanksgiving as a time to show off. I think that there are certain flavors and dishes my guests expect, and this is the time to give it to them.

The side dishes in this chapter are my versions of the dishes I ate as a child: Brussels Sprouts with Bacon (page 264), Glazed Carrots and Pearl Onions (page 266), Mashed Rutabagas (page 268), Savory Sweet Potato Pie (page 270), Concord Grape Tart (page 272), and Thankful Butterscotch Cake (page 275). Not only do I enjoy treating customers to the Telepan Thanksgiving Dinner, but my family has a relatively new tradition of dining on this holiday at the restaurant where I'm working, allowing me to enjoy the best of my past and my present at the same time.

Planning Ahead

There's no other meal that strikes fear into a cook like Thanksgiving dinner. As an amateur runner, I'm a big believer in pacing, and the key to making Thanksgiving fun for the cook as well as the guests is pacing yourself. If you want to make all of these dishes, as my family did every year, you can do all of the prep work a day before, chopping all of the vegetables and refrigerating them in individual packages with damp towels over them.

The brussels sprouts, cranberries, and sweet potato pie can be made the day before. If you're *really* organized and disciplined, you can make the butterscotch up to one week ahead of time.

Wine

Beth recommends just one or two wines for the entire Thanksgiving meal.

The white should be on the riper, richer, full-bodied side, such as a slightly aromatic viognier. Something a bit richer in style would come from California, such as Arrowood's Viognier from Saralee's Vineyards on the Russian River.

For the red, a fruity Beaujolais is often suggested for Thanksgiving, but for this holiday Beth likes to go "all-American" and serve a gamay from Oregon. Brick House Gamay Noir has the fruit and the spicy notes for this meal.

Brussels Sprouts with Bacon

SERVES 8

There's a small club of misunderstood foods that have been stigmatized as unlikable for generations. Its charter members include liver, broccoli, and the subject of this recipe: brussels sprouts. This recipe has converted more than a few sprout detractors, earning the vegetable their affection and respect. The sprouts turn tender and sweet when stewed in stock complemented by rich, salty bacon. Here the sprouts are kept whole, rather than breaking them up into leaves as many recipes do.

1 tablespoon canola or other vegetable oil

½ pound sliced bacon, cut crosswise into thin strips

½ cup minced onion

2 cloves garlic, minced

½ cup dry white wine

2 pounds brussels sprouts, ends trimmed

5 cups Chicken Stock (page 343), Vegetable Stock (page 344), or water

1   Warm the oil in a heavy-bottomed pot set over medium heat. Add the bacon and sauté until it has rendered its fat and turned crisp, about 8 minutes. Add the onion and garlic and sauté gently until softened but not browned, 5 to 7 minutes. Add the wine, raise the heat to high, and bring to a boil, stirring to scrape up any flavorful bits of bacon stuck to the bottom of the pan.

2   When the wine has nearly evaporated, about 5 minutes, add the brussels sprouts. Add the stock, bring to a boil, then reduce the heat and let the stock simmer until the sprouts are easily pierced with a knife, 12 to 15 minutes.

3   To serve, transfer the sprouts to a bowl and serve family style.

Glazed Carrots and Pearl Onions

SERVES 8

ne of the first surprises my culinary education had in store for me was how many of the ingredients that show up on a plate looking as though they had been cooked together had actually been cooked separately and then tossed together just before serving. The reason for this is about as fundamental as you can get: unless ingredients cook through at the same rate, cooking them separately is the surest way to get each one exactly right. Take something as simple as carrots and pearl onions. Many of my contemporaries grew up on frozen versions of this dish, and others grew up eating a mush of vegetables that had been cooked together. If you are like them, following this simple recipe will be a revelation.

4 medium to large carrots, cut into ½-inch pieces

2 tablespoons sugar

Salt

2 cups pearl onions, peeled (about a 10-ounce bag)

2 tablespoons cold butter, cut into small pieces

Freshly ground black pepper

1   Bring a pot of salted water to a rolling boil. Add the carrots, return to a boil, and blanch the carrots for 30 seconds. Drain the carrots in a colander and set aside.

2   Place 1 tablespoon of the sugar in a small deep-sided sauté pan set over high heat and cook until the sugar is a dark caramel color, 4 to 5 minutes, then quickly (or the sugar will burn) add the carrots and enough water just to cover, about 1 cup. Season with salt, and cook at a low rolling boil until the liquid is reduced to a glaze and the carrots are tender, 8 to 10 minutes.

3   Meanwhile, place the remaining 1 tablespoon sugar in another sauté pan. Set the pan over high heat and cook until the sugar is a dark caramel color, then quickly (or the sugar will burn) add the onions and enough water just to cover, about 1 cup. Season with salt, and cook at a low rolling boil until the liquid is reduced to a glaze and the onions are tender, 8 to 10 minutes. If the carrots or onions are not cooked enough, add ¼ to ½ cup more water and cook down again.

4 Add the onions to the pan with the carrots and toss together. Stir in and melt the butter. Season with salt and pepper.

5 To serve, transfer to a bowl and pass family style at the table.

Mashed Rutabagas

SERVES 8

ike cauliflower (page 221), rutabagas have a cabbage flavor that I just adore.

4 pounds rutabagas, peeled and cut into medium dice

8 tablespoons (1 stick) butter

Salt

Freshly ground black pepper

2 tablespoons finely chopped chives

1　Place the rutabagas in a large pot and add cold water to cover by 2 inches. Salt the water and bring to a boil over high heat. Lower the heat and let simmer until the rutabaga is easily pierced with a sharp, thin-bladed knife, 10 to 15 minutes. Be very careful not to overcook the rutabaga or it will fall apart and lose its texture.

2　Drain the rutabaga and put in a pan set over medium heat. Cook, stirring, until the pieces are dry, about 3 minutes.

3　Add the butter and, using a fork or wire potato masher, mash well. Season with salt and pepper, sprinkle with the chives, and serve.

Cranberry-Orange Sauce

ere's my *very* traditional recipe for cranberry-orange relish. As easy as it is, it produces something far better than any canned version you might buy, and the large, triangular orange pieces add an appealing visual element and bursts of flavor.

One 12-ounce bag cranberries

¾ cup sugar

½ cup freshly squeezed orange juice

1 orange, peeled and sectioned, sections cut into ½-inch triangles

1   Combine the cranberries, sugar, orange juice, and ½ cup water in a saucepan. Bring to a boil over high heat. Lower the heat and let simmer until the cranberries are cooked and a few of them start to burst, about 20 minutes.

2   Taste and add more sugar if too tart. Remove the pot from the heat and stir in the orange segments. This can be cooled, covered, and refrigerated for 2 to 3 days. Reheat gently before serving.

3   To serve, transfer the cranberries to a bowl and serve family style.

Savory Sweet Potato Pie

SERVES 8

his richly textured pie is not as sweet as many sweet potato pies. Make sure your sweet potatoes are firm with no "eyes." It's okay if they're dirty, as they usually will be from farm stands.

Crust

1½ cups flour

Generous pinch of kosher salt

8 tablespoons (1 stick) cold butter

1 egg

1   Combine the flour, salt, and butter in a food processor fitted with the metal blade, and pulse until crumbly. Add the egg and 1 tablespoon cold water, and blend until the mixture just comes together in a ball.

2   To make the dough without a food processor, flake the flour, salt, and butter into a bowl—rubbing bits of each together between your thumb and fingers and letting them fall into the bowl. In a separate bowl, whisk together the egg and 1 tablespoon cold water, and sprinkle this mixture over the dough flakes. Knead gently just until the dough comes together in a ball. Do not overwork the dough.

3   Form the dough into a disc, wrap in plastic wrap, and chill in the refrigerator for 1 hour or overnight.

Filling and Assembly

1 pound sweet potatoes

Flour for dusting work surface

¼ cup light brown sugar

¼ teaspoon salt

2 eggs

½ cup milk

½ cup cream

1 Preheat the oven to 400°F.

2 While the dough is chilling, place the sweet potatoes on a baking sheet and bake until soft, 45 minutes to 1 hour. Remove the sheet from the oven and set aside to let the potatoes cool.

3 Remove the dough from the refrigerator and let come to room temperature for 30 minutes to facilitate working with it. Dust a work surface with flour and turn the dough out onto it. Roll it out to fit a 9-inch pie plate. Line the pie plate with the dough and poke all over with a fork. Chill in the refrigerator for 45 minutes.

4 Peel the sweet potatoes and pass them through a food mill or ricer (see page 8) into a bowl. Stir in the sugar, salt, eggs, and milk. Transfer the mixture to a food processor fitted with the metal blade and process until smooth. Transfer to a bowl and stir in the cream.

5 Line the crust with waxed paper and fill with pie weights or dried beans. Bake until the bottom is just cooked and the edges just begin to brown, about 10 minutes.

6 Pour the sweet potato mixture into the crust and bake until the filling is set, about 45 minutes. Let cool for 15 to 20 minutes. The pie can be covered and refrigerated for up to 24 hours at this point. Let come to room temperature or gently reheat before serving.

7 To serve, cut the pie into wedges and present it whole, and let your guests help themselves.

Concord Grape Tart

SERVES 8

Concord grapes really aren't edible raw, because their pits are enormous and their skin is unpleasantly thick. But their juice is invaluable for making sorbets and other dishes that call for a big, almost winelike grape flavor. Their short season peaks around Thanksgiving, so I always have this dessert on my menu for the holiday.

Keep in mind that although their season is brief, the juice of Concord grapes can be frozen, so if you're making this, juice more than you need and save it for another day.

1¼ cups all-purpose flour, plus more for dusting work surface	⅔ cup plus 5 tablespoons sugar
½ cup whole wheat flour	¼ cup honey
1 teaspoon ground cinnamon	4 whole eggs plus 1 egg, separated, plus 1 egg yolk
½ teaspoon salt	4 cups Concord grapes
10 tablespoons (1 stick plus 2 tablespoons) butter, 8 of them cut into teaspoon-sized pieces	1½ teaspoons cornstarch
	1 small stem grapes, for garnish

1   Combine the flours, cinnamon, and salt in the bowl of an electric mixer fitted with the dough hook. Add the 8 tablespoons of cut-up butter and mix until crumbly but you can still see small butter lumps. Add 2 tablespoons of the sugar, the honey, 2 egg yolks, and 1 tablespoon of water. Mix until well blended. The dough will be soft. Pat the dough into an 8-inch circle, wrap in plastic wrap, and chill in the refrigerator for 1 hour.

2   While the dough chills, cook the grapes. Pick the washed grapes from the stems and place them in a medium saucepan. Add 1 cup water and cook over medium-low heat, stirring occasionally, until the water comes to a boil and the grapes break down and begin to boil. Let boil until no whole grapes remain.

3   Strain the pulp through a mesh basket strainer (not a fine-mesh strainer). Stir the grape pulp in the strainer with the back of a small ladle to help force the pulp through until only skins and seeds are left in the basket. Measure out 2 cups of the grape puree and set aside.

4   Preheat the oven to 350°F.

5   On a lightly floured surface, roll the dough out into a 14-inch circle. Lay a 10-inch tart pan with a removable bottom next to your work surface and transfer the rolled dough to the pan. Press the dough into the corners of the pan and cleanly trim the top edges. Chill the crust-lined tart pan in the refrigerator for 30 minutes.

6   In a small bowl, beat 1 egg together with 1 tablespoon water. Collect the dough trimmings and reroll them ⅛ inch thick. Cut out 5 to 7 leaves with a grape leaf cookie cutter and place around the raised rims of a baking sheet. Lightly score the centers of the leaves to emulate veins and brush with the egg wash. Bake until lightly browned and sandy. Cool for 2 to 3 minutes and loosen from the rims of the baking sheet. Let cool completely on the sheet.

7   Line the tart shell with waxed or parchment paper and fill with beans, barley, or pie weights. Bake for 15 minutes and remove from the oven. Lift off the paper and weights. Brush the interior of the crust with egg wash. Return to the oven and bake until lightly browned, about 12 minutes. Set aside and continue with the filling.

8   In a small saucepan, combine the 2 cups of grape puree, ⅔ cup of the sugar, and the cornstarch. In a medium bowl, lightly beat 3 eggs. Cook the grape mixture over medium heat, whisking slowly yet constantly. Bring the mixture to a boil and let boil for 1 minute. Remove the saucepan from the heat and whisk in the remaining 2 tablespoons butter. Slowly, in a thin stream, add the hot grape mixture to the beaten eggs, whisking the eggs all the while. When completely combined, place the crust on the oven rack and pour the filling into the crust. Gently position the tart in the center of the oven and bake until set, 15 minutes. Let cool to room temperature, then remove from the pan.

9   In a small bowl, beat the egg white until foamy. Put the remaining 3 tablespoons sugar in a small dish or bowl. Lightly brush the grapes on the stem with the foamed whites. Be sure to coat them completely, as the sugar will adhere only to the egg white. Put the stem in the center of the sugar, sprinkling the surrounding sugar over the grapes.

10 Arrange the "grape leaves" and frosted stem of grapes decoratively around one side of the crust and serve.

Thankful Butterscotch Cake

SERVES 16 TO 20

his is a very adult dessert; it includes a quantity of rum that does *not* get cooked out. It's so rich that very thin slices are the way to go. Most people think of Thanksgiving leftovers as being confined to the savory offerings, but this cake will last forever. If you store it in the refrigerator and can restrain yourself, you can snack on it for up to two weeks. But beware, you might not be able to resist.

You will need a candy thermometer for this recipe.

Butterscotch Filling

1¼ cups dark brown sugar	3 cups cream
1 cup granulated sugar	¼ teaspoon salt
⅓ cup corn syrup	1 tablespoon vanilla extract
8 tablespoons (1 stick) butter	3 tablespoons dark rum

1   Put all of the filling ingredients except the vanilla and rum into a large heavy-bottomed saucepan. Have another pot of a similar size ready and on the side. Over medium-high heat, melt the sugars, stirring continuously until the butterscotch boils. Once the mixture comes to a boil, stir frequently, taking care not to scrape any sugar crystals from the sides. Cook at a full boil until the mixture reaches 242°F.

2   Immediately pour the butterscotch into the empty pot. (Do not scrape the sides or bottom of the cooking pot, which would cause the filling to crystallize.) From a height, add the vanilla and rum. It will steam (and burn you if you aren't careful) right away. Stir to combine. Cool the filling for 20 minutes. It should be thick yet pourable.

(continued)

Cake Layers

3⅓ cups flour

¼ teaspoon baking soda

¼ teaspoon baking powder

1 teaspoon salt

½ teaspoon freshly grated nutmeg

18 tablespoons (2 sticks plus
2 tablespoons) butter, softened
at room temperature

2¼ cups granulated brown sugar
(Domino Brownulated or very fine
turbinado)

4 eggs

2 teaspoons vanilla extract

¼ cup dark rum

1 cup milk

1 Cut ten 8-inch circles of parchment or waxed paper. The baking will progress more quickly if you have at least three 8-inch cake pans. Preheat the oven to 350°F.

2 Combine the flour, baking soda, baking powder, salt, and nutmeg in a medium mixing bowl. Whisk lightly to combine. Using an electric mixer fitted with the paddle attachments, cream the butter and sugar until light and fluffy. Add the eggs one at a time, beating after each addition. Lower the speed and add half of the flour mixture. Blend well. Add the vanilla, rum, and milk. When the liquid is just combined, add the remaining flour mixture and beat until smooth.

3 Fill each cake pan, three at a time, with a heaping ½ cup of batter. Use a spatula to evenly spread the batter in the bottom of the pans. Bake for 15 to 18 minutes, or until the cakes spring back when lightly touched. Cool the layers in the pans slightly, remove, wipe the pan sides clean, and continue to fill and bake. You will need 9 layers.

4 Line the inside of a clean, dry cake pan with plastic wrap. If the plastic wrap sticks out above the rim of the cake pan, fold it over the outside of the pan. Peel the paper from one cake layer and place the layer upside down in the pan. Ladle about ¼ cup of warm filling over the cake. Top with another cake layer, paper removed. Continue ladling the filling evenly over each layer. The cake will grow higher than the cake pan as you fill. Don't worry if the edges of the cakes are a bit ragged; they will be trimmed before coating the outside of the cake. Just make sure the cake layers are evenly stacked. It's difficult to move a layer once it has been placed on the filling. If the butterscotch filling becomes too thick to pour easily, heat on low. Do not top the last cake layer with butterscotch. Chill the cake for at least 1 hour; it must be completely chilled to trim the edges.

5   Place an 8-inch circle of parchment on top of the cake. Carefully invert the cake onto a cake cooling rack. Remove the pan and lift off the plastic wrap. Hold a long sharp knife against the side of the cake. Trim off about ¼ of an inch evenly all around, making sure you are not tilting the blade. The size should be uniform, not wider at the bottom than the top.

6   Gently reheat the butterscotch and pour over the top and sides of the cake. Let stand until the coating is firm. Slide a metal spatula under the cake and place on a serving platter. Keep chilled, but serve at room temperature. This cake is best if made a day ahead, and keeps beautifully for 5 days.

Make-Ahead Menu

Veal Braised with
Celery Root and Potatoes

Cranberry Cobbler

This menu packs a very effective one-two punch: a rich, creamy main course followed by a tart cobbler.

The centerpiece of the dinner is a recipe based on *blanquette de veau,* a French "white" stew made with veal, cream, and vegetables. It borrows *gremolata*—a mixture of lemon zest, garlic, and herbs—the garnish from another classic veal dish. The acidic flavor of celery root wakes up the other flavors, the same way a squeeze of lemon juice perks up a fish dish.

For dessert, there's a cobbler that can be made ahead for any occasion and will last a long time in the refrigerator. It's also a delicious addition to the Thanksgiving dessert table.

Veal Braised with Celery Root and Potatoes

¾ cup dry white wine

½ medium carrot, thinly sliced

1 small onion, thinly sliced

1 stalk celery, thinly sliced

3 cloves garlic, crushed

1 sprig thyme plus 1 teaspoon chopped thyme

2 pounds center-cut veal shank, at least 2 inches thick (osso buco cut)

1½ cups Chicken Stock (page 343) or water

½ cup russet potato, peeled and cut into ½-inch dice

10 ounces celery root, peeled and cut into medium dice

6 tablespoons cream

Salt

Freshly ground black pepper

6 tablespoons cold butter, cut into small pieces, plus 3 tablespoons at room temperature

½ pound mixed wild mushrooms (e.g., shiitake, chanterelle, hedgehog, black trumpet), washed, ends trimmed, and cut into ⅛-inch slices

Grated zest of 1 lemon

1 teaspoon chopped chives

1 teaspoon chopped flat-leaf parsley

1 teaspoon chopped rosemary

1 recipe Egg Fettuccine (page 23) or ½ pound store-bought dried fettuccine

1   In a large bowl, mix together the wine, carrot, onion, celery, garlic, and thyme sprig. Add the veal, cover, and let marinate in the refrigerator at least 8 hours or overnight.

2   Remove the veal from the marinade and set aside on a plate.

3   Place the remaining vegetable mixture in a large heavy-bottomed pot, bring to a boil over high heat, then lower the heat and let simmer for 5 minutes. Add the stock and the veal to the pot. Raise the heat, bring to a boil, then lower the heat, cover, and let simmer until the veal is fork-tender, about 1½ hours.

(continued)

4   While the veal is cooking, put the potato and half of the celery root in a pot and cover with water by 1 inch. Lightly salt the water, bring to a boil over high heat, then lower the heat and let simmer until tender, about 10 minutes. Drain the potato and celery root and mash with a fork or potato masher. Stir in the cream and set aside.

5   Use tongs to remove the veal from its cooking liquid, season with salt and pepper, and set aside to cool.

6   Strain the cooking liquid through a fine-mesh strainer set over a pot and bring to a boil over high heat. Boil until reduced to 1½ cups. Add the celery root mixture, bring to a boil, remove from the heat, and whisk in the cold butter a piece at a time. Season with salt and pepper, then strain through a fine-mesh strainer, pressing on the solids until as much liquid as possible has been extracted.

7   Melt 2 tablespoons of the remaining butter in a large sauté pan set over high heat. Add one variety of mushroom, season with salt and pepper, and sauté until golden brown and tender, 5 to 6 minutes. (Times will vary based on type of mushroom.) Repeat with the other mushrooms, cooking each variety separately. Reserve them together for garnish.

8   Cut the remaining celery root into ¼-inch dice. Melt the remaining 1 tablespoon butter in a sauté pan set over high heat, add the celery root, season with salt and pepper, and sauté until lightly browned and tender, about 3 minutes. Set aside.

9   Combine the lemon zest, chives, parsley, rosemary, and chopped thyme—the *gremolata*—and reserve for garnish.

10 Break the veal into bite-size pieces with your hands or a fork.

11 Bring a pot of lightly salted water to a boil. Add the fettuccine and cook until al dente, about 2 to 3 minutes for fresh, 8 to 10 minutes for dried. Drain.

12 Place the veal, mushrooms, sautéed celery root, and the sauce in a pot set over medium heat, and cook until warm, about 2 minutes. Taste and adjust seasoning with salt and pepper.

13 Divide the fettuccine among four warm bowls, spoon the veal and sauce over the noodles, and sprinkle with the *gremolata*. Serve immediately.

Cranberry Cobbler

Topping

6 tablespoons butter	Grated zest of 1 orange
⅔ cup sugar	1 teaspoon baking powder
2 eggs	½ teaspoon salt
2 teaspoons vanilla extract	1 cup flour

Cream the butter and sugar together. (You can use an electric mixer, but a wooden spoon works fine.) The butter should be well combined with the sugar but not fluffy. Add the eggs, vanilla, and orange zest, and beat to combine. Add the baking powder, salt, and flour, and mix well. Set aside while making the filling.

Cranberry Filling and Assembly

6 cups fresh cranberries (from two 12-ounce bags)	1¼ cups sugar
	Grated zest of ½ orange
1 cup cranberry juice	

1   Preheat the oven to 350°F.

2   Place all of the ingredients in a 2-quart ceramic or Pyrex baking dish and stir to combine. Drop tablespoonfuls of the topping all over the top. Bake on the center rack of the oven until the topping is browned and the filling is bubbling around the edges, about 1 hour.

3   Keep the cobbler in the refrigerator until ready to serve. I recommend serving it warm the first day and serving leftovers cold or simply rewarmed in the microwave.

Wine

The tart cranberry notes would be better paired with a less sweet wine such as the moscato rosa from Abbazia di Novacella from the Alto Adige region of northern Italy.

Winter

When I think about winter cooking, I imagine myself hunkered indoors on a cold, windy day with some good music on the stereo or a football game on TV, or just hanging out with my wife, Beverly, and daughter, Leah. There's a soup or stew simmering away on the stovetop, or some beef braising in the oven, and although I'm not spending a lot of time in the kitchen, there's no question that I'm cooking: nurturing a slow-cooked dish and savoring the potent, homey smells that surround us are just as important to my enjoyment of the day as whatever entertainment I happen to be taking in.

People don't hibernate in the winter, but we do spend most of our time indoors, and much of it can be pretty solitary. But I find that you're never alone when you're cooking—you're with those people you'll be welcoming to the table later in the day, or with memories of other winter meals.

The best winter food, especially home-cooked food, is reassuring and welcoming. In a season when the foods that can be eaten right off the vine or the tree have disappeared until spring, we have no choice other than to turn to root vegetables like celery root, parsnips, rutabagas, and turnips, and the meats and fish that, like them, are well suited to long, slow cooking, whether it's braising, roasting, or stewing.

The word that sums up winter for me is *anticipation*—anticipation for dishes to finish cooking, anticipation for the holidays, and—finally—anticipation for the spring and the annual food cycle coming full circle.

Surprisingly Satisfying Vegetarian Menu

Egg Fettuccine
with Walnut Pesto

Root Vegetable
and Barley Stew

Pear-Pecan
Hamantashen

It's natural to build a winter menu around stewed chicken, braised beef, or roasted fish, but this dinner takes a different approach, bringing together lots of deep, dark flavors in a vegetarian menu.

Egg Fettuccine with Walnut Pesto (page 286) uses a cold-weather version of the Italian condiment, with parsley in place of basil, walnuts in place of pine nuts, and roasted garlic in place of raw garlic. The main course, Root Vegetable and Barley Stew (page 289), gets quite a bit of heft from the vegetables. Some might put tofu or another meat substitute in a dish like this, but I find it unnecessary: the vegetables are "meaty" enough on their own.

The dessert, Pear-Pecan Hamantashen (page 291), is my version of the Jewish pastry traditionally served as part of the Purim celebration. Pears are perhaps the sweetest fruit of the season; their delicate flavor is a refreshing contrast to the other flavors of this menu.

Egg Fettuccine with Walnut Pesto

SERVES 4

ike the salad on page 207, the pesto in this dish demonstrates that parsley—so often taken for granted—can be a powerful, central ingredient in its own right. This walnut pesto is Italian in spirit because it uses ingredients that you always have around the house. This is especially appealing in the winter, when a trip to the market is more unwelcome than it might be in other seasons.

Just as basil pesto is a perfect stir-in addition to soups and brothy pastas, this pesto is a great convenience during the colder months of the year. It's especially delicious tossed with gnocchi (page 209).

Walnut Pesto

³/₄ cup walnuts, or ¹/₂ cup if making pesto in advance

¹/₄ cup packed flat-leaf parsley

3 tablespoons freshly grated Parmigiano-Reggiano cheese

1 clove roasted garlic, or 1¹/₂ teaspoons roasted garlic puree (see Note, page 96)

¹/₄ cup extra-virgin olive oil

Salt

1 Preheat the oven to 350°F.

2 Spread the walnuts out on a cookie sheet. Place the sheet in the oven and toast the walnuts for 5 minutes, or until lightly browned and fragrant. Remove the sheet from the oven and set aside to let the nuts cool. If not making the pesto in advance, chop ¹/₄ cup of the walnuts and set aside for finishing the dish.

3 Transfer the walnuts to a food processor fitted with the metal blade. Process until finely chopped. Add the parsley, cheese, and garlic, and process until finely chopped and well integrated. With the machine running, slowly add the olive oil in a thin steam until fully incorporated. Transfer the pesto to a small bowl and season to taste with salt. (This pesto can be made in advance and stored in an airtight container in the refrigerator. It will keep for up to 2 days. Let come to room temperature before using.)

(continued)

Fettuccine and Assembly

¼ cup walnuts, or reserved toasted, chopped walnuts from preparing pesto, (page 286)

¼ cup freshly grated Parmigiano-Reggiano cheese

¼ cup packed flat-leaf parsley

1 recipe Egg Fettuccine (page 23) or ½ pound store-bought dried fettuccine

½ cup Vegetable Stock (page 344)

1 If you made the pesto in advance, you need to toast the walnuts. Preheat the oven to 350°F. Spread the walnuts out on a cookie sheet. Place the sheet in the oven and toast the walnuts for 5 minutes, or until lightly browned and fragrant. Remove the sheet from the oven and set aside to let the nuts cool. Chop the nuts and set aside.

2 Bring a pot of lightly salted water to a boil. In a small bowl, stir together the walnuts, cheese, and parsley, and set aside.

3 When the water boils, add the fettuccine and cook until al dente, about 2 to 3 minutes for fresh, 8 to 10 minutes for dried. Drain in a colander and set aside.

4 Place the stock in a wide, deep-sided sauté pan and bring to a boil over high heat. Stir in the pesto, add the fettuccine, and toss to coat. Transfer to a large serving bowl and top with the Parmesan-walnut-parsley garnish. Serve family style from the center of the table.

Wine

Serve this with a rich, round white, possibly a white Burgundy (chardonnay) with earthy notes from the village of St. Romain. The Domaine Vincent Girardin "Sous le Château" is a good choice.

NOTE: Though this recipe calls for only 1 clove of it, *roasted* garlic is essential in this pesto. I suggest roasting an entire head of garlic (see Note on page 96 for instructions on making and storing) and saving the rest for enhancing soups and stews.

Root Vegetable and Barley Stew

SERVES 4

any restaurants treat vegetable plates as a grudging concession to dieters and vegetarians. Nonmeat options often aren't listed on the menu and, when requested, turn out to be nothing more than an assortment of vegetable preparations from other dishes.

Because I have such respect for vegetables, my vegetarian offering is a carefully composed plate. At times, I've also served "one-pot" vegetarian dishes that have as much flavor as any other offering on our menu, like this stew, which is thickened with potato. The white wine lifts all the flavors in the dish.

1 small head savoy cabbage

½ cup barley

3½ cups Vegetable Stock (page 344) or water

Salt

Freshly ground black pepper

2 tablespoons butter

1 small onion, minced

1 clove garlic, minced

1 cup dry white wine

½ pound Yukon gold potatoes, peeled and cut into ½-inch dice

1 medium carrot, cut crosswise on the diagonal into ½-inch pieces

1 small parsnip, peeled and cut crosswise on the diagonal into ½-inch pieces

1 medium turnip, peeled and cut into ½-inch dice

½ small rutabaga, peeled and cut into ½-inch dice

1 small celery root, peeled and cut into ½-inch dice

1 medium leek, white and light green parts only, cut into ½-inch rings, well washed in several changes of cold water, and drained

1½ teaspoons chopped chives

1½ teaspoons chopped flat-leaf parsley

1 Remove and discard any damaged outer leaves from the cabbage. Peel off about one-quarter of the layers of cabbage leaves and save the rest of the cabbage for another use. Stack the leaves in batches, roll them, and cut them into thin ribbons. Set aside.

2 Put the barley and 1½ cups of the stock in a pot set over medium-high heat. Bring to a boil, then lower the heat and let simmer, uncovered, until the barley is tender but still

al dente, about 20 minutes. Taste, season with salt and pepper, and set aside. (Do not remove the barley from the pot; it will absorb more flavorful liquid as it cools.)

3   Melt 1 tablespoon of the butter in a large heavy-bottomed pot set over medium heat. Add the onion, garlic, and a pinch of salt, cover, and cook for 5 minutes. Pour in the wine, raise the heat to high, bring the wine to a boil, then lower the heat and let simmer for 5 minutes. Add the potatoes, the remaining 2 cups stock, and a generous pinch of salt. Raise the heat to high, bring to a boil, then lower the heat and let simmer for 15 to 20 minutes, or until the potatoes are tender. They are done when a sharp, thin-bladed knife pierces easily to the center of a piece of potato.

4   Transfer the potatoes and liquid to a blender and puree until smooth. Set aside.

5   Melt the remaining 1 tablespoon butter in a large pot set over medium heat. Add the carrot, parsnip, turnip, rutabaga, celery root, and a generous pinch of salt, cover, and cook for 10 minutes, removing the cover occasionally to stir the vegetables. Add the leek, cabbage, and a pinch of salt, and cook, covered, for 5 minutes, removing the cover occasionally to stir the vegetables. Add the pureed potatoes, bring to a simmer, and cook for 10 minutes. If making this stew in advance, let it cool completely, then transfer to an airtight container, or simply cover the pot with plastic wrap, and refrigerate. Let come to room temperature before reheating. If it looks especially thick, stir in a few tablespoons of water before reheating.

6   To serve, stir the chives and parsley into the stew, divide the barley among four bowls, and spoon some stew over the top.

Wine
Serve this with the same white Burgundy as the previous dish (page 288).

Pear-Pecan Hamantashen

SERVES 4

amantashen are triangular filled pastries served during the celebration of the Jewish holiday of Purim. They are traditionally made with different fillings, including prunes, nuts, apricots, and my favorite, poppy seeds, which contrast magnificently with the dry pastry. My version is made with sweet pears.

Pear Filling

4 ripe but firm Bosc pears

3 tablespoons sugar

Juice of ½ lemon (grate zest before juicing; you'll need it for the crust)

1   Preheat the oven to 300°F.

2   Cut off the long stem halves of the pears ¼ inch below where the wide, lower half of the fruit begins. Put the stem ends upright on a baking sheet. Bake until the pears are cooked through, 45 minutes to 1 hour, depending on the size and ripeness of the pears. When they are done, the pears should give a bit when squeezed, just like a baked potato.

3   While the pears bake, make the sauce. Peel and core the remaining pear halves, chop finely, and put them in a medium saucepan with the lemon juice, 2 tablespoons water, and the sugar. Cook over low heat, stirring occasionally, until cooked through and pulpy. Transfer the compote to a blender, puree until smooth, and set aside.

Crust

1 cup flour

⅛ teaspoon baking powder

¼ teaspoon salt

2 tablespoons sugar

4 tablespoons (½ stick) cold butter, cut into teaspoon-sized pieces

1 egg yolk

3 tablespoons sour cream

Grated zest of ½ lemon

½ teaspoon vanilla extract

½ teaspoon bourbon

(continued)

Put the flour, baking powder, salt, and sugar in a medium bowl and whisk briefly to combine. Work in the butter with your fingertips until the mixture resembles cornflake crumbs. Add the egg yolk, sour cream, lemon zest, vanilla, and bourbon, and work the dough with the palm of your hand until smooth. Divide the dough into 4 pieces, roll them into balls, wrap individually in plastic wrap, and chill in the refrigerator for 30 minutes.

Filling and Assembly

1 cup pecans	1 teaspoon bourbon
¼ cup sour cream	Flour for dusting work surface
5 tablespoons sugar	

1   Spread the pecans out on a cookie sheet and toast them in the oven until fragrant, about 10 minutes. (You can do this while the pears are in the oven.) Transfer the pecans to a blender or food processor fitted with the metal blade and grind them to a powder. Add 2 tablespoons of the sour cream, the bourbon, and 3 tablespoons of the sugar, and process just to combine. Set aside.

2   When the pears are done, remove them from the oven and set aside to cool for 15 to 20 minutes.

3   Lightly flour a work surface and roll each ball of dough into a 6-inch circle. Trim each to a perfect 5-inch circle, using a cookie cutter, small plate, or lid. (The circle must be even for both the appearance of the dessert and the evenness of baking.)

4   Divide the pecan filling among the dough circles, mounding it into 2-inch flat patties in the center. Place a pear half on each mound. Dip your forefinger in cold water and run it around the edge of the dough. Visually mark the circle into three arcs. Bring the arcs of dough up around the pear and pinch lightly at the joining edges to make a point. The dough surrounding the pear should be triangle shaped.

5   Place the hamantashen on a baking sheet. Combine the remaining 2 tablespoons sour cream with 1 tablespoon water and brush the dough around each pear. Sprinkle generously with the remaining 2 tablespoons sugar. Bake the hamantashen on the middle rack of the oven until pale blond, 35 to 40 minutes.

6   Let cool to lukewarm and serve with the pear sauce.

Wine

The delicate pear flavors are wonderful with the floral notes of the muscat de Beaumes-de-Venise from Domaine de Fenouillet in the southern Rhône region of France.

Ray-of-Light Menu

Sunchokes and
Grapefruit Salad

Parsley-Breaded
Diver Scallops
with Broccoli Rabe,
Meyer Lemon, and
Black Pepper

Clementine Pudding

I don't usually take vacations in the winter, but I do find myself daydreaming about Florida and California, which inspires me to use a lot of citrus in my menus. This menu brings some of my favorite citrus dishes together: Sunchokes and Grapefruit Salad (page 296), Parsley-Breaded Diver Scallops with Broccoli Rabe, Meyer Lemon, and Black Pepper (page 298), and a Clementine Pudding (page 301).

This menu will introduce you to some fruits that may be unfamiliar, like the super-sweet Meyer lemon, and teach you some unusual uses for familiar ones like grapefruit and clementines. You can use different varieties of grapefruits, lemons, and oranges in these recipes as well, depending on what is available in your local market.

Sunchokes and Grapefruit Salad

SERVES 4

Sunchokes, or Jerusalem artichokes, have a natural affinity with citrus fruits. Here they are paired with grapefruit, which coaxes out their understated acidity. The most interesting aspect of this salad is that it uses two vinaigrettes made from very similar ingredients, but one is emulsified and one is broken. The emulsified vinaigrette clings to the chicories; the broken vinaigrette helps focus the flavors of the raw vegetables without overwhelming them.

½ cup freshly squeezed orange juice

1 large ruby red grapefruit

2 tablespoons freshly squeezed lemon juice

½ cup plus 2 tablespoons extra-virgin olive oil

Salt

Freshly ground black pepper

3 cups mixed chicories (frisée, radicchio, endive), cut into small pieces

6 ounces sunchokes (Jerusalem artichokes), peeled and thinly sliced on a mandoline or sliced by hand as thinly as possible

1 teaspoon chopped chives

1   Pour the orange juice into a sauté pan and bring to a boil over high heat. Boil until it is reduced to a syrup, 5 to 7 minutes. Remove the pan from the heat and set aside to cool.

2   Remove the grapefruit peel and pith with a knife, and section the fruit by cutting off the membranes and carefully removing the seeds. Squeeze 2 tablespoons of juice from 1 section into a small bowl and set aside.

3   In a bowl, whisk together 1 tablespoon of the lemon juice, 1 tablespoon of the reserved grapefruit juice, and the reduced orange juice. Slowly add 6 tablespoons of the olive oil in a thin stream, whisking to make an emulsified vinaigrette. Season with salt and pepper. Set aside.

4   Mix together the remaining 1 tablespoon lemon juice, 1 tablespoon of the reserved grapefruit juice, and the remaining ¼ cup olive oil to make a broken (i.e., non-emulsified) vinaigrette. Season with salt and pepper.

5   To serve, toss the chicories with
    6 tablespoons of the emulsified vinai-
    grette, taste and adjust seasoning, and
    divide among four chilled plates. Toss
    the grapefruit sections, sunchokes,
    and chives with the broken vinai-
    grette, taste and adjust seasoning, and
    place on top of the chicories. Drizzle
    with the remaining vinaigrettes.

Wine

For this dish, choose a clean fresh dry
white with citrus notes and an herbal
character. Try the Brundlmayer Grüner
Veltliner "Kamptaler Terrassen" from the
Kamptal region of Austria.

Parsley-Breaded Diver Scallops with Broccoli Rabe, Meyer Lemon, and Black Pepper

SERVES 4

eyer lemons are supremely sweet, with a seductive perfume and taste almost like candy. Every part of the fruit is used here: the zest and juice flavor the sauce, and the lemon itself is tossed with the broccoli rabe, offering a bright balance to the green's bitterness.

Make this dish with meaty, diver-harvested scallops if you can get them, although "regular" sea scallops will also be delicious. Avoid scallops stored in preservatives, which soak up excessive amounts of liquid that keep the fresh mollusks from searing properly.

The sauce here is a "mother" fish sauce, meaning that it can be adapted in any number of ways (see page 301).

Scallops and Bread Coating

2 tablespoons butter	Freshly ground black pepper
6 to 8 slices brioche, crusts removed, cut into 1-inch cubes	3 eggs
	1 cup flour
¼ cup chopped flat-leaf parsley	16 sea scallops, preferably diver scallops
Salt	

1   Melt the butter in a small pan set over high heat. Remove the pan from the heat and set aside.

2   Put the brioche cubes in a food processor fitted with the metal blade. Process to form crumbs about the size of coarse-salt crystals. Transfer the crumbs to the pan with the melted butter. Add the parsley and stir the ingredients together. Season with salt and pepper and set aside.

3   Beat the eggs lightly, whisk in 2 tablespoons water, and season with salt and pepper. Spread the flour out on a plate. Dredge the scallops in the flour, then in the eggs, then in the crumbs. Place the scallops on a baking sheet and chill in the refrigerator for 30 minutes. (There is no need to cover them for such a short time.)

Meyer Lemon-Butter Sauce

1 Meyer lemon

7 tablespoons butter

1 small shallot, thinly sliced

1 clove garlic, thinly sliced

½ cup dry white wine

½ cup Chicken Stock (page 343)

3 tablespoons cream

1 teaspoon cracked black pepper

Salt

1   Grate the zest off the lemon with the fine holes of a box grater or a microplane and set aside. Halve the lemon lengthwise. Peel one half and separate it into segments (see Step 3 on page 41). Set them aside for use in the broccoli. Juice the other half of the lemon; you will need 2 tablespoons.

2   Melt 1 tablespoon of the butter in a sauté pan set over medium-low heat. Add the shallot and garlic and sauté until the shallot is softened but not browned, about 5 minutes. Add the wine, raise the heat to high, bring to a boil, and let boil until the liquid has evaporated, about 6 minutes. Add the stock, bring to a boil, and let boil until reduced by half, about 3 minutes. Add the cream, lower the heat, and let simmer for 5 minutes.

3   Whisk in the remaining 6 tablespoons butter and strain the sauce through a fine-mesh strainer set over a bowl. Blend the sauce with an immersion blender or in a blender. Season with salt. Add the lemon juice, lemon zest, and cracked black pepper, and set aside, covered, to keep warm.

(continued)

Broccoli Rabe

2 tablespoons extra-virgin olive oil

¼ sweet onion, thinly sliced

1 clove garlic, thinly sliced

Salt

1 bunch broccoli rabe (about 12 ounces), thick stems removed

1 cup Vegetable Stock (page 344) or water

Freshly ground black pepper

Segments of ½ Meyer lemon (see sauce Step 1, above)

Warm the olive oil in a large sauté pan set over medium-high heat. Add the onion, garlic, and a pinch of salt, and sauté, stirring occasionally, until softened but not browned, 5 to 7 minutes. Add the broccoli rabe and sauté for 1 minute more. Add the stock and season with salt and pepper. Cook, turning the broccoli occasionally with tongs, until the liquid has almost evaporated and the broccoli is tender, 5 to 6 minutes. Stir in the lemon segments and set aside, covered, to keep the broccoli warm.

Assembly

¼ cup olive oil

1   Preheat the oven to 450°F.

2   Warm the olive oil in a large ovenproof sauté pan set over high heat. Add the scallops and sear until the edges start to brown, about 2 to 3 minutes, then cook in the oven for 3 to 5 minutes, until the crumbs are golden brown. Remove from the oven, flip the scallops, and let sit in the hot pan for 30 seconds. Transfer to a warm plate.

3   To serve, divide the broccoli rabe among four dinner plates, mounding it in the center of the plates. Place 4 scallops on top of the broccoli on each plate. Drizzle some sauce over and around the scallops and broccoli.

Wine

A tangy New World sémillon from Australia would stand up to the scallops yet balance with the lemon and black pepper notes. The Cockfighters Ghost Sémillon from the Hunter Valley in Australia is a great choice.

FISH SAUCE OPTIONS

If you omit the Meyer lemon juice and zest and pepper from the sauce recipe, you will be left with a versatile basic sauce that can be adapted for various uses. Add roasted garlic puree (see Note, page 96) for a poultry sauce, or the herb purees on pages 102 and 132 to accompany white-fleshed fish. You can also replace the chicken stock with lobster stock (see page 252) for seafood dishes, or store-bought mushroom stock for poultry and meats.

Clementine Pudding

SERVES 4

To me, the sight of clementines in the supermarket signals the beginning of the holiday season. Ever the optimist, I begin looking for them at the beginning of November, though they often don't show up until later, and I continue to buy them throughout their short season.

I love clementines eaten out of hand, but I've also always loved the combination of citrus and custard, from lemon curd to lemon meringue pies to tarts. This recipe marries clementines and custard, which is harder than it might sound, because it's difficult to remove the membranes without pulling away too much fruit. Here, you make the juice, then the pudding. No muss, no fuss.

Serve this with your favorite store-bought pound cake.

2 cups freshly squeezed clementine juice	¼ teaspoon grated clementine zest
2 cups cream	1⅓ cups sugar
¼ cup cornstarch	½ teaspoon vanilla extract
4 egg yolks	4 blood oranges

1 Pour the clementine juice into a saucepan and bring to a boil over high heat. Lower the heat to medium-high and let boil until reduced to 1 cup, about 7 minutes.

(continued)

2   Meanwhile, in a medium bowl, whisk together the cream, cornstarch, and egg yolks until smooth.

3   Add the clementine zest and sugar to the juice and stir to dissolve.

4   Add half of the juice to the bowl with the yolk mixture, whisking to combine. Pour this mixture into the pot with the remaining juice, stir in the vanilla, and let simmer over low heat for 2 minutes. Remove the pot from the heat and let cool, then chill for at least 1 hour in the refrigerator.

5   Peel and separate the blood oranges into segments (see Step 3, page 41), working over a bowl. Squeeze the juice from the white portion of the oranges and save the segments in the juice.

6   To serve, divide the pudding among four bowls and top each serving with blood orange segments.

Wine

The citrus notes in this dish are an excellent match with a lighter-in-style version of a Sauternes, such as a sweet sémillon from the nearby village of Cadillac in Bordeaux.

A Fresh Taste of Winter

Chicory Salad with Pear, Blue Cheese, and Hazelnuts

Lamb Shanks with Mashed Parsnips, Caramelized Shallots, and Dried Cherries

Sticky Fudge Pudding

This menu tweaks classic winter dishes to make them feel new again.

The Chicory Salad with Pear, Blue Cheese, and Hazelnuts (page 304) is based on a timeless combination but turns to an American cheese rather than the traditional French (Roquefort) or Italian (Gorgonzola), and hazelnuts rather than the more conventional walnuts. Similarly, the Lamb Shanks with Mashed Parsnips, Caramelized Shallots, and Dried Cherries (page 305) uses sour cherries, more often paired with duck or venison, and parsnips in place of the more predictable potatoes.

Best of all is the Sticky Fudge Pudding (page 309), which I eat year-round. It's a decadent cross between pudding and cake that—I swear to you—is reason enough to have bought this book.

Chicory Salad with Pear, Blue Cheese, and Hazelnuts

SERVES 4

On a trip I took to Italy a few years ago, I enjoyed a salad of pears and pecorino. The memory of that salad inspired this one, which also matches pears and blue cheese, a truly sublime combination. The give-and-take between the bitterness of chicory and the sweetness of pear is the glue that holds this dish together.

½ cup chopped hazelnuts

2 tablespoons red wine vinegar

6 tablespoons hazelnut oil

Salt

Freshly ground black pepper

1 medium head radicchio

1 medium Belgian endive, cut into ¼-inch rounds

1 head frisée, core removed and torn into 1-inch pieces (about 2 cups)

2 ripe Bartlett pears, halved lengthwise and cored, each half sliced lengthwise into 4 pieces

1 cup crumbled blue cheese, such as Maytag

1 Put the hazelnuts in a wide, heavy-bottomed sauté pan and cook over medium heat, shaking them around to prevent scorching, until lightly toasted and fragrant, about 5 minutes. Remove the pan from the heat and set aside.

2 In a small bowl, mix together the vinegar and hazelnut oil and season with salt and pepper.

3 Trim the bottom core from the radicchio and remove and discard any damaged outer leaves. Remove 4 large outer leaves to use as cups and set aside. Tear remaining radicchio into 1-inch pieces; you should have about 2 cups of pieces.

4 In a large bowl, toss the radicchio, endive, frisée, and three-quarters of the hazelnuts with the vinaigrette.

5   To serve, place 1 radicchio cup on each of four chilled plates. Divide the salad among the cups. Arrange the pears around the cups and sprinkle with the remaining hazelnuts and the blue cheese.

Wine

A Spanish Priorat Blanco "Brugeres" from Coneria Scala Dei, made from the garnacha grape, has just the right Old World character to blend with the variety of ingredients. A Châteauneuf-du-Pape blanc would also do.

Lamb Shanks with Mashed Parsnips, Caramelized Shallots, and Dried Cherries

SERVES 4

Parsnips aren't nearly as well known or adored as potatoes. Because parsnips become remarkably creamy when cooked and mashed, they offer a lower-fat alternative to mashed potatoes. Each serving of mashed parsnips contains less than 1 tablespoon of butter, but everyone eating them will find them rich and satisfying. Part of the secret is slowly stewing the parsnips in a combination of butter and water. You can use the same technique for any vegetable you plan to puree, such as celery root, turnips, or the Mashed Rutabagas (page 268) in the Thanksgiving menu.

(continued)

½ cup dried sour cherries

1 cup red wine

6 tablespoons canola or other vegetable oil

4 lamb shanks, about 1 pound each

1 small onion, halved and thinly sliced

½ cup diced carrot

½ cup diced celery root

4 cloves garlic, thinly sliced

¼ medium orange, peeled, peel and flesh reserved separately

2 allspice

1 whole star anise

½ teaspoon black peppercorns

½ teaspoon ground coriander

2 cups Brown Chicken Stock (page 343)

1 Put the cherries in a bowl. Add the wine and let the cherries soak for 3 to 4 hours or overnight.

2 Preheat the oven to 325°F.

3 Pour ¼ cup of the oil into a 6-quart Dutch oven set over high heat. Put 2 shanks in the pot and sear them on all sides until well browned, about 20 minutes. Remove them to a plate and set aside. Repeat with the remaining 2 shanks.

4 Add the remaining 2 tablespoons oil to the pot and lower the heat to medium-high. Add the onion, carrot, celery root, and garlic, and sauté until well caramelized, about 15 minutes.

5 Drain the cherries, using a fine-mesh strainer set over a bowl. Set the cherries aside. Add the wine, orange peel, orange flesh, and spices to the pot with the vegetable mixture, raise the heat to high, bring to a boil, and let boil for 3 minutes. Add the stock, return to a boil, then add the shanks and cover. Put the Dutch oven in the oven and braise the shanks until tender, about 2 hours. Periodically check on the liquid to be sure it is just barely simmering. If it's simmering aggressively, lower the oven temperature to 300°F. The meat is done when it comes off the bone with the tug of a fork.

6 Use tongs or a slotted spoon to transfer the shanks to a plate. Cover them with aluminum foil to keep them warm.

7 Strain the braising liquid through a fine-mesh strainer set over a pot. Discard the solids and set the pot over high heat. Bring to a boil and let boil until reduced to 1 cup, about 30 minutes.

8 Add the cherries to the pot with the sauce, then add the shanks and warm over low heat.

Caramelized Shallots

1 tablespoon butter   Salt

8 large shallots

1 Preheat the oven to 325°F.

2 Melt the butter in a small ovenproof sauté pan set over medium heat. When the butter turns bubbly, add the shallots and cook, shaking the pan to ensure even cooking, until the shallots are lightly browned all over, about 10 minutes.

3 Carefully drain the butter from the pan. Season the shallots with salt and cover with aluminum foil. Place the pan in the oven and roast until the shallots are soft (a sharp, thin-bladed knife should easily pierce to their center) and glazed, about 40 minutes.

Mashed Parsnips and Assembly

3 tablespoons butter   Salt

1½ pounds parsnips, peeled and roughly chopped into small dice

1 In a 3-quart pot with a cover, melt 1 tablespoon of the butter over medium heat.

2 Add the parsnips and 2 tablespoons water, and sprinkle with salt. Cover the pan and cook until the parsnips are tender, about 15 minutes.

3 Remove the pan from the heat and use a potato masher or large spoon to mash the parsnips with the remaining 2 tablespoons butter. Season with salt.

4 To serve, spoon some parsnips on each of four warm dinner plates, divide the shallots among the plates, placing them on the parsnips, and lean a lamb shank against the parsnips.

Wine
Beth favors a syrah with lamb, but more mellow braised lamb calls for a smoky syrah from the northern Rhône village of St. Joseph, from Dard & Ribo.

JOHN JAMISON

JAMISON FARM
LATROBE, PENNSYLVANIA

I've been doing business with John Jamison, the soft-spoken lamb king of the New York restaurant world, since the mid-1990s. The farm that John runs with his wife, Sukey, and daughter, Eliza, exemplifies the passion and perfectionism I seek out in the farmers with whom I work. Jamison Farm is the only one in the United States that processes lamb at its own plant, which gives the Jamisons total control over their product. The 212-acre hill farm is situated along the westernmost ridge of the Allegheny Mountains, and the superior grass that grows there, on which the lambs feed, is the secret ingredient to the farm's success.

John's system of "intensive rotational grazing" requires that he and his team constantly shepherd between four hundred and five hundred lambs from two-acre patch to two-acre patch. The lambs eat all of the grass, along with copious amounts of wildflowers and water, over two days, then they move again. This cycle is repeated from March 29 until mid-January every year. The lambs are exercised as they move up and down the hills, which leads to the perfect texture of their meat.

Sticky Fudge Pudding

SERVES 4

've never served this dessert in my restaurant, but it's a favorite with my friends and family. It isn't quite a cake and it isn't quite a pudding. It bears some resemblance to those warm chocolate soufflé cakes that everyone was serving in big-city restaurants a few years ago, only more dense and decadent.

Once you make this dessert and see how easy and delicious it is, you'll make it over and over. The recipe is very forgiving; even if it falls, it's good, and it makes for delicious leftovers.

Oh, and here's a little secret I'm happy to share: the chocolate sauce alone is the perfect topping for a quick sundae.

1 cup flour	1 egg
½ teaspoon salt	6 tablespoons melted butter, plus 4 tablespoons (½ stick) at room temperature
2 teaspoons baking powder	
1¼ cups plus ⅔ cup sugar	2 teaspoons vanilla extract
⅓ cup plus ½ cup cocoa powder, preferably a high-quality brand, such as Valrhona	½ cup cream

1 Preheat the oven to 400°F.

2 Put the flour, ¼ teaspoon of the salt, the baking powder, 1¼ cups of the sugar, and ⅓ cup of the cocoa powder in a medium mixing bowl. Whisk to combine and to remove any cocoa lumps. Beat the egg lightly in a small bowl. Add the melted butter to the egg and whisk briefly to combine. Add the egg mixture, 1 teaspoon of the vanilla, and 1 cup warm water to the dry ingredients. Blend well.

3 Pour the batter into a soufflé dish, preferably a round one, with a 5-cup capacity. Tent the soufflé dish with aluminum foil. Place a larger baking dish into the center of the oven and place the soufflé dish into the middle of the dish. Pour hot water halfway up the sides of the soufflé dish. (The water need not be painfully hot; tap water is fine.) Steam for 1 hour in the oven.

(continued)

4   While the pudding steams, make the sauce: Place the remaining ⅔ cup sugar and
    ½ cup cocoa powder in a medium saucepan and whisk to combine. Add the cream
    and the remaining 4 tablespoons butter and ¼ teaspoon salt. Bring the mixture to a boil
    over medium-high heat, stirring constantly. Remove the pan from the heat and stir in
    the remaining 1 teaspoon vanilla with 3 tablespoons water. Set aside, covered, and keep
    warm until the pudding is done.

5   Remove the dish from the oven. Carefully peel back the tented foil and test for doneness
    by touching the pudding lightly; it should spring back. Pour half of the warm fudge
    sauce over the hot pudding. Reserve the other half. If the sauce has cooled by serving
    time, add 1 or 2 tablespoons of water before reheating.

6   To serve, let the pudding cool slightly and slice or spoon into four dishes. Serve with
    the warm sauce alongside.

Wine

The tawny port–like fortified wine from the appellation Maury, made from grenache
grapes from a village near the famed Banyuls in the south of France, would pair well.
Highly recommended is the Mas Amiel 10 Ans d'Age Cuvée Spéciale, aged for ten years.

The Last Hurrah

Warm Sea Urchin with
a Shrimp, Leek, and
Potato Stew

Butter-Braised Wild
Striped Bass with a
Leek Fondue and Caviar

Roasted Squab with
Foie Gras, Black Truffles,
Fingerling Potatoes, and
Celery Root

The New Year's Mint
Chocolate Soufflé
and Friends

Here's a menu that pulls out all the stops. You could serve it on New Year's Eve, or for a special winter occasion such as an anniversary or cherished annual get-together. It's full of luxurious ingredients like truffles, caviar, and foie gras, all of which are set against big, buttery flavors that will match up beautifully with your best wines. It's a menu that will reward your energies with a feeling of tremendous satisfaction and your guests with a meal to remember.

The feast begins with Warm Sea Urchin with a Shrimp, Leek, and Potato Stew (page 313), then moves on to Butter-Braised Wild Striped Bass with a Leek Fondue and Caviar (page 315). The main course is Roasted Squab with Foie Gras, Black Truffles, Fingerling Potatoes, and Celery Root (page 317). Dessert is a showy spectacle: The New Year's Mint Chocolate Soufflé and Friends (page 320).

Warm Sea Urchin with a Shrimp, Leek, and Potato Stew

SERVES 4

This is the most sensual dish I've ever cooked, thanks to the uniquely silky sea urchin. It uses a quick fish stock made by simmering shrimp shells in vegetable stock. If you can't procure sea urchins, purchase sea urchin roe and top the stews with it.

8 sea urchins

6 large shrimp, peeled, deveined, and halved lengthwise, shells reserved, shrimp kept covered in the refrigerator

¾ cup Vegetable Stock (page 344)

4 tablespoons (½ stick) plus 1 teaspoon butter

1 cup leek, white and light green parts only, thinly sliced, washed in several changes of cold water, and drained

2 tablespoons minced celery

2 tablespoons minced onion

Salt

½ cup Yukon gold potato, cut into medium dice

3 tablespoons cream

Kosher salt for a bed

1 teaspoon chopped flat-leaf parsley

1 teaspoon chopped chives

8 sprigs chervil

1 Preheat the oven to 400°F.

2 Clean the sea urchins: Cut out a small disk on the flatter top side and scoop out the roe and discard innards. Rinse the shell under gently running cold water. Return the roe to the shell, set on a plate, cover with a clean, damp towel, and keep in the refrigerator.

3 Put the shrimp shells in a small pot and pour in the stock. If the stock does not cover the shells, add some additional stock or water. Bring the stock to a boil over high heat and let boil for 1 minute. Turn off the heat, remove the pot from the stove, and let the shells sit in the stock for 20 minutes. Strain the stock through a fine-mesh strainer set over a bowl and set aside. Discard the shells.

(continued)

4   To make the sauce, melt 2 tablespoons of the butter in a pot set over medium heat. Add ½ cup of the leek, the celery and onion, plus a pinch of salt. Cook, covered, until tender, about 5 minutes. Add ¼ cup of the potato, then add the fish stock and let simmer until the potato is tender, 8 to 10 minutes. Add the cream and return to a simmer. Puree the vegetable mixture in a blender or food processor fitted with the metal blade, then return to the pan. Whisk in 1 tablespoon plus 1 teaspoon of the butter, adjust seasoning if necessary, and set aside.

5   Melt the remaining 1 tablespoon butter in a small sauté pan set over medium heat. Add the remaining ¼ cup potato and cook for 2 minutes, stirring occasionally so the potato does not stick together. Add the remaining ½ cup leek and a pinch of salt. Cover the pan and cook until tender, 5 to 7 minutes.

6   Add the cooked potato and leek to the sauce. Add the shrimp and warm over low heat for 3 to 4 minutes. Make sure to cook the shrimp, but do not let the sauce boil.

7   In the meantime, place the sea urchins on a bed of coarse salt in a baking pan and warm the roe in the oven for 5 to 6 minutes.

8   To serve, divide the warm salt among four plates. Add the parsley and chives to the sauce, and spoon 3 shrimp halves and some vegetables and sauce into each sea urchin shell. Set 2 sea urchins atop the salt on each plate and top each with a sprig of chervil. Provide your guests with small spoons.

Wine

A viognier from the famed Rhône village of Condrieu in France would be an elegant choice to match the full flavor of the sea urchins. Try La Petite Côte from Domaine Yves Cuilleron, which is also sold in half bottles.

Butter-Braised Wild Striped Bass with a Leek Fondue and Caviar

SERVES 4

Bass has more fat than other white-fleshed fish, which allows it to survive a relatively long braising in butter to render it meltingly tender and uncommonly rich. It's complemented here by an equally luxurious leek fondue, made by stewing leeks over a long period of time and finishing them with a cleansing dose of vermouth. The dish is topped with a flourish of osetra caviar.

1 cup cream

2 pounds (4 sticks) cold butter, cut into pieces, plus 2 tablespoons at room temperature

6 medium leeks, white and light green parts only, sliced into ⅓-inch rounds, well washed in several changes of cold water, and drained

Salt

½ cup dry vermouth

Freshly ground black pepper

4 skinless wild striped bass fillets, 6 ounces each

¼ cup Vegetable Stock (page 344)

1 tablespoon thinly sliced chives

Coarse sea salt

1 ounce osetra caviar

1　Make a beurre monté: Put the cream in an ovenproof pot. Add 1 cup water and set the pot over high heat. Bring the mixture to a boil, then whisk in the cold butter, one piece at a time. Blend the mixture in a blender or with an immersion blender and set aside, in the pot, covered, to keep warm.

2　Sprinkle the leeks with salt and let sit for 10 minutes.

3　Melt the remaining 2 tablespoons butter in a large sauté pan set over medium heat. Fill a bowl wide enough to accommodate the sauté pan to a depth of 2 inches with ice water. Add the leeks to the sauté pan and slowly stew them over medium heat until completely tender, about 15 minutes. Pour in the vermouth and cook until reduced by half. Taste and season with salt and pepper. Chill immediately by setting the pan in the bowl of ice water.

4　Preheat the oven to 300°F.

(continued)

5   Season the bass with salt and pepper.
    Set the pot with the beurre monté over
    medium heat and bring to a simmer.
    Carefully add the bass to the pot and
    return to a simmer. Cover the pot and
    place it in the oven for 10 to 15 minutes,
    depending on the thickness of the fillets.
    Remove the pot from the oven.

6   Pour the stock into a pot, add the leeks,
    and warm them through. Add ½ cup
    of the fish cooking liquid and stir in
    the chives.

7   Divide the leeks and sauce among four
    warm fish bowls. Using a flat spatula,
    place 1 fillet on top of the leeks. Sprinkle
    each serving with coarse sea salt and
    top with a scattering of caviar.

Wine
A pinot blanc from the region of Alsace in
France, specifically, the Herrenweg vineyard
of François Baur, would stand up admirably
to the leek fondue.

Roasted Squab with Foie Gras, Black Truffles, Fingerling Potatoes, and Celery Root

SERVES 4

One of the great dishes three-star chef Alain Chapel made was a galette—a sort of pancake—of black truffles and celery root that he served with roasted veal. I don't mind saying that I never would have thought of pairing celery root with black truffle, but I learned from Chapel that they were meant for each other. This recipe produces such a crispy skin on the squab that you may spot a guest or two nibbling on the bones by hand, the ultimate compliment.

Have your butcher bone and butterfly the squab, and save the bones, livers, and hearts.

4 squab, butterflied, all bones removed from the body (wing bones and leg bones will still be intact), with bones, hearts, and livers reserved

1 tablespoon chopped shallot

½ teaspoon chopped garlic

6 tablespoons butter

¼ cup ruby port

2 tablespoons red wine vinegar

1 cup Brown Chicken Stock (page 343)

¼ cup truffle juice (see Mall Order Sources, page 345)

Salt

Freshly ground black pepper

2 tablespoons canola or other vegetable oil

1 medium celery root, cut into ¼ by 2-inch batons

¾ cup Vegetable Stock (page 344) or Chicken Stock (page 343)

½ pound fingerling potatoes, sliced into ½-inch rounds

½ pound foie gras (page 185), cut into 4 pieces

1 small black truffle, julienned

1 Preheat the oven to 450°F.

2 Chop the squab bones, hearts, and livers into small pieces. Set the hearts and livers aside. Put the bones in a roasting pan and roast in the oven until golden brown, 20 to 30 minutes.

(continued)

3 Melt 1 tablespoon of the butter in a sauté pan set over low heat. Add the shallot and garlic and cook slowly until caramelized, about 6 minutes. Add the squab bones, hearts, and livers, and sauté until the hearts and livers turn gray, about 10 minutes. Add the port and vinegar, raise the heat to high, bring the liquid to a boil, and let boil until dry, about 6 minutes. Add the brown chicken stock and 2 tablespoons water and reduce to ¾ cup, about 7 minutes. Add the truffle juice. Strain the liquid through a fine-mesh strainer set over a bowl. Discard the solids. Taste the liquid and season with salt and pepper. Set aside.

4 Heat the oil in a large ovenproof sauté pan set over high heat. Season the squab with salt and pepper. Put them, skin side down, in the pan and brown for 3 minutes. Add 1 tablespoon of the butter to the pan and transfer to the oven for 3 minutes. Remove the pan from the oven, turn the squab over, and fold the breast up over the legs. Continue to roast the legs for 1 to 2 minutes more.

5 Melt 1 tablespoon of the butter in a sauté pan set over medium heat. Sprinkle the celery root with salt, add it to the pan, and sauté until just tender, about 5 minutes. Add ¼ cup of the vegetable stock and cook for 5 minutes. Taste and adjust seasoning.

6 Melt 2 tablespoons of the butter in an ovenproof sauté pan set over high heat. Add the potatoes to the pan and brown them on both sides, about 4 minutes per side. Add ¼ cup of the vegetable stock, a pinch of salt, and cook in the oven until the potatoes are tender, about 4 minutes. Taste, adjust seasoning, and set aside.

7 Heat a sauté pan over medium-high heat. Season the foie gras with salt and pepper. Sear the foie gras on both sides, 2 to 3 minutes per side. Remove the pan from the heat, transfer the foie gras to a baking dish, and cook in the oven until just soft, 5 to 7 minutes. Remove the pan from the oven and season the foie gras again with salt and pepper.

8 Add the celery root, potatoes, the remaining ¼ cup vegetable stock, the remaining 1 tablespoon butter, and the truffle to the pan in which you seared the foie gras. Cook, shaking the pan, over medium-high heat so that a glaze forms, about 4 minutes. Taste and adjust seasoning.

9 To serve, divide the potatoes among four plates, place the celery root and truffle over the potatoes, top with the squab and then the foie gras. Drizzle some sauce over the entire dish.

Wine

A classic pairing with the foie gras and truffles would be a red Burgundy made from the grape pinot noir. A good match would be "Les Longeroies" from Domaine Bernard Coillot Pere & Fils, from the village of Marsannay, in France. Or select the Domaine Bachelet Gevrey-Chambertin.

The New Year's Mint Chocolate Soufflé and Friends

SERVES 4

This is probably the most ambitious recipe in the book, and it's worth every minute of effort for the pleasure it will give you and your guests. I've broken it down into very detailed steps to allow you to pace the cooking to suit your own schedule. My suggestion? Go for it!

The dessert has five components, but it's really two desserts served side by side. One side is the warm mint chip soufflé with a rich chocolate bottom. The other is a cold version with similar textures and flavors. The fudge ice is on the bottom, topped with the chocolate chip mousse. The mint leaves surround the sides of the chocolate ice like an attractive, edible cup. If you have four rectangular plates, you need only one per person. If not, you will need two small bread and butter plates per person, one for the underliner of the soufflés and the other to plate the cold portion of the dessert.

Soufflés are not difficult to make, but timing is all-important. It will be easier if you portion the mousse with a small ice cream scoop or tablespoon ahead of time onto a plastic-wrapped dish. Then you need only transfer the mousse to the ice.

Ideally, you should use Valrhona Equatorial chocolate for this recipe, which is about 55 percent cocoa. Varieties with a higher proportion of cocoa will not have enough sweetness or will be excessively acidic when paired with the mint. If you can't obtain Valrhona, my second choice would be an El Rey chocolate with a similar percentage of cocoa. As for the white chocolate, anything would work except for white chocolate chips.

Fudge Ices

2 tablespoons excellent cocoa, such as Valrhona or Scharffen Berger

¾ cup milk

2 ounces chocolate (see headnote)

½ teaspoon vanilla extract

2 egg yolks (if making on the same day as serving, reserve the whites for use in the soufflé)

3 tablespoons sugar

1   Put four 3-ounce paper cups in the freezer. (To mold the ices, you may use stainless timbale molds, but 3-ounce small Dixie cups work fine.) In a small saucepan, whisk the cocoa and milk together. Finely chop the chocolate and put it in a small bowl.

2   Bring the cocoa and milk to a boil over medium heat, stirring. As soon as it boils, immediately pour the mixture over the chopped chocolate and stir to melt and combine. Set the mixture aside at room temperature.

3   Rinse out the saucepan, fill it halfway with hot tap water, and set it over medium heat. Put the egg yolks and sugar in a bowl larger than the pot and set the bowl over simmering, but never boiling, water, and whisk briskly to blanch the yolks. Continue to whisk until warm to the touch, the sugar has dissolved, and the mixture has tripled in volume. Pour the chocolate mixture into the blanched yolks and whisk to combine.

4   Divide this mixture among the four frozen cups, cover with plastic wrap, and freeze until firm. These ices may be made and kept frozen for up to 1 week.

Ganache

2½ ounces chocolate (see headnote)

⅓ cup cream

NOTE: You will need four 5-ounce soufflé molds

1   The day before your dinner party, finely chop the chocolate for the ganache and place in a small bowl.

2   Bring the cream to a quick boil and pour over the chocolate, whisking as you pour. Spoon the ganache into the bottom of the soufflé molds, avoiding the sides. The ganache can be prepared and chilled for up to 24 hours.

White Chocolate Mousse

5 ounces white chocolate	1 egg white
1 cup plus 2 tablespoons cream	¼ cup sugar
1 ounce chocolate (see headnote)	½ teaspoon freshly squeezed lemon juice

(continued)

NOTE: I suggest that you make this early on the morning of the day you will serve it. It could be made the night before without losing too much air, but any earlier will result in a too-dense mousse. The mousse recipe makes a bit too much for the dessert, but frozen scoops of the leftover mousse are heavenly in hot coffee. If you own an electric handheld mixer, this is the time to use it. The meringue can be made in a standing mixer, but you must lift one edge of the bowl so the whisk will touch the bottom.

1   Chop the white chocolate and melt it with 2 tablespoons of the cream in a microwave or over a simmering water bath in a double boiler.

2   Finely shave the chocolate and set aside. Whip the remaining 1 cup cream to medium peaks, but do not overwork it; too stiffly whipped cream will make for a grainy mousse. Chill the whipped cream in the refrigerator.

3   Whisk together the egg white and sugar in the bowl of an electric mixer or in a mixing bowl if you are using a handheld mixer. Put the bowl over a simmering water bath similar to the one in the fudge ice recipe and whisk until warm to the touch, the sugar has dissolved, and the mixture has doubled in volume. With the mixer, whip the mixture to soft peaks.

4   The meringue should still be slightly warm. Whisk in the lemon juice. Fold the still-warm white chocolate into the meringue. Fold one-third of the white chocolate meringue into the whipped cream. Fold the cream mixture into the remaining meringue mixture. With the last turns of the spatula or tip of the whisk, sprinkle the chocolate shavings into the mousse. Gently transfer to a clean bowl, cover with plastic wrap, and chill in the refrigerator for up to 12 hours.

Soufflé Base

6 sprigs mint

½ cup milk

2 tablespoons sugar

2 egg yolks (reserve the whites for use in the soufflé)

2 teaspoons cornstarch

¼ teaspoon peppermint flavor, *absolutely not the supermarket variety,* or 2 teaspoons good peppermint schnapps

1   Break and crush the mint sprigs in your hands, then place them in a small stainless steel saucepan. Add the milk and sugar and bring to a boil. Remove from the heat and let steep for 30 minutes.

2   In a mixing bowl, whisk the egg yolks and cornstarch until smooth. Strain the mint milk and combine it with the yolks. Pour the mixture back into the saucepan and cook over low heat, stirring constantly. Cook the mixture until thick and pudding-like. Be careful not to brown or scorch the bottom. A quick finger taste should have no starchiness.

3   Immediately transfer the mixture to a bowl, mix in the peppermint, cover, and chill until ready to serve. The soufflé can be made to this point and refrigerated up to 24 hours in advance.

Chocolate-Covered Mint Leaves

1 ounce chocolate (see headnote)

20 fresh mint leaves, washed and dried

1   Melt the chocolate in the pot of a double boiler set over simmering water. Place a small plate in the freezer to chill.

2   Wash and dry the mint leaves. Using a pastry or artist's brush, brush the tops of the leaves evenly with the melted chocolate. Place on the plate in the freezer to set the chocolate. Repeat, coating the undersides of the leaves. The underside will be the visible side of the garnish. Once the chocolate is firm, line up the leaves in a tightly sealed plastic container until ready to serve. Do not make these more than a few hours ahead of time; the chocolate will absorb the "freezer flavor" if left unsealed for too long.

Okay, now all the prep work is finished. All that needs to be done is the plating and, of course, the last-minute soufflé. The egg whites for the soufflé should be at room temperature; remove them from the refrigerator just before dinner.

The main course has been cleared from the table. Allow your guests to finish their wine while you start the coffee and prepare the dessert.

(continued)

Soufflé and Assembly

1 tablespoon butter

⅓ cup plus 1 tablespoon sugar

4 egg whites (the reserved whites from preparing the fudge ice and soufflé base)

½ ounce chocolate (see headnote), finely shaved and set aside at room temperature

1 Preheat the oven to 375°F. Put a baking sheet in the oven. Set out your serving plates, four on your work space, four by the oven. Remove the ganache-bottomed soufflé molds from the refrigerator. Butter the sides and coat with 1 tablespoon of the sugar, tapping out the excess sugar.

2 Remove the soufflé base from the refrigerator and whisk it in a large bowl to loosen it. Put the egg whites in the bowl of an electric mixer and whip on medium speed to very soft peaks. Slowly pour the remaining ⅓ cup sugar into the whipped whites. When all the sugar is incorporated, raise the speed to medium-high. Whip only to medium peaks. (Stiff peaks will overextend the protein of the whites, causing the hot soufflés to sink more quickly.) With the tip of the whisk, fold one-third of the whites into the soufflé base. Then fold the lightened base into the remaining whites.

3 Fill the molds to the top. You will have more than enough. Run your thumb around the inside edge of the rim of each mold to ensure no mixture sticks to the sides, which will result in a lopsided soufflé. Put all 4 soufflés into the oven at once. Set the timer for 7 minutes, it will take 8; consider the timer to be a warning bell.

4 As soon as the soufflés are in the oven, remove the fudge ices from the freezer. Leave on the counter for 5 minutes and then unmold onto the plates; a soft squeeze is all that's needed to unmold. Top with scoops of mousse. Place the mint leaves, undersides out, around the ices, pressing lightly to attach. At the sound of the timer, check the soufflés; they should be risen but with no color. Begin serving the finished plates. Return to the kitchen to plate the soufflés. Slide a wide spatula under each soufflé mold and steady with two fingertips of your other hand (the molds won't be too hot, but you could use an oven mitt or pot holder if you wish). Quickly place the mold, spatula, and all on the underliner plate. Slide the spatula out and repeat with the other three. Serve at once. Happy New Year!

Make-Ahead Menu

Braised Beef Short Rib
Borscht with Horseradish Oil

Roger's Coconut Cake

This is the fanciest make-ahead menu in the book, but if you follow the instructions, you'll see that the main course, Braised Beef Short Rib Borscht with Horseradish Oil (page 327), can be made component by component and assembled to order. The horseradish oil can be made up to a week in advance, or prepared as you're making the borscht. The gnocchi can be made up to two weeks ahead of time and frozen.

The one thing everyone knows about borscht—other than the fact that it lent its name to an entire school of bad comedy—is that it's made with beets, which gives this Eastern European soup its bright, purplish-red character. But what you may not know is that borscht is traditionally made with beef stock. So the leap this recipe takes from borscht to *braised short rib* borscht is actually just a little hop. I use chicken stock so the meat comes out like boiled beef rather than an overly intense wine-based braise. The borscht can be enjoyed on its own, or served as a starter or side dish with firm-fleshed white fish such as bass (page 93) or halibut (page 31).

One of the charms of this recipe is that the beet and pickle juices can simply be drained from store-bought jars of pickled vegetables.

The dessert, Roger's Coconut Cake (page 330), is named for the guy who invented it, sort of. Most capable home cooks develop the ability to make logical substitutions for the ingredients called for in a recipe. But my friend Roger once exceeded expectations and made history among our circle when he was forced to substitute some ingredients and accidentally improved on the author's excessively sweet formula by making a cake that had coconut and icing in perfect balance.

You can skip the step of toasting the coconut and this will still be delicious, but I love the extra dimension of flavor that it adds. The recipe calls for a small quantity of flavored rum. If you don't usually keep this kind of rum in the house, ask your local liquor store if they have any "minis" for sale. It doesn't need to be a premium brand.

Braised Beef Short Rib Borscht with Horseradish Oil

SERVES 4

2 pounds Idaho or russet potatoes

4 medium red beets, top 1 inch cut off and discarded

1 tablespoon olive oil

Salt

Freshly ground black pepper

¼ cup finely grated fresh horseradish

1 tablespoon white wine vinegar

¼ cup extra-virgin olive oil

1 tablespoon chopped flat-leaf parsley

1 tablespoon chopped dill

¼ cup canola or other vegetable oil

4 pounds beef short ribs, flanken cut (about 8 ribs)

1 small onion, thinly sliced

4 cloves garlic, thinly sliced

2 medium carrots, cut into medium dice

1 celery root (about 12 ounces), peeled and cut into medium dice

1 quart Chicken Stock (page 343)

1¾ cups flour, plus more for dusting work surface

1 egg

4 tablespoons (½ stick) butter

2 cups shredded white cabbage (about ½ head cabbage)

6 tablespoons strained pickled beet juice or bread-and-butter pickle juice (see headnote)

6 tablespoons strained dill pickle juice (see headnote)

1 Preheat the oven to 450°F.

2 Place the potatoes directly on the top rack of the oven and bake until tender when pierced with the tip of a thin, sharp-bladed knife, about 1 hour.

3 While the potatoes are baking, put the beets in a baking pan with the olive oil and ½ cup water, and season lightly with salt and pepper. Cover the pan with heavy aluminum foil and roast the beets on the bottom rack of the oven until tender when pierced with the tip of a sharp, thin-bladed knife, about 25 to 30 minutes. Remove the pan from the oven and set aside to cool.

(continued)

4 Make the horseradish oil: In a bowl, mix the horseradish with the vinegar and season with a pinch of salt. Stir in the extra-virgin olive oil, parsley, and dill, and let sit for at least 1 hour.

5 When the beets and potatoes have been removed from the oven, reduce the oven temperature to 325°F.

6 Warm 2 tablespoons of the canola oil in a large heavy-bottomed pot over medium-high heat until almost smoking. Add the ribs to the pot and sear until browned all over, 3 to 5 minutes per side. Transfer the ribs to a plate and set aside.

7 Repeat Step 5 with the remaining 2 tablespoons canola oil and the remaining ribs.

8 Add the onion, garlic, one-third of the carrots, and one-third of the celery root to the pot. Sauté, stirring occasionally, for 10 to 12 minutes, until the vegetables are well caramelized. Add the stock, raise the heat to high, and bring to a boil. Return the ribs to the pot and let the liquid return to the boil.

9 Transfer the pot to the oven, cover, and braise the ribs for 1 hour, then rotate the pot 180 degrees and braise for an additional hour or until the ribs are tender and the meat can be pulled away with the tug of a fork.

10 While the ribs are braising, peel the potatoes and pass them through a food mill or ricer (see page 8) into a large bowl. You should have about 2 cups of mashed potatoes. Add the flour to the potatoes, season with salt and pepper, and stir to combine. Beat the egg in a small bowl with a whisk and add it to the potato mixture. Squeeze together until the dough just comes together, but do not knead or overwork it. Form the dough into a ball, wrap it in plastic wrap, and chill in the refrigerator for 20 to 30 minutes to soften it and make it easier to work with.

11 Place the dough on a well-floured work surface and divide it into 8 equal pieces. Roll out one piece into a rope about ½ inch thick, working from the middle out and applying even pressure. (If the rope won't roll, wipe any excess flour from the work surface and roll using just enough flour to keep the dough from sticking.) Cut the dough into segments about ¾ inch long. Using the edge of a large, wide-bladed knife or a flat spatula, transfer the gnocchi to a well-floured baking sheet. Repeat with the remaining dough, then place the sheet in the freezer until the gnocchi harden, about 1 hour. (If preparing in advance, divide the frozen gnocchi among Ziploc-type bags and store in the freezer for up to 2 weeks.)

12 While the dough is resting, melt the butter in a sauté pan set over medium heat, but do not let it brown. Add the remaining carrot and celery root, and season with just a pinch of salt. Cover the pan and cook, removing the cover to stir occasionally, for 5 minutes. Add the cabbage and another pinch of salt, and cook, covered and stirring occasionally, until tender, about 12 minutes. Remove the pan from the heat and set aside.

13 When the ribs are done, remove the pot from the oven. Use tongs or a slotted spoon to remove the ribs, set them aside on a plate, and season with salt and pepper. Strain the braising liquid through a fine-mesh strainer set over a bowl. Discard the solids, pour the liquid into a pot, and set the pot over high heat. Bring the liquid to a boil, then lower the heat and let simmer until reduced by about one fourth, 10 to 12 minutes. Remove the pot from the heat and let the liquid settle for 5 minutes. Use a large spoon to skim off and discard any fat that rises to the surface. Set ½ cup of the liquid aside.

14 Peel the beets and cut into medium dice. Add the beets, carrots, and celery root to the skimmed braising liquid, stir in the pickle juices, taste, and adjust seasoning with salt and pepper. Add the ribs and bring to a boil. (If preparing in advance, wrap the ribs and vegetables in serving portions and freeze.)

Assembly (for each portion)

1 tablespoon butter	2 tablespoons chopped dill
2 tablespoons cooking liquid (see Step 14, above) or Vegetable Stock (page 344)	Salt

1 Bring a large pot of lightly salted water to a rolling boil. Add the frozen gnocchi and cook until they all rise to the top, about 2 minutes, then cook 1 minute more. Drain.

2 Put the butter and cooking liquid in a sauté pan set over medium-high heat. Bring to a boil and let boil until thickened and slightly reduced, about 2 minutes. Add the gnocchi, sprinkle with the dill, and toss to combine. Season with salt.

3 To serve, put the ribs and vegetables in the middle of a bowl, place a few gnocchi around the outside, and top with a dollop of horseradish oil.

Wine

A light pinot noir would be best to pair with this dish because the ribs are mellowed by braising, and the beet and horseradish flavors do not need a full-bodied red. A California pinot noir from the Santa Maria Valley, such as Byron's Hangtime Pinot Noir, would be a good choice.

Roger's Coconut Cake

SERVES 12

Cake

2 cups flour

¼ teaspoon salt

2 teaspoons baking powder

1 cup (2 sticks) butter, at room temperature

1 cup sugar

3 eggs

2¾ cups Coco López (cream of coconut)

2 tablespoons coconut-flavored rum, such as Malibu

½ cup freshly squeezed orange juice

3 cups finely grated unsweetened coconut

3 egg whites

1 Preheat the oven to 350°F.

2 Line two 8-inch cake pans with parchment or waxed paper circles.

3 Put the flour, salt, and baking powder in a bowl. Whisk them together and set aside.

4 Put the butter and sugar in the bowl of an electric mixer and cream on medium speed until fluffy.

5 Separate the eggs and add the whites to the other whites. Add the yolks one at a time to the creamed butter and beat on medium speed after each addition. Lower the speed of the mixer and add the flour mixture. Mix until just combined.

6 Place the Coco López in a securely covered container. Shake well and pour into a bowl. Stir in the rum and orange juice. Add this mixture to the batter one-third at a time, alternating additions with additions of the unsweetened coconut. Set the batter side.

7 In a very clean bowl, whip the 6 egg whites to soft peaks. Fold a large dollop of batter into the whites, then fold the whites into the remaining batter. Divide between the prepared pans.

8   Bake the layers until golden, about 1 hour; a toothpick inserted into the center of the cake should come out clean. Let cool until they are slightly above room temperature. Moving a small paring knife or metal spatula around the edges, release the sides of the cake from the pans. Invert, then peel off the paper and let cool completely (overnight is best).

9   If the cake layers are mounded in the center, trim them so they are flat and even. Slice each layer into two.

Icing

4 egg whites

1 cup sugar

Pinch of salt

12 ounces (3 sticks) butter, well softened at room temperature

2 cups very soft cream cheese

3 tablespoons coconut-flavored rum, such as Malibu

1   Put the egg whites, sugar, and salt in the bowl of an electric mixer. Set the bowl over a water bath over medium heat (the base of the bowl should not touch the water). Keep the water at a steamy simmer, but do not let it boil. Hand whip the whites until they are opaque and warm to the touch.

2   Place the bowl on the mixer and whip on medium-high speed to medium peaks; the whites should now be cool to the touch. Reduce the speed to low and add the butter in spoonfuls, mixing after each addition until combined. Continue with the cream cheese, adding it in small increments. Finish with the rum and continue mixing until incorporated.

Syrup and Assembly

One 7-ounce bag sweetened, shredded coconut

1 cup Coco López (cream of coconut)

2 teaspoons coconut-flavored rum, such as Malibu

1   Preheat the oven to 350°F.

2   Spread the coconut out on a cookie sheet and toast in the oven until tan, about 12 to 15 minutes.

(continued)

3   Put the Coco López, rum, and 2 tablespoons water in a saucepan. Bring to a boil over high heat and set aside.

4   Divide the icing into two batches. (You'll use half in between the layers and half to frost the cake.)

5   Place 1 layer of cake on a serving platter. Brush with the warm coconut syrup. Top the layer with one-third of the icing, spreading it evenly. Sprinkle with toasted coconut. Repeat with the remaining layers. Ice the top and sides of the cake and coat with the remaining coconut.

6   Chill the cake for at least 2 hours. Remove from the refrigerator 1 hour before serving. Although you may store the cake cold, it should be eaten only at room temperature.

Wine

A light floral sweet wine would do well with the coconut flavors. The late-harvest Cluster Select 2001 Gewürztraminer from Navarro Vineyards in Mendocino, California, or, on a more festive note, a demi-sec Champagne. Another possibility is Wölffer Late Harvest Chardonney, from Wölffer Estate Vineyards and Stables, in New York State, on Long Island's South Fork.

Cabbage Classics

Apple Cider Sauerkraut

Red Cabbage with Cider and Pears

Spicy Coleslaw

Káposzta Teszta (Mom's Cabbage and Noodles)

I dedicate this section on cabbage to my mother, who taught me and my siblings to appreciate this often maligned vegetable. Because I grew up on cabbage, it was one of those things I always knew would make it onto my restaurant menu. And I guess I'm not alone, because I've worked in a lot of restaurants where the chefs featured it, including Gotham Bar and Grill and Le Bernardin.

If you're like most people, you probably don't cook much cabbage. For some reason, we as a country seem unable to think about it as anything more than the main ingredient in coleslaw. But I love cabbage. I love stuffed cabbage with meat and rice. I love Sauerkraut (page 336) and Apple Cider Sauerkraut (page 335).

I love that cabbage is very easy to cook with, a convenient way to bring a homey, rustic touch to a meal. I certainly love it cooked long and slow, as in Red Cabbage with Cider and Pears (page 337). And, above all, I love Mom's Cabbage and Noodles (page 340).

But cabbage is also great raw. In fact, it's one of my wife's favorite raw ingredients in a salad. One of my favorite cold uses is in Spicy Coleslaw (page 338). As for when to use which type of cabbage, generally speaking, savoy cabbage is best for braising, white cabbage is best raw, and red cabbage is the universal donor, delicious raw or cooked.

Apple Cider Sauerkraut

SERVES 4 AS A SIDE DISH

auerkraut is another one of those dishes that's been with me my whole life. We ate it when I was growing up; my mother made hers with grated apple. This dish, made with apple cider, is based on that flavor combination. On New Year's Eve at my house we followed the Hungarian tradition of serving sauerkraut with kielbasa and roasted pork, which is supposed to bring good luck for the next twelve months.

2 pounds homemade sauerkraut (recipe, page 336) or store-bought drained

4 ounces bacon, thinly sliced, then chopped

½ medium onion, minced

2 cloves garlic, minced

2 apples, peeled and grated

½ teaspoon caraway seeds, crushed

1½ cups apple cider

1½ cups white wine vinegar

1 Preheat the oven to 400°F.

2 Put the sauerkraut in a colander set over a bowl. Place in the sink and run cold water over the sauerkraut for 15 minutes. Let drain, then squeeze any excess moisture out of the sauerkraut.

3 Render the bacon in a large ovenproof pot with a lid over medium heat until just golden brown, about 5 minutes. Add the onion and garlic and sauté until softened but not browned, about 5 minutes. Add the apples, caraway seeds, cider, and vinegar, and reduce to a syrup over high heat, about 40 minutes. Mix in the sauerkraut, cover, and cook in the oven until the sauerkraut is tender, 30 to 40 minutes.

Sauerkraut

MAKES ABOUT 12 CUPS

3 medium heads white cabbage, about 8½ pounds total weight

5 tablespoons kosher salt plus more if necessary

1   Trim and discard any tough dark green or damaged outer leaves from the cabbage. Quarter the cabbage, remove the core, and thinly slice it crosswise.

2   Sprinkle the cabbage with the salt, tossing with your hands to ensure it's evenly coated. Put the cabbage in a large glass or ceramic crock, packing it in if necessary. Put a plate on top of the cabbage and weight it down with a few cans of food wrapped in plastic wrap.

3   Cover the crock with a clean towel and set it in a cool, dark place. Check it every other day for mold. If mold, scum, or dark leaves appear, remove and discard. The cabbage will bubble and ferment for between 4 and 6 weeks.

Red Cabbage with Cider and Pears

Because it's sturdier than the green variety, red cabbage is the one I turn to for winter braising, especially since it's more flavorful at that time of year, as are so many vegetables grown and harvested after the first frost. You want this side dish to be sweet, but with the balance provided by the slightly acidic wine.

This is an outstanding accompaniment to meats, especially game, and would be delicious with the lamb shanks on page 305 or as an addition to the Thanksgiving selections on pages 262–77. For a true revelation as to how much flavor fatty fish can stand up to, serve it with roasted salmon or trout.

4 tablespoons (½ stick) butter

¼ medium onion, minced

1 clove garlic, minced

Salt

1 large head red cabbage, quartered, cored, and sliced into thin ribbons

1½ cups dry white wine

1½ cups apple cider

1 large Bartlett pear, peeled and grated

1 Melt the butter in a wide, deep pot set over medium heat. Add the onion, garlic, and a pinch of salt, and sauté until tender, about 5 minutes.

2 Add the cabbage, season with salt, and cook, covered, removing the cover to stir occasionally, until the cabbage is wilted and tender, about 25 minutes.

3 In a small pot, bring the wine to a boil over high heat and immediately pour the wine into the pot with the cabbage. Stir, then add the cider and pear. Raise the heat to high, bring to a boil, and let boil until almost all of the liquid has evaporated, about 30 minutes. If not serving immediately, store in an airtight container in the refrigerator for up to 2 days.

Spicy Coleslaw

SERVES 4 AS A SIDE DISH

oleslaw's name comes from the Dutch words that mean "cabbage salad," which is appropriate, because cabbage is about the only ingredient that all coleslaws have in common. I've seen recipes that include sliced carrots or turnips, and even bacon and pineapple. For all of their diversity, most coleslaw recipes fall into two camps: those dressed with a vinaigrette, or even just vinegar; and those dressed with a mayonnaise-y coating (that may include vinegar as well).

My own personal coleslaw belongs to the mayonnaise camp but is distinctly spicy, with lots of fresh jalapeño pepper and the tangy, fresh flavor of lime juice. If you like your food insanely hot, leave in all of the jalapeño seeds; to moderate the heat, remove all or some of them.

I suggest making this a day before you plan to serve it so the flavors have a chance to marry. The sturdy savoy cabbage will have no trouble maintaining its texture overnight.

1 head savoy cabbage, coarse outer leaves removed	½ cup mayonnaise (recipe follows)
1 small red onion, halved and thinly sliced, ideally on a mandoline	¼ cup freshly squeezed lime juice
	¼ cup white wine vinegar
3 jalapeño peppers, seeds removed from 1½ peppers, minced (wear latex gloves to protect your hands)	½ cup extra-virgin olive oil
	Salt
	Freshly ground black pepper
2 tablespoons chopped cilantro leaves	

1 Peel off and reserve the large leaves of the cabbage until they start to become difficult to remove. Lay the peeled leaves flat and cut a V up their middles to remove the thick central veins. Stack the leaves and thinly slice them crosswise. Quarter the cabbage, remove the core from each quarter, and thinly slice the quarters crosswise. Collect the cabbage in a large mixing bowl. Add the onion, jalapeños, and cilantro, and toss well. Set aside.

2 Put the mayonnaise in a mixing bowl. Whisk in the lime juice and vinegar. Slowly add the olive oil in a thin stream to maintain the emulsification. Season with salt and pepper, add to the cabbage, and mix well.

3 Cover the cabbage with plastic wrap. Place a weight, such as a plate or a flat lid, on top of the cabbage to keep all of the cabbage in constant contact with the marinade. Chill in the refrigerator for at least 2 hours. If not serving immediately, store in the refrigerator for up to 2 days.

Mayonnaise

MAKES ABOUT 1 CUP

1 egg yolk, at room temperature

1 tablespoon freshly squeezed lemon juice, at room temperature

1/4 teaspoon salt

Pinch of pepper

1 cup canola or other vegetable oil

In a medium mixing bowl, whisk together the egg yolk, lemon juice, salt, and pepper. Whisk in the oil a few drops at a time to form a thick emulsion. After about 1/4 cup of oil has been added, whisk in the oil in a thin stream until all the oil has been incorporated. Thin to desired consistency with water.

NOTE: Eating raw eggs carries the risk of salmonella. Foods containing raw eggs should not be eaten by the very young, the very old, pregnant women, or anyone with a compromised immune system.

Káposzta Teszta (Mom's Cabbage and Noodles)

I've talked about my family quite a bit in these pages and—as I leave you—
I invite you to join me in reliving a great family moment. While I was writing
this book, I convinced my mother to share her legendary and very secret recipe
for Hungarian cabbage and noodles, a greasy, crunchy, starchy delight that's one
of my favorite things on planet Earth. To this day, when Mom makes this dish for
me and my siblings, we revert to adolescent behavior, moaning with delight and
anticipation.

On Christmas Day, 2002, we were all gathered for our annual festivities. I
knew my mother was going to share the recipe with me, and we decided to give
the revelation of this long-kept secret the pomp it deserved by staging a mock
talk show in the living room.

What follows is a transcript of that show. I play the part of the Host. The
Audience is my sister Cindy and her husband, Vito; my dad, George; my niece,
Brittany; and my nephew, Kevin. My mom, Evelyn Telepan, is played by herself.
The setting is my sister Karen's house in Freehold, New Jersey, surrounded by
the snow of a white Christmas.

HOST: Hello, good evening, and welcome to *My Show*.

[Audience applauds.]

HOST: Tonight we have a very special guest, the very famous Hungarian chef Evelyn Telepan. She's here to tell us the famous secret recipe for Cabbage and Noodles.

[Audience applauds.]

HOST: Please, Evelyn, proceed with the recipe.

EVELYN: Okay. This is how we make it.

[Audience moans in anticipation.]

EVELYN: First, we cut the cabbage in quarters. Then we grate it on the grater. Not the fine grater, the big-hole grater.

AUDIENCE: Ahhhhhhh.

HOST: So you grate the cabbage is what you're telling us?

EVELYN: Right.

HOST (sarcastic): I would've never thought of that myself.

EVELYN (dismissing Host, lovingly, of course): Okay. Then you sprinkle, no *smother*, it with salt.

AUDIENCE: Mmmmm. Ahhhhhhh.

EVELYN: And mix it, cover it, and let it stand for a good three hours.

HOST: Really?

EVELYN (deadly serious): Really.

HOST: So you really need to think about this—you can't just whip this up?

EVELYN (serious): No, you gotta think about this. Then, about three hours later, you take it and you rinse it and you squeeze it.

HOST: You're talking about quick sauerkraut here is what you're saying?

EVELYN: No.

HOST: Well, sorta like that.

EVELYN (humors the Host): Kinda. Then you take your frying pan and you use bacon fat.

[Audience applauds.]

HOST: The kids love bacon fat out there. Don't ya?

AUDIENCE: Yeah! [Biggest "yeah" from Vito.]

EVELYN: The bacon fat makes it. When you melt the bacon fat, you put two or three table-spoons in because you want that flavor to go [makes a gesture indicating "all over the place"] . . . You put the cabbage in there and brown it, let it get a little brown. Then you boil your noodles. You can use bow tie, that's what we usually use, or wide noodles.

HOST: Egg noodles?

EVELYN: Egg noodles would be good. After you boil the noodles and drain them, take the cabbage and mix it with the noodles.

HOST: And then?

EVELYN: And then you eat it. Isn't that delicious? Bacon and cabbage and noodles. It's out of this world.

[Audience applauds.]

EVELYN: And if you want me to do another one someday, I'll make you another Hungarian recipe.

HOST: Thank you very much.

EVELYN: Thank you.

Stocks

Chicken Stock

MAKES ABOUT 4 CUPS

6 pounds chicken wings

1 onion, roughly chopped into small pieces

1 carrot, roughly chopped into small pieces

1 celery stalk, roughly chopped into small pieces

1 head garlic, split

1 teaspoon black peppercorns

2 sprigs thyme

2 sprigs parsley

Put all of the ingredients in an 8-quart stockpot, add water to cover by 2 inches, bring to a boil, then lower the heat and let simmer for 4 hours, skimming any impurities that rise to the surface. Let cool at room temperature and skim off any fat that rises to the surface while the stock rests. Strain through a fine-mesh strainer, cover, and refrigerate for up to 1 week, or freeze for up to 2 months.

Brown Chicken Stock

MAKES 4 CUPS

2 tablespoons canola or other vegetable oil

1 onion, roughly chopped into small pieces

1 carrot, roughly chopped into small pieces

10 pounds chicken wings

1 head garlic, split

1 teaspoon black peppercorns

2 sprigs thyme

2 sprigs parsley

(continued)

1 Preheat the oven to 450°F.

2 Put the chicken wings in a roasting pan and roast, stirring occasionally, until dark golden brown, about 2 hours.

3 Warm the oil in a 12-quart stockpot set over medium-low heat. Add the onion and carrot and sauté until browned, about 20 minutes. Add the chicken wings, garlic, peppercorns, thyme, parsley, and water to cover by 2 inches.

4 Bring to a boil, then lower the heat and let simmer for 8 hours or overnight, skimming any impurities that rise to the surface. Let cool at room temperature and skim off any fat that rises to the surface while the stock rests. Strain through a fine-mesh strainer. Transfer to a clean pot and gently boil until reduced to 4 cups. Strain, cover, and refrigerate for up to 1 week, or freeze for up to 2 months.

Vegetable Stock

MAKES ABOUT 8 CUPS

¼ cup canola or other vegetable oil

2 medium leeks, trimmed, halved lengthwise, roughly chopped, well washed in several changes of cold water, and drained

2 medium fennel bulbs with tops, washed and roughly chopped

6 medium onions, halved, ends trimmed, and thinly sliced

1 bunch celery, washed and roughly chopped

4 heads garlic, halved crosswise

1 Heat the oil in a 12-quart stockpot over medium heat until hot but not smoking. Add the leeks, fennel, onions, celery, and garlic, and cook over low heat, stirring frequently, until tender, about 1 to 1½ hours. The vegetables will release their juices as they cook.

2 Add 2 quarts water, bring to a simmer, and let simmer, uncovered, for 20 minutes. Remove the pot from the heat and let rest for 20 minutes to develop the flavor. Strain through a fine-mesh strainer into a large bowl, pressing on the vegetables to release as much liquid as possible. Discard the solids. Use the stock at once or transfer to an airtight container and refrigerate for up to 4 days, or freeze for up to 2 months.

Mail-Order Sources

Anson Mills
803-467-4122
www.ansonmills.com
Grits.

Browne Trading Company
800-944-7848
www.browne-trading.com
Fish and shellfish.

D'Artagnan, Inc.
800-DARTAGN
www.dartagnan.com
Foie gras and other duck and game
products, caviar, and truffles.

Hudson Valley Foie Gras
845-292-2500
www.hudsonvalleyfoiegras.com
American foie gras and other
duck products.

Jamison Farm
800-237-5262
www.jamisonfarm.com
Lamb and lamb products.

JB Prince
800-473-0577
www.jbprince.com
Kitchen equipment.

Kalustyan's
800-352-3451
www.kalustyans.com
Middle Eastern food products.

Murray's Cheese Shop
888-692-4339
www.murrayscheese.com
Domestic and imported cheeses.

Niman Ranch
www.nimanranch.com
Beef, pork, and lamb.

Nueske's
800-392-2266
www.nueskes.com
Smoked bacon and other
smoked pork products.

Metric Equivalencies

LIQUID EQUIVALENCIES

CUSTOMARY	METRIC
¼ teaspoon	1.25 milliliters
½ teaspoon	2.5 milliliters
1 teaspoon	5 milliliters
1 tablespoon	15 milliliters
1 fluid ounce	30 milliliters
¼ cup	60 milliliters
⅓ cup	80 milliliters
½ cup	120 milliliters
1 cup	240 milliliters
1 pint (2 cups)	480 milliliters
1 quart (4 cups)	960 milliliters (.96 liter)
1 gallon (4 quarts)	3.84 liters

DRY MEASURE EQUIVALENCIES

CUSTOMARY	METRIC
1 ounce (by weight)	28 grams
¼ pound (4 ounces)	114 grams
1 pound (16 ounces)	454 grams
2.2 pounds	1 kilogram (1,000 grams)

OVEN-TEMPERATURE EQUIVALENCIES

DESCRIPTION	°FAHRENHEIT	°CELSIUS
Cool	200	90
Very slow	250	120
Slow	300–325	150–160
Moderately slow	325–350	160–180
Moderate	350–375	180–190
Moderately hot	375–400	190–200
Hot	400–450	200–230
Very hot	450–500	230–260

Index

(Page numbers in *italics* refer to illustrations.)